FROM THE
PATERSON STATION

FROM THE PATERSON STATION

The Way We Were

Douglas Kinnard

Copyright © 2000 by Douglas Kinnard.

Library of Congress: 2001116843
ISBN #: Hardcover 0-7388-5867-6
Softcover 0-7388-5868-4

All rights reserved. No part of this book may be reproduced or transmitted in any form or by any means, electronic or mechanical, including photocopying, recording, or by any information storage and retrieval system, without permission in writing from the copyright owner.

This book was printed in the United States of America.

To order additional copies of this book, contact:
Xlibris Corporation
1-888-7-XLIBRIS
www.Xlibris.com
Orders@Xlibris.com

CONTENTS

I. PATERSON (1926-1940)

1. THE TAXI	13
2. THE CONVERT	21
3. ST. JOE'S	33
4. THE GREEN YEARS	42
5. THE GHOSTS OF EASTSIDE HIGH	63

II. RENDEZVOUS WITH DESTINY (1940-1947)

6. NEW LONDON SWAB	101
7. WEST POINT AT PEACE AND WAR	133
8. THE FARTHEST EAST SEVENTY-FIRST	189
9. AN END AND A BEGINNING	246
10. THE BEST YEARS OF OUR LIVES	284

AUTHOR'S NOTES AND ACKNOWLEDGMENTS   315

TO THE AUNTS
ANNIE, FANNY, ROSIE

Other Books by Douglas Kinnard

The War Managers

President Eisenhower and Strategy Management:
A Study in Defense Politics

Ike 1890-1990: A Pictorial History

The Secretary of Defense

The Certain Trumpet:
Maxwell Taylor and the American Experience
in Vietnam

PART I

PATERSON (1926-1940)

". . . remember only for a fleeting moment . . . the song of the fox sparrow reawakening the world of Paterson."

William Carlos Williams
Paterson Book Five

1. The Taxi

The car was yellow, which struck me as odd, but in 1926 all cars were oddities of sorts, and in any case not seen in large numbers in West Paterson, New Jersey. Four of us were getting into the taxi, as my sister called it; besides me and one of my four sisters was one of my two brothers and my father. At age four, I was by far the youngest. The remainder of the family stood on the sidewalk in front of our McBride Avenue home early that April morning waving what seemed a rather definite farewell. It would be, in fact, the last time that the family would all be together.

The yellow cab proceeded at a leisurely pace and since it was the first automobile ride that I was conscious of, the excitement of the moment overcame whatever trepidations the departure had engendered. Soon the landscape turned from farms to buildings; and then a large and high waterfall flowing at great speed came into view, and across from it a large number of red brick factory-like buildings. We were entering Paterson: the falls were the great Passaic falls, and the buildings were what was left of Alexander Hamilton's Society for Useful Manufacturers.

Turning down the hill into the town center we could see at a great distance very tall buildings that my father identified as New

York City. I could not know it then, but I was looking across some sixteen miles of New Jersey—Passaic, Bergen, Essex, and Hudson Counties—to the ever dominant skyline of Manhattan, which has always loomed eastward over the New Jersey landscape, beckoning with greater possibilities.

Soon we were going up Market Street past a large new building. The driver said it was a high school to be called Paterson Eastside that would open in the fall. Shortly thereafter, we reached our destination. As we got out of the taxi, I saw a large three-story red brick building—austere and surrounded by a very tall iron picket fence. Excitement turned to apprehension. Over the entrance arch in large gold letters were the words "Paterson Orphan Asylum"!

The entrance formalities were over almost immediately. My father and sister Ruth had disappeared, probably to somewhere in the building. I found myself standing in a long hall with my brother Harry, who was being sent upstairs with the "older boys." Despite my roars of protest I was consigned to a large first-floor room that turned out to be a nursery. Suddenly, from one of a family of nine, I was completely alone, as a result—at least in my mind—of a ride in a taxi. In my mind's eye, even now over seventy years later, I can still see that long empty stairway up which my brother disappeared.

My protesting cries went on for the remainder of that long day. I was reasoned with, bribed, cajoled, threatened, and paddled—all to no avail until exhaustion took over. Through that endless first night in a crib I tried to come to grips with what was happening. One thing I knew was that I was alone and on my own, and I sensed whatever problems there were I would have to solve them myself. Reality took over at a very early age.

Why was this four-and-a-half-year-old beginning a new life in an orphan asylum in the days of Coolidge? I remember very little before that benchmark day, but to set this starting point in perspective let me make a brief digression into family background.

My paternal grandfather was born in London in 1847 of Scotch descent, the son of a judge. He was an artist who also taught art, and one of his younger pupils, Hettie Hudson, born in 1862 of English and French parentage, became his wife about 1877. My father was born in London in 1878 and named Frederick like his father. A couple of years later the family came to America, which offered a better market for my grandfather's paintings, and settled in what would become Hawthorne, New Jersey. Eventually my grandfather built and operated a hotel there, which bore his last name Kinnard, which had been modified from Kinnaird.

It was from here that my father at about twenty enlisted in the Army during the Spanish-American War. Being a good musician, specializing in flute and sax, he ended up in the Army band at Fort Adams, a Coast Artillery post in Newport, Rhode Island. Newport was then the principal port and base of the U.S. Atlantic fleet. It was here that he met my mother Mary Jane Toomey, who had been born in 1880 to Patrick Toomey—obviously Irish—and Marie McQuade, a native of Fall River, Massachusetts.

Until 1908 they remained in Newport where my four oldest siblings were born. The family returned to Hawthorne a few years before my father's parents died. For about ten years they remained there, and three more children were born. Sometime in that period my father became involved in the life insurance business, which in 1918 required him to move to Morristown, New Jersey.

It was here that I was born on Tuesday, September 13, 1921. As it happened, Daisy (note the artistic influence), one of my father's two sisters, and her husband, Reuben Kithcart, were unable to have children and they indicated an interest in adopting me. My parents, with six others (a sixteen-year-old sister had died the previous June) to care for, agreed, so I was off to the new home in Hawthorne and brought up as an only child. This lasted until early 1924 when Kithcart, at age thirty-eight, died following gall bladder surgery. At that point I was returned to my family who were now living at 52 McBride Avenue in West Paterson.

I have a few scattered memories of that location beginning about the summer of 1925: falling in the Passaic River while jumping between rowboats with some of my sisters; my sister Helen and her friend singing a new song, "Show Me the Way to Go Home," at which point my father complied with the friend's wishes and she was duly dispatched; my father chasing me through the house with a strap in hand and my escaping into the only bathroom, whose door I locked and where I stayed until my father left for work—without a shave.

What personal events between my parents led to the day of the taxi I never knew. Since my father later married his secretary, I have some general suspicions, but the reasons for the drastic nature of the breakup I never understood. Since, as we will see, I shortly became a member of an extended family of totally different makeup, I lost both the capability and the interest required to pursue the matter.

Of life in the Orphan Asylum, or "Home," as it was called, where I was destined to spend more than seven months, I have a few memories. The building itself sat on a grassy knoll surrounded by an iron picket fence on one of the main streets of Paterson. The first floor, in addition to housing the nursery, held the dining hall and, in front, a large visitors' reception room. The upstairs contained dormitory-type rooms for the older children. In September, the month I became five, I qualified as "older," and my sleeping quarters were relocated from the nursery to a cot in one of those rooms.

Exactly how I filled my time in the early months escapes me. I do recall occasionally talking to people through the fence, and once that summer we went to a large park for a picnic with families or friends of the Home. We must have been treated as well as the situation permitted, since I recall no particular traumas except a feeling of isolation, at least until I started to school.

From September on I was enrolled in Public School 15, a short walk from the Home. Located on a large hill in Sandy Hill Park, the school was new and well equipped. I was in the kindergarten that fall, which was to be the first of forty-three years I was to spend in schools in one capacity or another.

I can still see the precise layout of that schoolroom, but only a few incidents come back. A teacher disciplining me, a strong-willed brat, was subjected to having the buttons torn off her smock, for which I was duly dispatched to the principal. After a few minutes of attempted intimidation he gave up and I was returned "cleansed." Another event, which happened to me only once that I recall, involved a child who lived in a house contiguous to the Home property. As we walked four times a day to the school and back, naturally I befriended those walking with me, sometimes including those living nearby. One day a shocked mother, seeing me and her own five-year-old engaged in discussion, rescued him with the admonition not to fraternize with children "from the home." I got the uncomfortable impression that I represented something not high in the order of things—but I was too anxious to get to dinner to worry about it.

One final picture that comes back: the school was on a hill, and from the rear, where the kindergarten windows were, one could see over a great distance. Down below was a Catholic church, and one morning when we were on a stand-up break, the bell of the church started tolling as a funeral cortege entered. The teacher explained to us what was happening when we asked about the bell. As we watched from the window, we all felt duly sad. It was many years before I knew and understood the lethal significance of those very lethal words of John Donne: "Never send to know for whom the bell tolls, it tolls for thee." But whenever I see those lines I think of that scene.

Paterson of the 1920s and '30s formed my life for fourteen years and in a sense does so even today, more than seven decades later. Northern New Jersey is heavy with rivers and lakes, but no spot equals in visual impact that craggy spot in Paterson where the waters of the Passaic River plunge madly downward over the Great Falls. It was a mecca for tourists and honeymooners before the more spectacular Niagara Falls exerted its call. But the Great Falls meant more than spectacular natural beauty to Paterson for they were responsible for the actual founding of the city.

Paterson is an American city in the strictest sense; no creation of English colonization, it did not spring up till after the American Revolution. Alexander Hamilton, the first Secretary of the Treasury, urged the Congress to assure the new nation's independence. Promoting domestic industry would prevent another country from aggrandizing itself at American expense by withholding necessary manufactured goods. With this in mind he organized in 1791 the Society for Useful Manufacturers to build for the first time, a group of American factories. The waterfalls on the Passaic River were chosen as "the best situation in the world" for this venture, and the Society purchased seven hundred acres at that spot, naming the future city for the New Jersey governor who chartered the Society. The city was to play a crucial role in the history of American industrial development. This Society was a sort of forerunner of the quasi-public development corporations and authorities of later days.

In the nineteenth century, Paterson became an immense manufacturing city with cotton mills, locomotive factories, and above all, silk mills. By 1900 it was the fifteenth largest city in the United States with a population of 105,000, 40,000 of whom were foreign-born workers from almost every country in Europe.

Soon after, however, came an industrial turning downward, beginning with the closing of the locomotive factories. The silk industry though remained vigorous, and Paterson was known alternately as the "Silk City" or the "Lyons of America." But in February 1913, there came a dramatic turning point: the Great Paterson Silk Strike. The greatest textile strike in American history, it was brought on by years of smoldering resentment over low wages and miserable working conditions.

The strike involved 25,000 workers and was viciously repressed. It became the stuff of legend and the most famous leaders of the International Workers of the World were there: Big Bill Haywood, Carlo Tresca, Emma Goldman, Eugene Debs, Elizabeth Gurley Flynn. A magazine article at the time began, "There's a war in Paterson." The author was a young writer barely three years out of Harvard, John Reed, who was to become a hero to the labor movement. When I lived in Paterson in the 1920s and '30s there was still a John Reed Club.

The Great Strike lasted five months. Ultimately the strikers were defeated, but it was a pyrrhic victory for the mill owners who now faced bankruptcy. The workers were now destitute. Paterson never fully recovered from the after effects of the strike, although it did have a positive effect for American laborers. Many subsequent judicial decisions interpreting the Bill of Rights on behalf of the laboring sector were brought about by the 1913 Paterson strike.

While the city remained strongly industrial, the silk industry was reduced to such a level that Paterson was no longer known as the "Lyons of America." One new industry that came to Paterson only five years before my own arrival was the Wright Aeronautical Corporation. It became a great success early on with its Wright Cyclone engines of the type used by Lindbergh in his epic 1927 flight. This firm remained in Paterson until after World War II, employing some 47,000 people at its peak.

There is much more to Paterson's history, both industrial and in other ways, than can be covered in a brief sketch. For example, William Carlos Williams in his long poem *Paterson* depicts the richness, complexity, and diversity of American city life as he contrasts the inhuman industrial environment to the natural beauty of the physical landscape. I knew none of this, of course, one November day in 1926 when I left the Home, heading, as it turned out, for life in Paterson itself.

Thursday, November 18, 1926, is like the day of the Taxi—a stellar moment in my memory. The first thing that struck me as different that memorable day was that I was told I would not be going to school. Then after breakfast I was asked to dress "a little more uptown" than on a normal school day. At some point I was told I would be leaving later with my father (whom I had not seen since he had left me in the Home the previous April) to live with a "new family." My belongings, such as they were, were collected in a paper sack.

By late morning my brother Harry, now ten, and I were waiting together in the large front sitting room of the Home. He explained to me that our sister Ruth, now thirteen, had left the previous weekend. About noon my father arrived and there was considerable discussion about which of us would go first. Since Harry had the farther distance to go, it was decided that he would be first.

With some misgivings I watched my father and Harry disappear down the long walkway and steps in front of the building. Harry was headed for a place called Beaver Lake, in northern New Jersey, a stop on the Susquehanna Railroad, one of the three railroads running through Paterson at the time. The father of the family he would be living with was an engineer on that railroad and a friend of my family from the Hawthorne days.

For the time being, I was left to have lunch, to take an enforced nap, and to contemplate my unknown future. As the afternoon wore on I became bored with whatever diversions had been provided, and in any case mightily concerned with where from here. In the late afternoon as dusk began to fall on this cloudy November day, I stood looking out the front window of the Home, nose pressed against the large glass, anxiously watching for any sign of my father's return.

At last, when I could almost no longer see and the lights started coming on, he reappeared. We set out, with the paper sack of belongings clutched in my hand. Down the long steps to Market Street and left about two blocks, turning right on Graham Avenue. We passed a very large, formidable building, identified by my father as the Paterson Armory. On the next block we came into a neighborhood of houses; at the corner was a man on top of a small ladder lighting a gas lamp.

Shortly we turned up some steps to a house marked "415" and my father rang the bell. I was about to be introduced to my fourth living arrangement in the first five years of my life. As the porch light came on and the door opened, I was keen with anticipation. What next?

2. The Convert

Standing in the doorway was an attractive woman in her forties, tall and strong. She seemed to be expecting us, and we were ushered directly into her living room, where we continued to stand. The two adults had a brief conversation, ending when my father passed the strange woman an envelope and then quickly departed. This time he was gone from my life for more than two years; meanwhile, there would be no more envelopes.

Turning to me, the woman surveyed the new arrival and, smiling, told me to call her Aunt Annie. She led me into a large kitchen at the rear of the house. In the middle of the room was a long oak table set for eight. Aunt Annie ran a boarding house.

As she completed dinner preparations, she kept up a running commentary, telling me about the boarders while she sized up her new arrival. My only comment was, "I like you"—a fortuitous reflection that a pleased Aunt Annie often quoted to her friends. The Home had apparently developed some basic survival techniques in its graduate.

In her commentary Aunt Annie explained that all but one of her boarders worked in the silk mills, and though they finished work at five, the walk to Graham Avenue took about half an hour. One of them was a Johnny Bustard, with whom she said I would share a bedroom in the attic. She told me that most of the boarders had been "doughboys." From school discussions and pictures, this conjured up soldiers going "over the top" in France. The Great War had ended only eight years before.

The men soon began arriving. I noticed that, except for one, they were in their twenties or early thirties, quite old to a five-year-old. One was even older, about Aunt Annie's age, and dressed like a businessman. He was introduced as Ed Ridler, and his occupation was undertaker. In time he and Johnny Bustard were, in their own ways, to become close to me and, in the two years that were left to Ed, they became surrogate fathers.

The group was talkative and friendly, and as we sat down to dinner I found my place at the end of the table, noticing that the seat to my left was unoccupied. The group opined that the missing boarder had probably stopped for more than "one for the road" on the way home. Aunt Annie did not appear amused at the explanation.

Being new and more than two decades younger than any of the other boarders, I naturally received attention, comments, and jibes, the latter occasionally terminated by Aunt Annie, who ran a tight ship. All of this went on without any pause in eating. I made no comment but observed big-eyed, with an occasional smile.

One item that had caught my attention early was a serving of pumpkin pie in front of my plate. While the others were into seconds on the main dishes, I went to dessert without pause. At this point there appeared in the door at the rear of the kitchen the tardy boarder whose seat was next to mine. He was boisterous and staggering. A verbal altercation arose with Aunt Annie and she was on her feet in a moment. Some of the others also stood, all attention riveted on the noisy one.

While this was going on, I had finished my pie, and it was obvious to me that the adjacent seat was not going to be occupied. I eyed the pie in front of the empty plate. Why not? As the altercation reached its peak, I exchanged plates and was into my second piece of pie unnoticed by the others.

By now Aunt Annie, who was unusually strong for a woman, had the offender by the collar and the rear of his pants and literally threw him down the short flight of steps and out the back door, never to be seen by me again. All returned to their meal and began discussing who would get the ejected one's pie.

As the boarders turned toward the presumptive prize, their attention turned to astonishment at the empty plate. Then all eyes shifted to the new boarder who, without comment, was completing his second piece of pie. Chagrin, protest, and then laughter, led by Aunt Annie, ensued. The new boy, age five, a veteran of seven months of competition at the Home's dining room, was accepted into full membership at the boarding house. Not a bad start.

Graham Avenue turned out to be my home for two years, and Aunt Annie quickly became a surrogate mother. She belonged to an extended Irish Catholic family named McCue, though her surname was Murren, all that was left of a divorced husband. I doubt that she had ever gone past the elementary level in school, but she was remarkably good with numbers, especially those involving money. She wrote passably. Businesslike in manner, she was completely in control of her environment. The boarders had better be at dinner on time or else! With me she talked like a strict disciplinarian, but the threatened punishment for getting out of line rarely materialized into action.

Since Public School 15 remained within walking distance, I continued there without interruption the remainder of the kindergarten semester, and subsequently into what was then known as the primary grade, a kind of advanced kindergarten featuring reading and writing. When not at school, I was free to roam so long as I remained on the city block where the boarding house was located. Since the block had only one or two children even close to my age, many of my activities had to be self-generated.

The block was bounded on one side by Park Avenue, up which passed all the parades in Paterson. On Memorial Day there were still soldiers from the Grand Army of the Republic riding in open cars. The Armistice Day Parade, commemorating the end of the Great

War on the eleventh hour of the eleventh day of the eleventh month of 1918, was still staffed with former members of Pershing's AEF, a surprising number of whom still had their uniforms. Besides all the other customary holiday parades, there were many processions on Park Avenue for special occasions such as funerals of local dignitaries—in one memorable case the current mayor.

Another boundary of my free-roaming zone was the Paterson Armory, home of an infantry battalion of the 113th Regiment of the New Jersey National Guard. It was not this aspect of the Armory that interested me, but rather the large-scale special events held there, many lasting up to a week. The one I liked most was the Annual Paterson Food Show with its many display booths containing free samples of edible goods. Unfortunately, unaccompanied five-to seven-year-olds were not permitted past the entrance. After my trips with Aunt Annie and Johnny Bustard, I thus served as guide for any boarder I could talk into attending. Another week-long event was the Annual Car Show, but one trip sufficed on that. Other events that I especially enjoyed were the occasional circuses and the annual Boy Scout Rally of the Paterson Council.

Activity at the boarding house peaked each evening at dinner, the only time everyone was together. There were invariably discussions of the major news events of the day as featured in Paterson's three daily papers or on its radio station, WODA. Routinely covered in the dinner conversation was the fate of the three nearest baseball clubs: the New York Yankees and Giants and the Brooklyn Dodgers. During football season the fortunes of Notre Dame became the central sports topic.

The most dramatic news event of that period was Charles Lindbergh's flight in his monoplane, "The Spirit of St. Louis" from Long Island to Paris's Le Bourget in 1927. Like everyone else in the United States on the night of the twentieth of May when the "Lone Eagle" was still en route, that was all the boarders could talk about. The next day, when he landed, he became their greatest hero, and for many days all other stories were crowded out of the newspapers. On

June 13, the day of New York's tumultuous ticker-tape parade for him, all schools in Paterson closed at noon.

But one matter on which the citizens of Paterson took exception regarding the hero was the "Lucky Lindy" soubriquet given him by the press. The locals felt that he had eliminated the element of luck by powering his plane with a Wright "Whirlwind" engine. The Wright Corporation had been located in Paterson since 1921—as every resident knew well, since each evening at five the factory was allowed to test engines for thirty ear-splitting minutes.

In September the boarding-house regulars conducted many discussions on Gene Tunney's second defeat of Jack Dempsey based on the "long count." They heard the action blow by blow, huddled around Aunt Annie's upright Philco in the living room. The consensus was that Jack was robbed. Later in that September of 1927, the Babe's sixtieth home run of the season took over as the group's favorite topic.

By the early summer of 1928 politics dominated the nightly discussions. Coolidge having announced, "I do not choose to run," the Republicans had nominated Herbert Hoover. This all-Catholic group was solidly behind their fellow Catholic from the sidewalks of New York, Governor Al Smith. While they always favored a Democrat, in this case Smith had even more going for him as a "wet" at a time when the Eighteenth Amendment was still in force. Paterson, with a saloon on almost every downtown block, seemed to be in a legal zone of its own where the Volstead Act had very little relevance (a matter I was to have some personal experience with in a couple of years). Still, one never knew when some new official might decide to take the prohibition law seriously, even in Paterson.

My activities outside of Graham Avenue and school were largely determined by Johnny Bustard. He was related in some way to Annie's sister Rose's husband, and in his thirties at the time I met him. Johnny's education had stopped in elementary school and he was, I think, probably simpleminded as well. He had spent all of his working life as a weaver at the Paterson silk mills, and was a good one. Athletically built (he had played semiprofessional baseball for a few years), short, and wiry, he was already partially bald and definitely not a ladies' man. His enjoyments were walking and fishing expeditions; his indulgences, cigars and, increasingly as he grew older, beer. He was kind and generous to me, and during these years he was my best friend.

Almost every evening after dinner the two of us walked downtown, ending always at his cigar store. En route he usually treated me to an apple or other fruit at an open stand on Market Street. Sometimes I got a sweet at Klaties' delicatessen, usually on Friday, which was payday. The walk also entailed watching trains arrive and depart at the Erie Railroad Station in the center of town. Frequently, we met fellow weavers or other friends who continued the topics of conversation already covered at the dinner table.

Weekends were more interesting and the walks longer. We would go to Eastside Park where we fed the squirrels on previously purchased peanuts—my attempts to sample these in advance being usually frustrated. Longer walks involved following the railroad line of the infrequently used Delaware, Lackawanna, and Western Railroad that skirted Paterson. Sometimes we stopped walking to glance upward toward the distant drone of an airplane, still a novelty in the mid-1920s. On some Sundays we actually traveled on one of these trains to a fishing location for the day.

Occasionally, Johnny would take me to the movies—a real treat. Paterson's best movie house in those days was the newly opened Fabian Theater. Here I saw my first movie, one of the last of the memorable silent films, *Wings*; later, my first talkie, *The Jazz Singer*, starring Al Jolson.

About a month after my arrival at Graham Avenue, Aunt Annie decided that it was time to introduce me to her family. Taking advantage of a preholiday gathering at her sister's, Rose Bustard, the two of us set out one cold Sunday afternoon in mid-December down Market Street. Aunt Annie was decked out in her finest, and I was in a new blue suit with knickers she had bought for me the week before at Konner's—Paterson's finest for grade-school clientele.

En route she told me that Rosie was her oldest sister, who also had a few boarders. Rosie's husband, George, worked in the dye works and I was to refer to him as Uncle and to Rose as Aunt. A younger sister, Fanny, would also be there, as would Rosie's children George and Tootsie, who lived with their mother. Another daughter, Irene, who Aunt Annie implied was a bit uppity, would be there with her husband Walter from a town they lived in called Glen Rock. At this point my head was swimming with names, and I decided the best defense as usual would be the smile.

Just before we arrived at our destination we stopped in front of a large church with a school adjacent to it, which Aunt Annie identified as St. Joseph's. She talked in a way that made me think I would have some affiliation with it in the future. Little did I know! Across the street was Aunt Rosie's home, located on the second floor of a very long three-story building of masonry construction with a large porch at the rear from which we entered the kitchen.

There stood Aunt Rosie, all two hundred pounds of her, who, without warning, grabbed me in an embrace saying, "So you're the boy!" and insisting I meet everyone right then. Since each of these personalities was to play a part in my life from then on, I might anticipate events at this point and describe each as I now recall them rather than what was clear on that confused but exciting day in December 1926.

Aunt Rosie was jolly and a good cook as evidenced by her size, which also meant that she bossed her entourage around from a sitting position. In good weather her command post was the back porch, in other times a side window, and it was from here that she watched all and knew all that went on in the environs of St. Joseph's church and its school yard. No wedding or funeral escaped her notice. One of her culinary specialties was bread making and she so excelled at this that for a time she sold it to others—at one point I became one of her delivery boys. Despite her jolly manner, she was the boss of the manor, and all her siblings, as well as her husband, understood that. Uncle George Bustard was quiet; he apparently used most of his energies at work. He had little to say to me and accepted me as kind of an additional burden acquired by the family.

Mary Frances Bustard, or Tootsie, as I was told to call her, whom

I also met in the kitchen, was warm and friendly like her mother, and we became close friends despite the twenty-eight-year gap in age. At this point she was single, still living at home. During those years she always seemed to be ironing, cooking, or cleaning up the kitchen—though she also enjoyed a good time, including having a "trinkie," as she called it. She seemed amused by me, especially the manner in which I observed the family in action without comment but, at least in her eye, with some amusement mixed with puzzlement.

As Aunt Rosie moved me into the living room, a big boisterous individual, drink in hand, greeted me with a hearty laugh, a "hello, boy!," and a heavy slap on the back. This was Georgie, Aunt Rosie's only son, who was about thirty at this point. Divorced and on the Paterson police force (bad feet, so he rode as guard in the patrol wagon), a braggart, spendthrift, heavy drinker, he was controlled only by mama. For some reason I was wary of him; in response, he tried to impress me by extolling his virtues even more.

The final sibling and the one who would be in my life the longest (close to six decades) eyed me suspiciously. This was Irene, about thirty at this time, and the one Annie considered too uptown (but a person she was cautious with). I answered her few questions about myself while she studied me intently; Aunt Rosie broke in, "Let the boy alone, Irene, and introduce him to Walter."

Walter Nally, also Irish, was Irene's husband. He was about her age and late of the AEF. They had been married after the War in 1921. Walter was a stenographer and office assistant with a firm in New York City and was, Aunt Annie said, doing well. They lived some miles away on their own and kept their distance from Paterson. I liked Walter immediately and he seemed unusually interested in me.

Sitting by herself was the younger sister, Fanny, also divorced like Annie and also in her forties. She asked me to sit next to her, and as the others went back to their own concerns we talked together. I found out later that Fanny was also an excellent cook and had run a boarding house, but was now tied up with a Frank McAndrews, who owned a saloon farther down Market Street. They lived over this establishment, but she talked about a summer house she rented at a place called Lake Hopatcong and indicated I should come to see her there next summer. This confused me a bit, since I had no idea where I would be next summer—but, rather that going into that, I said that this would be fun.

It was now time for dinner at two big tables at which Tootsie, with some help from Irene, was serving the food. Aunt Rosie was busy with directions to everyone on where to sit. At this point a new personality appeared—Jimmy Owens, one of Rosie's boarders and the only one allowed to eat with the family on special occasions. What was unique about Jimmy—who also worked in the dye house—was his ownership of a car. This made him the one-eyed man in the land of the blind, since no one else was in that category. He was, in fact, Aunt Rosie's chauffeur. She liked to travel a bit, but understandably did not like walking.

The others made passing reference to Aunt Annie's other sibling, Andrew McCue. A successful tobacconist with his own firm and trucks, he lived on the more fashionable east side of Paterson and rarely saw the others. His daughter Claire was still in her teens and was away at a boarding school somewhere. That family was discussed in terms of distant deities—but with the intermittent irreverence that working-class Irish reserve for those who "put on airs."

After dinner, the group sang "My Wild Irish Rose," "Let Me Call You Sweetheart," and their other favorites accompanied by a bit of drinking and good fellowship. Then it was time to leave, and Aunt Annie and I headed back up Market Street under the street lamps. She mentioned that everyone liked me, which made me happy, but I was a bit puzzled. The question in my mind was, would I ever see this group again? I had no way of knowing that I had de facto become part of an extended Irish family that would guide my fortunes for the next fourteen years.

The first Christmas of which I was conscious was soon upon us. It came not only with a Christmas tree but also—to my surprise since I didn't know anything about Christmas—many small gifts from Annie, Johnny, Ed, and even Aunt Rosie and Tootsie. Understandably, they saw the need to expand on the clothing supply I had arrived with held in my single paper sack.

On that Christmas Day there was one other event whose significance escaped me at the time. I accompanied Aunt Annie to my first religious service—Mass at St. Joseph's. It seemed very spectacular, but of course I had no idea what was going on. As I studied the church, two things particularly puzzled me: the Stations of the Cross fastened to the walls and the confessional booths. Aunt Annie, in response to my queries, said that would all be explained to me later; by whom was not clear.

The winter/spring of 1927 was unremarkable to the extent that somewhere in that period I assumed that my living arrangements were permanent, especially since my own family had dropped out of sight. My shift in school from kindergarten to a reading curriculum was good for me, as I soon had a constant companion on lonely days—books. This was especially true after I was introduced to the Danforth public library. This elegant marble edifice, built in 1905 and still standing, was designed by the architect Henry Bacon, who later designed the Lincoln Memorial. Of main interest to this young reader was its very large and complete children's section.

School ended as June faded, and I lost my school friends, none of whom lived on the city block that was my roaming zone. I then especially looked forward to walks and occasional fishing expeditions with Johnny and Ed on evenings and weekends. I also anticipated more the early evening discussions at the boarding house table. The group was particularly incensed that summer (along with such notables as John Dos Passos, Dorothy Parker, Walter Lippmann, and H.G. Wells) with the approaching execution of Sacco and Vanzetti. Ed Ridler, more intelligent and articulate than the others, was especially worked up. I can recall his reciting on the day of the execution the words Vanzetti spoke after his sentencing by the Boston Brahmin Judge Webster Thayer. Some years later I looked them up: "That last moment belongs to us—that agony is our triumph." He was right.

Midsummer brought an exciting diversion. After much preparation Aunt Annie and I headed off via the Erie Railroad, Hudson

River Ferry, taxi, and Long Island Railroad to Rockaway Beach, then known as the Irish Riviera. There we were ensconced right on the shore at a tourist home for a week. I spent the days on the beach directly in front of our location, where a constantly changing group of boys and girls frolicked. From that summer there remains only one tangible souvenir: a picture an itinerant photographer took of me sitting on his pony in front of Annie's house. The pony looks much more at ease than I.

When the new school year began in September of 1927, everything seemed as before. With the same group of children reassembling, I felt comfortable, and there were only a few differences in routine—assemblies with the big children, an exercise period, and so on. The big change in my life came in early October.

On the first weekend of that month, Aunt Annie informed me that after dinner on Tuesday we would be going to St. Joseph's church, where I would be baptized; I would then be a Catholic. Aunt Fanny and Frank McAndrews were to be my sponsors. None of this made a great impression on this now-six-year-old. On the appointed evening, all dressed up, we proceeded down Market Street to the church rectory and met one of the priests. He was introduced as Father Gardner, and after some head patting on his part the sponsors arrived.

As the paperwork was being done, Father Gardner paused. Douglas, he stated, was not the name of a saint; thus I would have to be given another name. Much discussion ensued. Finally Frank asked the priest what his first name was. It was Leo. This seemed serviceable to the others, so henceforth my name would be Leo Douglas Kinnard. Although the others agreed, I was a bit uncomfortable since I had not been consulted. As the Bard himself said, "What's in a name?" If the choice is between Leo and Douglas the answer, I discovered, is everything. But it was half a lifetime before I got around to reclaiming my original name.

Soon the water and hands were laid on: "I baptize thee in the name of . . . ." Many congratulations to the new convert, as they referred to me. Whatever the merits of becoming a Church member, I could as my understanding of the language grew—think of many more precise words than conversion to describe how I arrived at my new religion, such as Catholicism by assimilation.

The stage was now set for a major change. Within a few days of the baptism Aunt Annie announced that I would soon be leaving the public school and would enroll at St. Joseph's, now that I was a Catholic. Action followed pronouncement, and on Monday, October 17, Aunt Annie accompanied me to School 15 to arrange the transfer. From there we set out across Sandy Hill Park to St. Joseph's Grammar School and the principal's office.

Greeting us as we entered was Sister Mary Arilda, the principal. I can still see her standing there, more holy-looking than human. Dressed like all the Sisters of Charity (the order that had run this school since its doors were opened in 1875), a black robe covered her mortal body, and white starched linen hid her hair. She and Aunt Annie exchanged brief greetings—and then Sister looked at me and said, "So you're Leo Kinnard." After studying me briefly, she told me to come with her and she would take me to the first grade to meet my teacher.

Apprehension, curiosity, and acceptance of the inevitability of more change were blended together in my mind as we walked to the first-grade classroom. When we got there, Sister Catherine Pierre appeared at the door while fifty pairs of eyes behind her strained to survey this late arrival in the school year.

3. St. Joe's

Sister Catherine introduced me to the roomful of owls and pointed toward an empty desk while handing me a book they had been reading. To my surprise I found it to be the one we had just completed at PS 15 At this point I became an owl myself.

As the period progressed, she covered the litany of names I was soon to get to know, calling on each in turn to read—Agnew... Farrell... McGuinness... O'Brien, and so on. Toward the end of the period she turned to me and asked if I would like to try. With all eyes—and occasional snickers—directed at the new boy, I read the next passage unassisted. When I finished, Sister said, "You've read this before." I reluctantly agreed; thus ended my only intellectual triumph that year.

St. Joseph's, better known as St. Joe's, was part of the most ambitious private system of education ever assembled in America, a nationwide network of brick, mortar, and nuns. In greater Paterson alone, there were at least ten Catholic schools. The oldest of this group, the chief rival of my new school, was St. John's at the center of the city. St. Joseph's parish covered those living on the slightly more affluent eastside of Paterson.

St. Joe's opened in 1875 with the Sisters of Charity in charge.

From a rented building it progressed to its own structure by 1888. The great Paterson fire of February 1902 destroyed the school and church, but within seven months there was a new building that expanded over the years. By the time I entered in 1927, the parish had built its own high school on the front of the building. Across the school yard were the convent and a very large, attractive church.

The students were mainly descendants of immigrants from the British Isles, with some from Italy and other Western European countries. Depending on the area, other Catholic schools had their own ethnic groupings; for example, the Italians at St. Anthony's. The families in St. Joseph's parish were mostly middle class. In my own class of 1935 there were daughters of two successive mayors of Paterson, besides children of a furniture store owner, car dealer, and funeral director. There were also a fair number of fathers who commuted to office jobs in New York City.

As I soon discovered, religion was central to the school's mission. The day started and ended with prayers, and the first period was always Christian Doctrine, which in the lower classes meant memorization of the Catechism. Q. Why did God make me? A. To know him, love him, and serve him in this world and to be happy with him in the next. Sister Catherine and her successors discussed with us each question and its many ramifications. Sometimes these discussions became rather farfetched. I recall a lengthy one on how a baptism could be handled on a desert if there was no water. It seemed to me that if one were on a desert without water, there might be some more immediate concerns.

Moderately stern in manner, Sister Catherine projected an image quite different from that of my public-school teachers. One of her techniques was to use a clicker, a low-tech, handheld instrument to clue the class's precise genuflection when we prayed in church. And during my first days in class I could not help but focus on the strange movement of her right hand as she monitored our individual work. From her black cincture dangled rosary beads that her fingers rotated while she silently said Hail Marys and other prayers until reaching the crucifix, which she held before releasing. Soon, if she was not about to lecture to the class, the ritual began all over again. Another item I noticed were the letters AMDG in gold atop the middle blackboard. On querying, I was told that these were the Latin initials for "All for the Honor and Glory of God," which appeared in all the classrooms. In a couple of years we began to translate this irreverently as "Aunt Maggie Drinks Gin."

Occasionally, as connected with some event in the church year, one of the priests would visit the class. Perhaps once in the school year the pastor, Father McDonald, came. Before these visits we sat nervously and silently, but maybe whispering a little as the moment approached. The purpose of the visit was presumably to get us fired up for some period of sacrifice or extra effort ahead, like the four weeks of Advent before Christmas or the forty days of Lent preceding Easter.

Christmastime meant, besides church services and visits to the crib, a bit of Santa at a school assembly. This celebration, though low-key by today's standards, was something to look forward to in the late 1920s and early 1930s. There was no actual auditorium but rather an open room in which chairs were constantly put up or taken down according to the event. On Thursday afternoons, for instance, Mr. McGinnis, the choir director and organist, sat behind a grand piano that had seen better days and directed our rehearsal for Sunday's hymns. McGinnis, a rather florid white-haired fellow who imbibed on the side, had numerous hideouts in the organ loft and the school basement. He was nice enough when sober—a condition that became rarer as the years went by.

The Christmas party would take place about 10:30 on the last day before the school vacation, which for some reason always began at noon (11:45). After the usual lower-class recitals, we all sang. Soon Santa appeared, and it was not until years later that I realized that simultaneously McGinnis had disappeared. The old reprobate was probably Santa—for once able to reel about and chuckle without anyone's knowing he was tight. He had one other advantage; not much padding was required.

The high point was the presentation to each of us of a small box of hard Christmas candy from the friendly Loft (Candy Company) people. I now see that it was good advertising and, of course, a tax writeoff. Cynicism aside, I know that it was still fun, and even today when I see a box of Loft's candy I think of a little boy clutching a box of hard Christmas candies all the way home in the Paterson of the late 1920s.

About two months later came the painstaking Lenten preparation. In Catechism the various possibilities of the hereafter were emphasized—Purgatory, Heaven, Hell, and Limbo with special attention on achieving the first two and avoiding the third. Apparently, our group had already avoided the Limbo possibility by being baptized. The culmination of Lenten preparation was Holy Week, requiring daily attendance at Mass, and then time off for celebrating Easter.

The month of May was dedicated to the Blessed Virgin Mary. On the first day of May we wrote down our petitions to Mary, sealed them in an envelope, and placed them in front of her statue in the classroom. Throughout the month there was discussion of Mary's role, and toward the end of May the petitions were transferred to the feet of a large statue of Mary in the school yard. On the last great day of the month we formed a procession—the girls in white and the boys in blue serge—for a ceremony conducted by the pastor. At the conclusion the petitions were burned while we all sang, "O Mary, we crown thee with blossoms today, Queen of the angels, Queen of the May."

The final religious events of this first year took place in June, leading up to our first confession and first Holy Communion. Instruction in early June focused mostly on confession and the various ways the commandments could be broken; on the degrees of sin—venial and mortal; and how confession confers forgiveness. We approached that event nervously and, once alone in the confessional with the priest, began, "Bless me, Father, for I have sinned; this is my first confession." Then came the recital of sins a six-year-old could commit—whatever they were. Next day was our procession into church for first Holy Communion. I still have a photograph taken that day (June 20, 1928) by Leo Studio on Main Street in Paterson. I am wearing a blue serge suit with knickers, a high collar with large white tie, a ribbon on my arm, and a boutonniere. In my left hand are rosary beads.

I have emphasized the school's religious instruction because it is what I recall of that year—and what had the most significant effect on my later life. We did, of course, learn other subjects, similar to those in my public-school experience. The difference was stricter discipline and more individual attention, actually more than we wanted.

During my first year at St. Joe's, life continued in the established pattern at Graham Avenue, but with some minor variations. Because the school was near Aunt Rosie's home I usually went there for lunch, a high point of my day. She and Tootsie were good cooks who kept up a running, frequently humorous dialogue. They also subscribed to New York papers with different comic strips. On days when Georgie was in attendance he tended to monopolize the conversation. At the height of his bombasts Tootsie and I would exchange glances and occasional smiles.

Another aspect of my new routine, now that I was a Catholic, was my required attendance at Mass on Sundays and holydays. This called my attention to an interesting anomaly; no one else at either Annie's or Rosie's attended Mass except on special occasions like Christmas and Easter, although all professed to be strong Catholics. In class Sister Catherine emphasized that not attending Sunday Mass was a mortal sin. The fires of Hell that awaited seemed to hold no terror for either Aunt Annie or Aunt Rosie.

The summer of 1928 opened up a new possibility for adventure. About an hour's drive from Paterson are the gently rolling Ramapo Mountains and, nestled into the many valleys, numerous lakes. Here perhaps 20 percent of Paterson's population spent part of the summer. The largest lake, Hopatcong, was famous for its boating and swimming; it even had its own amusement park, Bertram's Island.

The lake's shoreline of about forty-five miles contained many small settlements, including one called Sperry Springs. Here Aunt

Fanny and Frank McAndrews rented a two-story cottage from a Mr. Sutton, owner of the area's one general store. Though the cottage had a sink and a small stove, it lacked indoor plumbing in the usual meaning of the term. As the alternative severely tested my somewhat fragile stomach, I frequently became acquainted with the flora and fauna nearby until someone noticed my routine disappearances into the woods.

The cottage was sparsely furnished, but Frank had brought along an old upright wind-up record player and many of his records that covered the World War I period up to the present. I played some records over and over; those I remember at this remove are "Over There"; "Oh, How I Hate to Get Up in the Morning"; "My Buddy"; "April Showers"; and one new title I never heard again: "I Love to Dunk a Hunk of Sponge Cake."

Besides members of the extended family who came and went, there were other guests of Aunt Fanny's. That first summer the Flaherty family, right out of an Evelyn Waugh satire, came to Hopatcong. The family had no boys, just three girls, the youngest of whom was my age. The eldest sister decided that she would introduce me to a new activity, which I did not fully understand and for which my libido was not yet adequately developed. I had a vague feeling that I had violated the Sixth Commandment as Sister Catherine had explained it, but decided not to pursue the matter until later in confession—which time never came.

My stay that summer was only two or three weeks; too soon I was back on Graham Avenue, getting ready for the second grade. The discussions at dinner now centered on the Hoover-Smith presidential campaign, with frequently expressed doubts that Al Smith could be elected, not because of his stand on Prohibition repeal but because he was a Catholic.

Soon after my return home—and definitely by the time school started in September—I was aware of a subtle shift in the tone of the boarding house. When two of the boarders left—one to be married and another to return to his home in New England—they were not replaced. There was talk of a move to the second floor of a building on the corner of Graham Avenue and Market Street. This materialized in early November, with another boarder lost in the process.

Instinctively, I did not like the new location, but the worst news was that it would no longer be necessary for me to go to Aunt Rosie's at noontime. I would now have lunch at home, since the new location was at the end of one long city block that encompassed St. Joe's and involved no crossing of streets. My last lunch at Aunt Rosie's was in the gloomy atmosphere of a day or two after the 1928 presidential election. The man in the brown derby had put up a valiant fight, but his opponent, Herbert Hoover, received about 60 percent of the popular vote with his promise that "we shall soon be in sight of the day when poverty will be banished from this nation," presumably during his tenure.

Walks with Johnny and Ed continued as before, but now there appeared a new personality, Bob Marion, a friend of Aunt Annie's. For some reason I did not like him and sensed that the feeling was mutual. In early December Ed became ill; he was so tired that I had to go rouse him for dinner. Then on the 11th the doctor arrived and Ed took to bed with, I was told, pneumonia. I was no longer allowed in his room. On Sunday morning the 16th the doctor was called; Ed was in extremis and by midday he was dead at age forty-nine.

Johnny was immediately charged with taking me on a long walk. Even though it was December, we were out at least three hours, much of the time along the railroad tracks of the Lackawanna. When we returned, Annie was standing in the living room with the undertaker, a Mr. Blauvelt. Ed, lying very quietly on a cot while awaiting the casket, was embalmed and dressed for the final journey. It was my first experience with the American way of death. I was both shocked and saddened at the loss of one of my best friends. What followed at the boarding house was to be even more traumatic.

Soon after the funeral Aunt Annie began acting oddly. Bottles with Gordons Dry Gin labels began to show up in the house. Bob Marion's appearances became routine; frequently, he and Aunt Annie would go out to a nearby Market Street saloon. One day, when Johnny had a fight with him, Johnny was banished. Where he went was not announced.

Meals became irregular, and the remaining boarders left. There would be no real Christmas that year. For the holidays Aunt Annie and I went to Haledon, a countrylike suburb of Paterson, where we stayed with some people who ran a nearby tavern—a place where Aunt Annie spent a good deal of her time.

When we returned to Paterson in time for school, life was strange. I recall a couple of weekends in a bar owner's apartment over his bar and my giving a lecture from a bar stool to a couple of astonished beer drinkers on a seven-year-old's version of the meaning of the unknown. Fortunately, it was not recorded.

Somehow life went on, though it was lonely outside of school, and a new boarder even appeared for a short while. One day in February, perhaps a Sunday afternoon, I was alone in the house. As I glanced out the window and saw Bob Marion approaching the rear entrance, I became panicky. Retreating to the living room I hid in a narrow space between the fireplace and the wall. In a minute he was wandering around the house, searching, I assumed, for the absent Annie. Suddenly, as I peered out, he was heading across the room with a malevolent look that I will never forget. Was he heading for me or for the exit? I did not know. Luckily, he did not see me, I assume, and left without a word.

I was still alone that evening and sitting in the kitchen when I heard someone on the steps. As it was too late to hide, I was petrified. The door opened and I saw a little gnomelike lady I remembered meeting at Aunt Rosie's once or twice at lunch. It was Mrs. Lappin, who "told fortunes" by reading tea leaves. She sensed or knew about the neglect, and soon I was pouring out the details of the situation. She took me to a nearby grocery, where she brought me some bread, ham, and fruit, and we returned home. Before she left, she told me not to be afraid, but I still was.

A few days later was Ash Wednesday. Sister Alice Ucarry, my second-grade teacher, had warned us about not eating meat that day. When I went home to lunch, no one was there. I had some bread and then eyed the last piece of ham. The present dilemma was more pressing than future fires; down went the ham.

I walked slowly back to school with vague feelings of guilt. No sooner had the afternoon class gotten underway than Sister Mary Arilda, the principal, was at the classroom door. I was told to go with her. Surely, I thought, I would not be punished so soon for the meat. And how could she know, anyway? Silently we walked to her office. Standing there was my father, whom I had last seen twenty-seven months before. "You are to go with your father," Sister said. We headed toward the front door without a word. Now what? I did not want to go back to Aunt Annie's; on the other hand, I did not want to go with my father. Mostly, I did not want to leave my school, which at this point was the only anchor left in my life.

4. The Green Years

As we exited the school, my father cleared up my questions—at least for the moment. Pointing at Aunt Rosie's house, he said, "We are going over there, and you will be living with Mrs. Bustard for now." What a relief! In a few minutes we were in the kitchen with Aunt Rosie and Tootsie; and, as soon as my father left, both threw their arms around me.

"Look at that boy," Aunt Rosie exclaimed. "He needs a haircut and clean clothes." Had I had lunch? After much clucking over my having eaten ham on Ash Wednesday, I was given a hearty meal. Then came the explanations for my new location—Rosie and Fanny had been behind the shift and Mrs. Lappin was sent as a scout to Aunt Annie's; it was her report that initiated the aunt's call to my father.

By the end of lunch I had all the details of the new arrangement. As Johnny Bustard was already boarding there, he and I would share an attic room in a house across the school yard owned and occupied by the Shannon sisters. My meals would be at Aunt Rosie's, and that would be my home, except for sleeping, until the end of the school year. After that I would live with Aunt Fanny.

Tootsie concocted a plan whereby Johnny would retrieve my

clothes from Aunt Annie's, surreptitiously if possible. Action followed plan, and by that evening I joined Johnny at the Shannons'. The sisters' home was an attractive red brick building directly opposite the church. On the first floor they ran a kind of elegant dress shop. An open stairway to the second floor led to their living area, which they shared with their brother. The third floor belonged to Johnny and me.

The arrangements were very convenient not only to church and school but also to Sandy Hill Park across the street. Next to the park was Lessig's candy store, a new temptation held in abeyance only by a lack of funds. Also down the street was a small grocery store where several newspapers on a rack in front kept passersby informed of major events of the day. The owner was a Syrian named by Aunt Rosie and known afterward as Dirty Face Charlie, in part because he seemed always to need a shave.

Immediately next to the building in which Aunt Rosie lived on Market Street stood a slightly lower one with a very impressive exterior. The word STUDIO was carved just over the first floor. One day, as Johnny and I walked by, I asked him what was there. He told me that it was now the Italian-American Club, but that before the War it had been the studio of a famous sculptor, Gaetano Federici. Johnny reminded me that the family I had met in the flat below Aunt Rosie's was named Federici; the father, Tony, was the sculptor's brother.

Later I was fortunate enough to meet the sculptor, who was indeed famous in the Paterson area. He had come to the United States from Italy as a child in 1887 and after apprenticeships with some of New York's most eminent sculptors, he had established himself as Paterson's "master artist" and resident sculptor. By the time of his death in 1964 the Paterson vicinity contained, and still does, some forty monuments that he executed.

Federici's works contributed in no small way to Paterson's need for civic myth making as a complex and volatile American city with its interplay of ethnic, religious, and political groups. Besides depicting local notables who had built up Paterson, Federici also made several hundred smaller works that made him something of a local icon.

One that I saw frequently was a large altarpiece of the Last Supper in St. Joseph's Church.

The four months at Aunt Rosie's were pleasant and fun. I was now totally assimilated into the extended family and, in effect, under the protection of the "Irish Mafia." Even Uncle George had an occasional smile for me, perhaps out of inevitability. Soon, though, it was time to move in with Aunt Fanny, my sixth living arrangement in my first seven years. Though no one foresaw it at the time, this arrangement was to last over nine years. Fanny and Frank McAndrews had relocated their saloon, over which they lived, to a small building on Straight Street just off Market and a few blocks from Aunt Rosie. I arrived there in June 1929, this time without Johnny.

Life at 278 Straight Street was different. The two-floor apartment over the saloon provided plenty of room; and Aunt Fanny's furniture, in which she took great pride, was impressive compared to her sisters'. She was also, when she cared to be, an excellent cook. As for the bottom floor, on the first day I was told the rules: when the saloon was closed and Sparky the bartender was cleaning up, I could read the papers there but could not play the slot machines. Other times, stay out. (In most other cities a saloon would, because of the Volstead Act, be a speakeasy type, but in Paterson the law was generally ignored, and saloons were the same as other stores.)

Frank was a quiet individual; indeed, for a saloon keeper a bit aloof. Like Uncle George he accepted me as a given, but I was never close to him. During his World War I service in the AEF he had taken in a touch of gas and required frequent trips to a veterans hospital elsewhere in New Jersey. Frank was intelligent and, I suspect, a good businessman. I can still recall two of the titles on his bookshelf: that greatest of all World War I novels, *All Quiet on the Western Front*, and Richard Halliburton's *The Royal Road to Romance*.

Aunt Fanny, who retained the last name of a former husband, "McNally," had—like Rosie and Annie—run a boarding house before becoming involved with Frank. She, too, had a quiet manner but showed affection to me. What I did not know for a couple of years was that Aunt Fanny could neither read nor write.

Almost as soon as I moved in with her, she introduced me to the Gallaghers, a nearby family who lived in a large second-floor flat up a long cobblestone alley facing Market Street. Conveniently for Mr. Gallagher, who was a conductor on the Erie Railroad, they were only one block away from the Paterson railroad station. Mrs. Gallagher was friendly, voluble, and a good cook. There were four children: Jim, the elder brother; George, my age; and two sisters. I was rapidly accepted as one of the family—like, say a cousin. Jim and Georgie soon took me on my first forays into downtown Paterson not sponsored by an adult. Some were old locations, but Jim provided new insights and perspectives, merging fact and fiction rather well.

About once a week Mr. Gallagher took us on an early evening ride in his open Model T. Usually this was to one of the areas surrounding Paterson, such as Clifton, in those days largely undeveloped. What they did contain were large truck farms which in season provided vegetables and fruits to the metropolitan area including northern New Jersey and New York City.

Before I was fully settled into the new environment, we were off to Sperry Springs for the summer, chauffeured there by Jimmy Owens on temporary loan from Aunt Rosie. Allowed to bring one of the Gallagher boys for the first two weeks, I chose Georgie (also called Red). Summer brought the usual extended family; Walter and Irene were my favorites since I could always count on an outing in their car. It was the beginning of a lifelong friendship, ending only with their deaths late in the century.

A new activity I discovered nearby was a small boxing camp where it was exciting to watch teenage future Golden Glovers mix it up. One day the owner, a friendly type, asked Georgie and me if we would like to have a go at it. Red got the better of it until the owner gave me a few tips on leading with my left and keeping my right in a threatening position for occasional use. After that I held my own.

Another event new to me was the weekly visit by canoe of the Boy Scouts from Camp Altaha to take on the Sperry Springs Nine in baseball. The camp, operated by the Paterson Boy Scout Council, was reachable by canoe in about thirty minutes. I looked forward to their visits almost as much as Mr. Sutton did. He owned the only outlet for snacks and soft drinks, mainly Moxie and Birch Beer.

When school opened in September, a bit of Irish logic deemed me still within St. Joe's borders. The walk was a bit longer, but compensated for by passing Lessig's candy store and Dirty Face Charlie's, where I became an expert in current events by a free study of the headlines. Lunch was at Aunt Rosie's.

Life on Straight Street was different in other ways from that on Graham Avenue. When Frank was there, we frequently dined out for dinner at one of the many ethnic restaurants in Paterson, especially at Fanny and Frank's favorite German or Italian places. Most of their evenings were spent in the saloon, so I was left upstairs to my own devices or, on non-school nights, at the Gallaghers'. On some evenings I read at home, the beginning of a lifelong habit.

Saturdays during school months meant the Jim Gallagher-led forays into town, almost always ending at one of the movie theaters. By 1929 Paterson had no less than eight downtown, nine if you counted the off-limits Orpheum, a burlesque house. Early on, these trips took us to the Grand and the Dalley, as the price tag was only five cents. Since the movies were silent, piano players provided the background music. Sometimes the pianist livened up one of the frequent westerns by bringing down a fly swatter on a stack of papers when the screen depicted pistol shots. One of the Grand's silent movies in 1929 made a permanent impression on me: *Ten Days That Shook the World*, based on John Reed's book of the same title. Reed, by then deceased and buried in the Kremlin wall, was still something of a local folk hero for his role in the great Paterson silk strike of 1913.

When I attended movies with adults, we went up the scale of the local theaters, which by then were moving into talkies. Frank took me one Sunday in 1930 to *All Quiet on the Western Front*, based on Erich Maria Remarque's great novel. Watching the extraordinary performance of Lew Ayres, I was caught up in the emotion of this movie, which was shown at Paterson's premier theater, the Fabian. Opened in 1925 it was opulent by the standards of the day with boxes, a mezzanine in front of the balcony, and a very high-ceilinged auditorium. During the 1930s I saw many exciting movies at the Fabian. An added attraction on weekends and holidays was an organ that came up out of the floor during intermissions while the organist entertained from a versatile repertoire.

On a Sunday in late September of 1929 I was introduced to my first Democratic Party activity via Duffy's Outing, an annual event held in Idlewild Park on the banks of the Passaic River in West Paterson. Reaching the park by trolley, the faithful gathered from about noon until well after dark. Besides eating, drinking, and dancing (needless to say, the Volstead Act was not operative there), the event featured free merry-go-round rides and other activities for the young. Since it came about six weeks before elections, the outing was a good opportunity for lining up local Democrats for electioneering chores. In all, I attended about seven years in a row, but I never did find out who Duffy was.

That same fall of 1929 began what was to be one of the most profoundly disturbing events of the twentieth century—the Great Depression. On Thursday, October 24, the stock market collapsed, and thousands of Americans were immediately wiped out. As an eight-year-old I did not at first understand what was happening, but like everyone else I would soon feel its impact. Frank McAndrews owned some stock but not enough to affect our life directly; the secondary effects took a while to develop.

The Depression marked the end of the roaring twenties and the beginning of the two major crises that my generation was to face. The other, was of course, that watershed of the twentieth century, the Second World War, which merged with the end of the Depression. The Depression did not reach its most acute phase until 1931-1932. By then American industry was operating at half of its 1929 maximum, and one out of four workers was unemployed. A minor diversion distracted people from the sadness of the Depression. The boom started in Florida in the winter of 1929-1930 and by spring had spread north to New Jersey: miniature golf. In May a course appeared in an empty lot almost directly across Straight Street from the saloon; by June it was attracting crowds, particularly in the evenings.

The game was rather simple. You knocked a golf ball along an artificial greensward through little holes in wooden barriers, over bridges, and through pipes. Jim Gallagher soon hit on the idea of our getting tips as caddies for "older" (say, 35) people, especially women. This was absurd from a utilitarian viewpoint, as the job consisted only of picking up the player's ball when finally maneuvered into each hole and of keeping score—it was a form of dole. But I soon discovered that the size of the tip was proportionate to my ability to keep the player both pumped up and amused. I often made thirty or forty cents an evening—not bad for an eight-year-old in Depression days. This career ended, however, in July when we headed up to Sperry Springs for, as it turned out, the last summer that Aunt Fanny could afford a cottage.

In the fall of 1930 came the slow reentry of my own family into my life. There were one or two visits from my father with the gift of a few books. More significant was the contact made by my sister Daisy, whom I did not remember. Eighteen years older than I, she was by nature an activist. She was employed by an insurance company and was soon to be married to Steve Evinger, who owned a car. Their mobility provided me with a trip to Morristown to see another of my sisters and an older brother.

Later, that same car took me on a trip that really pleased me—to Beaver Lake. There I got to spend the weekend with my brother Harry, whom I had not seen since the day we had left the Home four years earlier. All this family reemergence brought about some primitive letter writing on my part. (Thanks to Daisy, I still have the originals from the fall of 1930, signed Duglas.)

While I enjoyed seeing my family, things were not the same. I had been separated from them when I was so young that I did not identify with them nor have any desire to live with them. I had bonded with an extended Irish family and was by now a de facto member. I had my school and my friends and had no wish to change anything—nor, apparently, did anyone else.

During those years epidemics of polio (infantile paralysis) spread fear and anxiety throughout the country as they had for the two previous decades. In the summer of 1930 Paterson had an unprecedented number of cases, involving many deaths or permanent paralysis in some part of the body. There was no cure so the safest precaution seemed to be to avoid those locations where there might be carriers of the disease. To that end movies were avoided, swimming pools closed, and school openings delayed in Paterson for most of September that year.

When my fourth grade finally did sit at the end of September, there were two changes. Our original class had grown too large—to about sixty—and was thus split in half; it remained that way throughout my grammar school years. For a nine-year-old the extra attention by the teacher was at first uncomfortable; I could not hide if, for example, I had not done my homework. In time, though, the closer rapport of the group and the increased opportunity to express opinions in class more than compensated.

The second change was at first not evident. Our teacher, Sister Edward Paula from the novitiate, was only about nineteen. I felt very much at home with her—I had not with her predecessors—and apparently she did with me. It was my only experience at St. Joe's as a nun's favorite, almost like her younger brother. There were disadvantages, of course, like the extra chores assigned me and the ragging of my classmates. Still, it was such an unusual experience for me that I never forgot it, particularly my 90s average, achieved only one other year in grammar school. Sister Edward Paula remained at St. Joe's one more year and I never saw her again after that. She spent her life as a teaching nun in other New Jersey schools until her retirement in 1985 when she was seventy-four.

However good school was that year, the shadow of the Depression was beginning to be visible even to nine-year-olds. Grown men, who a year before had commuted daily to New York, were selling apples on street corners. Adults were becoming cynical about the system, and pronouncements of the leadership were no help. Former President Coolidge was credited with a truism that drew guffaws: "The final solution of unemployment is work." To a prophecy made by President Hoover, "Prosperity is just around the corner," the query came: "Yeah, but what corner?"

For Aunt Fanny, too, things were starting to tighten. Frank McAndrews was increasingly ill and absent for treatment; business was down and by 1931 a move from Straight Street was inevitable. A new general post office was to be built on a large area that included the lot occupied by the saloon. One change among a wave of belt-tightening measures was that there would be no Lake Hopatcong the following summer. On that score, though, luck intervened for me—surprisingly at my school.

St. Joe's had a city nurse who occupied a large room in the school basement; there students received such things as vaccinations and first aid. I served that year as sort of an occasional messenger between Sister Edward and the nurse, Mrs. Van Houten. On one of my visits in midwinter she was tacking up a poster featuring young campers on a hike and in big letters the name Camp Christmas Seal. When this caught my eye, I queried Mrs. Van Houten, who filled me in.

About five years before, the Paterson Tuberculosis League had founded a summer nutrition camp at Lambert's Castle, a prominent brick structure on the side of Garrett Mountain overlooking Paterson. (Lambert, a Scottish immigrant himself, was a legendary exploiter of workers in his silk mills. He was brought down by the great silk strike of 1913 and was later immortalized by William Carlos Williams in his epic poem *Paterson*.) The previous summer the camp had been moved to a more rural setting and was being expanded to handle two one-month encampments for the summer of 1931.

Since Hopatcong was impossible that summer, the idea of the camp intrigued me; thus, on some pretext, I visited Mrs. Van Houten again to express an interest. Eventually, I became St. Joe's quota, the only price being a tonsillectomy at Paterson General Hospital. On the first of August I lined up with 140 anxious campers from all over Passaic County, and we were off by bus to Camp Christmas Seal. On arrival we were assigned to one of seven cabins based on age. Since each cabin had two counselors, we were further divided into small groups of ten boys each.

The routine reminded me in some ways of the Home. From wake-up at 7:30 a.m. to lights-out at 8:00 p.m. our activities were carefully structured. Probably because I turned out to be the best swimmer in my group on our initial test, I was designated chief of our tribe of ten, called the Wanaques. As we marched between activities, the counselors led us in the camp song: "Against a line of jolly campers full of pep and zeal, up on our mountain Camp Christmas Seal . . . ."

There was also plenty of time for reading. Among a good supply of books were many from those boys' series that were turned out on an assembly-line basis at fifty cents a copy. This was the summer that I discovered Tom Swift in his adventures in the Big Dirigible. I went on to join him in many of his other adventures, all of which included his good friend Ned Newton and the blushing Mary Nestor. Tom's scientific discoveries and adventures make our moon landing in 1969 pale by comparison. Other series on the camp's bookshelves included Franklin W. Dixon's *Hardy Boys* (Frank and Joe) and Laura Lee Hope's *Bobbsey Twins* (Bert, Nan, Freddie, and Flossie). Years later I learned that all these authors' names were pseudonyms—there were sixty-five in all—developed in a syndicate by Edward Stratemeyer to turn out more than eight hundred books by the contract writers. In the summer of 1931, though, none of this mattered—only the adventure and escape these books gave to me and many of my colleagues.

All in all, the camp built up my personal confidence. This was just as well, since there was news from Johnny Bustard when he met my return bus. Frank McAndrews had died from his lung problems, and Aunt Fanny had moved to 321 Market Street, where she and I would live in a flat over the saloon, now called Fanny's Place.

This arrangement with Aunt Fanny went on for over seven years—the first four connected with the saloon. Sparky the bartender ran the place but Aunt Fanny was there every evening. Our eating-out days were over, but she was an excellent cook and, as "man of the house," I was frequently given menu preferences. My responsibilities were a bit greater as well. Sometimes I had to read and sign papers for her, since, as previously mentioned, she could neither read nor write. When it came to signing my report card from St. Joe's, this signing chore was not a bit onerous.

One of my duties was, I suspect, somewhat illegal. I was custodian of the Internal Revenue stamps that, for reasons still not clear to me, needed to be pasted atop each bootlegged bottle. The gin was delivered in very large glass bottles and placed in an upstairs closet. Tommy Owens, who cleaned the saloon, was assigned the task of transferring the gin with a suction hose from the large to the small bottles as I stood by ready to affix the stamps. Tommy routinely left the chore in a much happier mood than when he arrived. On one occasion as I stood there, Tommy passed out. After removing the hose from his mouth, I had to get Sparky to help revive him. Thereafter, Tommy's services were restricted to only cleaning the saloon.

My fifth-grade teacher at St. Joe's was Miss McGreen, and the ambiance was much to my liking, making for my best year at St. Joe's. One new subject for me that year (fortunately not graded) was penmanship, beginning several years of struggle with the Palmer Method. The goal was that, by the eighth grade at the latest, each of us should qualify in penmanship enough to receive a Palmer Diploma. Eventually, 75 percent of us did, but meanwhile we were subjected to daily drills that for me have rarely been surpassed for boredom in anything else I have encountered in the decades since.

The method had been around for almost a half-century when I was introduced to it in the fall of 1931. Austin Norman Palmer, apparently a born penman, began teaching the subject at a business college in Iowa. His particular contribution to the American schoolboy was to reduce all letters to five basic strokes, which—if the neophyte repeated them over and over in various ways—would in time become automatic. When I encountered the method in 1931, Palmer had gone to his reward, but he left a legacy of workbooks at levels going right up to the eighth grade. In desperation I finally qualified in the seventh.

By the sixth grade in the fall of 1932 my luck ran out as to highly compatible teachers and I returned to my struggle with the nuns to retain my individuality. Naturally, my grade point average dropped—once as much as ten points. Still, I liked St. Joe's and by now knew each of my thirty classmates so well (we had been together since the fall of 1927) that the group was like a daytime extended family. Our first experience in losing a colleague came that year; on a bleak February day we attended the funeral of Gertrude Gatti, who had been struck by a train.

The church remained an essential part of our school experience. When we went to confession individually on Saturday afternoons, there were long lines at the confessional of Father Francis Xavier Daisey, who gave three Hail Marys as the penance for almost any offense. There were very short lines at Father Carleton Smith's confessional, where even a few "dirty thoughts" cost a lap around the rosary.

The high point of the church year for those of us in the sixth grade was our Confirmation, scheduled for Friday, May 19, 1933. Months before, on one afternoon a week in the school auditorium, priests began our instruction. Each of us was periodically called upon to stand up in front of the group and answer a question or two. All one had to do, of course, was to repeat back what was stated in the Catechism—with a little emphasis for sincerity.

Finally, the big day arrived. His Excellency, the bishop of Newark, Thomas J. Walsh—whom we knew by name only—was to preside. My sponsor, who would stand behind me, was Walter Nally, scheduled to leave work early and to commute to Paterson for the occasion. There was one catch to my Confirmation, though; again, it was the name Douglas. An extra name—that of a saint—had to be added for Confirmation; Sister Regina Margaret selected Francis for me.

For the ceremony, attended by Aunt Fanny, Aunt Rosie, Tootsie, and the others, I was decked out in a blue serge suit with a red ribbon on my arm. The bishop began with token questioning of the group; then we moved forward to the altar rail. Walter was nowhere in sight, so a proxy was brought from the congregation. As the bishop approached me, Walter came down the aisle on the double (his train had been late) and relieved the proxy just as His Excellency placed his hands on my head and intoned, "Strengthen, O Lord, your servant Leo Francis Kinnard with your Holy Spirit . . . Amen."

In my new location on Market Street, my world began to move

outward. Our location on a very large city block meant proximity to many families with children of my own age. To the Gallaghers were added Johnny Sproverie, Darwin Hillegas, Bradner Riggs, and so on. The welcome by their families was always warm and friendly. Our group was adept at scaling back yard fences, and on a whim we could move across the entire block without using the street. Pick-up games of baseball and football flourished on non-school nights. Most of us were allowed out after dinner until dark, heading home with the final greeting "see you after."

Saturday afternoons with one or more of this group were still reserved for the movies. Those in the early 1930s that I recall at this remove are the type that would make an impression on ten-and eleven-year-old boys of that time. In 1931 I saw Bela Lugosi in his most famous role in Bram Stoker's *Dracula* and Boris Karloff in Mary Shelley's *Frankenstein*. In 1932 it was Karloff again in *The Mummy*, spiced up by Bramwell Fletcher's maniacal laugh as the mummy's hand began to move; and in 1933, *King Kong* stood on the newly built Empire State Building.

By 1933 two of these movies inspired us to a series of Sunday adventures in New York. Since the family of Mr. Gallagher, a conductor on the Erie Railroad, was treated to a permanent pass, it was not hard for me to convince Georgie that on Sunday the two of us could take the train to New York if I assumed the identity of his brother Jim. Our immediate goals were the observation tower of the Empire State (Kong's domain) and the Egyptology collection (abounding with mummies) of the Metropolitan Museum of Art on Fifth Avenue. New York was safe in those days, and during the next two years we were joined by other friends, who paid their railroad fare. Our trips expanded to the Aquarium at the Battery, the Statue of Liberty, the Museum of Natural History, and even, once, the Bronx Zoo.

Though Fanny and I lived alone in those days, I kept daily contact with Aunt Rosie. Uncle George was dead, but she carried on as before, but for a time without Tootsie. One evening, arriving at Fanny's for dinner, Tootsie had with her an energetic baldheaded man named

Clyde Griffith, whom she was going to marry in a few days. Clyde was a "big operator," and the honeymoon involved flying to Washington, big stuff then. They subsequently lived in an apartment in the center of Paterson, where Clyde seemed to have a lot of contacts and interests. It turned out that he was a bookie. I learned this not from Tootsie but from being with Clyde at events he took me to. One night it was professional boxing matches; another was a wrestling match featuring Jim Londos, one-time world champion. When we visited Jim in his dressing room, his conversation with Clyde seemed more to involve horses than wrestling. Clyde simply disappeared one day; so did the agency where he worked. Tootsie returned to live with Aunt Rosie, and eventually her marriage was annulled.

Nineteen thirty-two has been called the cruelest year of the Depression. Certainly by then evidence of that was seen in many parts of Paterson: many vacant stores; breadlines and soup kitchens; among my schoolmates fewer fathers commuting to work in New York and more staying home. I witnessed many bonfires at the empty silk mills, "mysteriously" started but resulting in large insurance settlements.

As people stayed home more, radio played a growing role in their lives. Families listened to Morton Downey's singing of "Carolina Moon"; to Kate Smith's "When the Moon Comes Over the Mountain"; and to many renditions of "Brother, Can You Spare a Dime?" The radio also showcased the increasingly discordant voices of critics such as Father Charles Coughlin from Detroit's Shrine of the Little Flower, drawing large Sunday audiences. To top off everything, in the summer of 1932 came radio reports and newspaper accounts of the Bonus Marchers in Washington. The heroes of 1918 had become, at least in the eyes of the Hoover administration, the bums of 1932.

Into all of this came Hoover's challenger for the presidency, Franklin Delano Roosevelt, who seemed new and exciting to this eleven-year-old and many others of my age group. The outcome of the election was evident long before the event itself, but the margin of victory was staggering: Hoover carried six states with 59 electoral votes; Roosevelt, the remaining with 472. That winter of 1932-1933, when the old administration fell to the New Deal, marked the end of an era and the beginning of another for all of us.

With this change came that unforgettable day, Saturday, March 4, 1933, raw and blustery on the East Coast. I sat with a classmate, Jim McLaughlin, and his family in their living room listening to the first Roosevelt inaugural. Jim's father, who spoke with a burr, had been a mechanic in shipbuilding in Scotland. The family emigrated when Jim was a baby, and now the father was out of work as a mechanic and was trying to establish a small ice and coal outlet. We heard the oath being administered by Chief Justice Charles Evans Hughes and then that strong, confident voice we all got to know very well in the years ahead. Shortly into FDR's inaugural address came these words that I can still hear in my mind as though it were yesterday: ". . . let me assert my firm belief that the only thing we have to fear is fear itself." Then came the "Hundred Days," described in detail in multitudes of books, beginning with the bank holiday and a special session of Congress. Their effect was not to solve the Depression but to dissipate the panic atmosphere attendant to it. The resulting actions were aided by the new president's fireside chats that began a week after his inauguration. A kind of confidence seemed to return to the people I knew, including my own adopted family.

The summer of 1933 turned out to be my last one with one of the aunts at Hopatcong. This time, for the whole summer, I was at Aunt Rosie's cabin, replete with indoor plumbing. The activities included reading, swimming, boating, and entertaining frequent visitors. Walt and Irene often came to visit, and this meant many side trips for me. Rosie's son George had to be tolerated during his two-week vacation, but by now I had figured out how to get along with him and could count on his largesse for a Moxie or ice cream from Sutton's almost every day. All too soon came the mellow days of late August. Jimmy Owens arrived to help close up and to drive Rosie and me back to Paterson.

One of the changes that seventh grade brought was Sister Cecilia de Paul. I became aware of the price of not getting along with one's superiors—this was the year my average dropped ten points. During many after-school sessions I had to write on the blackboard five hundred times, "I must not . . ." (in effect, "be Doug"). Also that year my activities outside of school were becoming increasingly important to me.

Like many of my friends I became a paper delivery boy with my own route. This meant delivering the *Paterson Morning Call* very early and the *Paterson Evening News* directly after school. Inevitably, my afternoon duties conflicted with Sister Cecilia's board-writing assignments. One day I walked out before completion—with predictable results—and I never tried that again. What I learned from the incident, though, was the art of compromise was a two-way street: Sister Cecilia found other ways to penalize me for my "attitude," while I was free after school to pursue my job.

The most interesting aspect of my paper route was the chance to meet many different families during my collections each Saturday. While some were strictly business, others were friendly and conversational; some even provided a cookie or other goodie. One very large house on my route had a plaque stating that this had been the home of Garret Augustus Hobart, William McKinley's vice president. Noting that he died in office in 1899, I had the thought that if he had lived, he would eventually have succeeded the assassinated McKinley. There would have been no President Theodore Roosevelt, at least at that point. It was my first musing on a counterfactual of historical import.

With the paper route I could now pay my own way to the weekly movie. One that made a strong impression on a twelve-year-old was *David Copperfield*, a movie that seemed to have it all: plot by Dickens, Mr. Micawber played by W.C. Fields, and David brought to life by dimpled Freddie Bartholomew, who was even younger than our crowd but with whom we could all identify. He became the male child star of the mid-1930s, for a time second only to Shirley Temple in earning power.

It was the newsreels, though, that had the most lasting impact; I still retain their images of the world of the Great Depression. On the domestic scene there was one Francis Townsend of California discussing the feasibility of pensions to all citizens of a certain age (our elders payed close attention but we were bored). Then there was the Louisiana Kingfish, Huey Long, by then in the United States Senate and its greatest filibusterer. By 1934 Americans were listening in desperation to anyone promising an economic miracle that would end the Depression. Long's "Everyman a King" program, however improbable, made him an interesting and formidable demagogue, even on film, until he was cut down by an assassin's bullet in September 1935.

Sometime in the spring of 1933 Fanny's Place was for some reason finally padlocked by a nonlocal agency charged with enforcing the soon-to-die Volstead Act. Sparky the bartender took "the rap," not a serious one; and after some arrangements the solution was simply to move the saloon to an adjacent store, then empty, in the same building. Simultaneously, we moved across the hall to a flat over the new saloon. So much for the seriousness with which the Volstead Act was taken in Paterson!

In his 1932 campaign Roosevelt had explicitly stated that the 18th Amendment (Prohibition) should be repealed; and even before he took office Congress had, in February, voted to repeal. Finally, on December 5, 1933, Utah became the last of the required thirty-six states to ratify the 21st Amendment effecting the repeal. Though there was much great celebrating in Fanny's Place that night, eventually the repeal brought the demise of marginal liquor outlets like hers. Gradually, larger places and restaurants were to take over the dispensing of spirits.

During the spring of 1934 a few of my classmates kept encouraging me to join them in the St. Joe's Boy Scout troop, but for a time I was indifferent to the idea. In early June I finally agreed to attend a meeting. I was instantly hooked, but there would be only one more meeting until fall. When I was told that there was no time to take the Tenderfoot test, required for enrollment, I prevailed on the Scoutmaster, Gus Rauchenbach, to help me. During the next week I was able to satisfy him on the required knots and Tenderfoot knowledge: "Be prepared"; "Do a good turn daily"; and the Boy Scout oath. Thus, at the last meeting of the academic year I was duly enrolled as a member of Troop 35 Boy Scouts of America and assigned to the Flying Eagle Patrol.

Before the month was out I purchased, with Johnny Bustard's help, my neckerchief and Scout shirt complete with Tenderfoot badge. Since there would be no Hopatcong with an aunt this summer, I soon visited the Paterson Council of the Boy Scouts to inquire about Camp Altaha. The cost was seven dollars a week, underwritten by Aunt Rosie for one week. In August I headed for Hopatcong with a group of campers; and even though the seven days were cold and rainy and I was not well prepared for the activities, I enjoyed the experience. I met a number of new personalities, in particular Chief Lotee. H.A. Lotee, a big, friendly man who took a personal interest in each of us, had been head of the Paterson Council since 1917. To my astonishment he recalled that my brother Jim—whom I scarcely knew—had been a Boy Scout in Hawthorne (perhaps while living temporarily with my aunt) in the early 1920s.

The eighth grade brought a new format that was much more interesting than that of the past; there were four teaching nuns rather than one. Sister Rita Cecilia was by far the most outstanding as teacher and friend. Because her face was colorless, we called her "the Ghost." She told us that if anything "happens to me during class, just get the bottle of pills out of the top drawer of my desk and put a pill under my tongue." It was scary but we listened and were prepared to act.

We hung on every word of her teaching; as she took us through Sir Walter Scott's *The Lady of the Lake* with its sixteenth-century setting, she transported me from Paterson to the Scottish highlands. I can still recall her leading up to that dramatic moment when the sentry confronts Fitz-James with the words "and I, dear sir, am Roderick Dhu!" But we learned more than our lessons from Sister Rita. She helped us all along the road of our early years and beyond, both in temporal and spiritual life.

Sister Rita kindled in us a special interest in St. Therese of Lisieux, the Little Flower. Therese Martin lived from 1873 to 1897 in Lisieux, France—the last nine years in the Carmelite convent. Here she developed her practice of the "little way." Canonized by Pius X in 1925, she appealed to people in all walks of life as the saint of the times. In my years, St. Joseph's had a novena to her each fall; we were required to attend all nine sessions "on our own time." After a year or two the novena began to drag for me, but then with Sister Rita's discussions I developed an empathy with the Little Flower. Three decades later, when I was living in Paris, I made several visits to Lisieux, in particular the places where she lived and died. Whatever one's beliefs—and my own have changed over the years—the message of Therese's "little way" is that "there is no misery too small to be accommodated by it, nor any stress too large to be comprehended by it."

By the fall of 1934 I began to think, with mixed feelings, about high school. Most of my friends would be going to St. Joe's, but the curricula offerings were limited and tended toward the classical. Walter Nally had long recommended that I take a commercial course; he felt that it would give me job opportunities in areas where he could assist me. St. Joe's High had no commercial program, but Paterson Eastside did—and it was a good one. Given my circumstances the thought of college had not at that point crossed anyone's mind, including mine.

There was also a larger appeal to Eastside High. It was in the same city block as St. Joe's, and I knew a number of its students. Eastside had opened in 1926, shortly after I arrived in Paterson, and, like most children, I was fascinated by its appellation, "The Ghosts" (it had been built on the site of an old large cemetery). Directly in front of the school was the football field, where my colleagues and I had spent many Saturday afternoons watching the home games. Normally, we did not have the fifteen cents for admission, but the under-fence tunnels that we prepared in late summer took care of that. We had so many tunnels that if one or two were discovered by the lone school policeman Tony, it really did not matter. I suspect that Tony knew exactly who we were and how we got in; he was possibly even a bit sympathetic.

What impressed me about Eastside was its size (about four thousand students), the variety of its offerings, the ethnic diversity of the student body, and the flexibility of the daily schedule. Another plus for Eastside—but something I did not appreciate until later—was that in the 1930s it was probably one of the top high schools in the country, on a par, for example, with Brooklyn Boys High. By the winter of 1935 I had made up my mind that I would be one of the few from my class who would go to Eastside rather than St. Joe's High.

Though the newsreels of the period still emphasized domestic happenings—the dust storms in Oklahoma, the capture of Bruno Richard Hauptmann, the arrival of the *Normandie*, and the birth of the Dionne quintuplets—early in 1933 European events began to capture my attention.

I can still recall the newsreel from Berlin showing the aged President Von Hindenburg standing at night in the window of the chancellery. In the adjacent window was Adolph Hitler, the newly named chancellor, watching the torchlight parade of storm troopers. In rapid order over the next few years the films depicted Hitler's assumption of the presidency combined with Von Hindenburg's elaborate funeral procession, the return of the Saar to Germany, the German departure from the League of Nations, and the beginning of conscription in Germany. All this caught my interest enough so that I began to read related newspaper accounts; still, everything seemed far away. Little did I know.

By the winter of 1934-1935 Fanny's Place was having a hard time surviving the post-Prohibition competition. Attempts to hold on included free lunches, occasional Saturday night corned beef "dinners," and a Saturday evening piano and singing duo, "The Boys." This helped somewhat, but in desperation a boarder, Mrs. Pettigrew, was added to our apartment when her children wanted a place to deposit her. In the end, nothing could save Fanny's Place, scheduled to close on June 29. Fanny and I and Mrs. Pettigrew were to move a few days later to the corner of Market and Rose streets, not far from Aunt Rosie and opposite St. Joseph's Church.

Meanwhile, in that spring of 1935, other changes were occurring. My sister Daisy and her husband, now living in Orange, New Jersey, initiated little get-togethers for family at their apartment. There

I also spent several weekends with my brother Harry, now about to graduate from high school in northern New Jersey. These visits were always a treat, but my feeling was one of being with cousins rather than with my own family. For better or worse, nine years had elapsed since the Day of the Taxi, and nothing could dispel its impact.

The main excitement that spring was at St. Joe's: the class of 1935 was preparing to graduate. As our eight-year-long group prepared to say goodbye, the autograph books were full of corny and sometimes warm messages. Then began the rehearsals for the big night.

Friday, June 21, dressed in St. Joe's Blue for the last time, we marched in to Loret's "Marche Heroic." The diplomas were presented by our favorite priest, Francis Xavier Daisey, who also gave the graduation address, "Sacred Heart of Jesus Pleading." After the Benediction we filed out to Kretchner's "March Coronation." From there we went our several ways.

That night in the back room of Fanny's Place I was feted at my only graduation party ever. For the ceremony and party Rosie had rounded up all the family who could make it: besides Fanny there were Rosie, Georgie and his new wife Bela, Tootsie, Walter and Irene, Jimmy Owens, and, of course, Sparky—everyone but Annie, who was, however, to return to my life before long.

5. The Ghosts of Eastside High

The summer of 1935 was a season of change. Life at 6 Rose Street, without the saloon, was one of limited means and semiboredom for Aunt Fanny. Besides me, her only companion was the boarder, Mrs. Pettigrew, who had a very restricted range of interests. One of Mrs. Pettigrew's frequent comments, "It all comes to those that wait," was merely repeated when I asked just what she meant. Before long, Mrs. Pettigrew needed a practical nurse, and to our relief a Marie Riley moved in for that purpose. An interesting person, Marie had a repertoire of stories to tell, especially in the evenings when she and Aunt Fanny sat down with a "little trinkie."

Because Aunt Rosie lived nearby, I spent as much time at her place as I did on Rose Street. At that time I also began to see my mother occasionally; she now lived in an apartment in downtown Paterson with her second husband, Tom Ruddy, a nice guy. They were, of course, strangers to me, as I was to them. Brother Harry was now working as an apprentice in the building trade, having for some reason turned down a scholarship to Drew, a college in Madison, New Jersey. Since his work frequently brought him to the Paterson area, I saw him from time to time. Several times I was his guest at big league games at the Polo Grounds, especially when his favorites, the New York Giants, played mine, the Brooklyn Dodgers, then an unintentionally comical team.

Aunt Rosie sponsored me to two weeks at Camp Altaha that August, but I then returned to shocking news—she had died suddenly a day or two before. On the evening of the very day of my return, I attended the Irish wake at her home and next day the funeral at St. Joseph's. Because the distance from her home to church was short, the casket, with family following, was carried up Market Street to the High Requiem Mass. It occurred to me during the service that, except for my Confirmation and grammar school graduations, this was the only time I recall Aunt Rosie being in church. The interment brought together the entire family, including Aunt Annie, whom I had not seen in more than six years. Afterward, she placed her arm around me and talked briefly. Before too long she was again to be an important part of my life, although I had no inkling at the time.

On Tuesday, September 3, I entered a new world, Eastside High. On the same city block as St. Joe's, it was a world apart. For its time Eastside was a large school with over four thousand students and two graduations each school year. The facilities were still comparatively new, as the school was only ten years old.

What struck me immediately at the opening assembly (where there were over five hundred of us) was the diversity of the student body. Though a law in 1920 had halted the flow of immigrants, many of my new classmates were children of those who had come in the last surge. I was no longer in a predominantly Irish group; the largest number of classmates by nationality were probably Italian, German, and Poles. Another diversity, not at first apparent, was that of religion. Though there were many Catholics, there were also Protestants of various denominations (I gave up in time trying to figure out the differences among them) as well as a substantial number of the Jewish faith. This diversity turned out to be an important part of my education at Eastside, especially regarding the Jewish students, among whom I developed many acquaintances.

The school offered five major fields of study. In addition to my own field, Commercial, comprising over 50 percent of the class, there were Classical, General, Mechanical Arts, and Household Arts. Since all programs required four years of history and English, we had for part of the day a useful and interesting interaction with students of different majors. Because facilities were already too small for the student body, flexible scheduling was a necessity. This, too, was advantageous for diversity since it meant that even within a major, classmates changed around.

Eastside had two facilities that I used daily that were not available at St. Joe's, a good school library, and a first-rate gymnasium. The library was the precinct of Mrs. Grimshaw, who was constantly on watch for talking between students. I was once banned from the library for a week for not heeding her warning; after that I kept quiet. Gymnasium was a required daily subject, always beginning with a tough series of calisthenics, followed by games, sometimes outdoors, or workouts on one of the pieces of apparatus such as the high bar, rope climb, and parallel bars. Directing or closely supervising all this was Bob Diamond, head football coach, or his assistant Hank Rumana, whose jacket sported a big "I" from his days a few years before as a varsity football player for the University of Illinois.

The student body came from all over the east side of Paterson and its eastern suburbs. Because of this geographical spread and individual school scheduling, I did not acquire outside friends at Eastside. Most of my close friends continued to relate in some way to St. Joe's. A few had come to Eastside with me, but most of my contacts were those who remained in the Catholic school. This came about partly through church services but increasingly through the St. Joe's Boy Scout troop. Somewhere along the line the Knights of Columbus chapter, allied with St. Joe's, started a junior group called the Columbian Squires, in which I became a charter member. This opened up a nice clubhouse to us, as well as a chance to participate in their junior athletic teams. All in all, the church remained a big influence in my life—especially in nonreligious matters.

There were aspects of this that I sometimes found restrictive, for example the Legion of Decency. As a fairly frequent moviegoer I was expected by the church to read over the Legion's movie ratings before making my weekend selection. These ratings began around 1934 when some church officials decided that they could not depend on Hollywood's good graces in presenting what were to them morally acceptable films.

The Legion rated films in categories: A—"approved"; B—"objectionable in part"; or C— "condemned." I have forgotten now in what subcategory of a "B" rating I would be committing sin if I viewed the film. The whole thing seemed to me an overreach on the part of the church; for example, I wanted to see *Dodsworth*, a Sinclair Lewis story in which Walter Huston had starred on Broadway and was now in a film directed by William Wyler. As the Legion had rated the film "objectionable in part," a couple of my Catholic friends dissuaded me from attending. This bothered me more than I admitted at the time, and afterward I adopted an approach known today as "don't ask, don't tell."

By the fall of 1935 the Depression had become a semipermanent way of life, and although most people fared a bit better than they had a few years before, the situation remained serious, the New Deal notwithstanding. Millions of people looking for some solution tuned in each Sunday evening to Father Coughlin's broadcasts, from Detroit's Shrine of the Little Flower, to hear his combination of religious-economic doctrine. He had by now become anti-Roosevelt and his approach seemed to combine Catholicism, socialism, populism, and occasional anti-Semitism.

There were, fortunately, lighter diversions in those mid-Depression years. The Christmas market of 1935 presented the world with a board game—bearing New Jersey street names—that became an instant hit—Monopoly. Those who could not earn much money in the real world could with luck become millionaires with the game's play money. Another fad about that time required one to be always ready with a clever answer to the question "Knock knock, who's there?" This initiated an exchange that went on until the punch line. An unwritten rule required the original respondent to ask the same introductory question of the other party, starting all over again in mirror-image fashion with a new riposte. With some enthusiasts one had almost to scream for mercy in order to end the exchange.

By the spring of 1936, with presidential politics in the air, FDR was a heavy favorite with everyone I knew. What I remembered about his acceptance speech at Philadelphia's Franklin Field in late June was one short paragraph (as reprinted in the next day's *New York Times*), in particular its closing sentence: "This generation of Americans has a rendezvous with destiny." (How right he was in ways no one could have then known!)

Roosevelt's opponent, Governor Alfred Mossman Landon of Kansas, was a nice-appearing man with all the sparkle of Calvin Coolidge. The *Literary Digest*'s prediction of a Landon victory was puzzling to the people I knew who reflected on such things, but then none of us knew much about polls. In the end, of course, the *Digest* was totally wrong when Roosevelt won by a landslide. His opponent won only Maine and Vermont, prompting a revision of the old adage to, "As Maine goes, so goes Vermont."

Sparked by newsreels, my interest in European affairs intensified in the fall of 1935 as, in a dark theater, I witnessed the Italian invasion of Ethiopia. I saw, too, how the League of Nations was unable to react. My earlier interest in such matters had by now been heightened by discussions in high school civics class and by the wide variety of newspapers available in the high school library. Also about then the Fabian Theater carried a monthly film documentary, Henry Luce's "The March of Time," with a deeply serious narrator's voice reporting on international and other matters. The documentary was always ended by the narrator with an even sterner voice, announcing: "TIME . . . marches ON!"

In school we discussed the 1935 and later the 1936 American neutrality laws and their significance for American foreign policy. Like almost everyone I knew at the time, I accepted the American impulse toward isolationism as a given. Still, one could not view on the screen and read about events such as the March 1936 German occupation of the Rhineland without feeling somewhat apprehensive. Of course, most of my interests at the time were on less weighty matters; the German situation was not yet even a small cloud on my personal horizon.

I did, though, follow closely the XI Olympiad, for which Germany was the host country in 1936. The reoccupation of the Rhineland occurred between the winter Olympics in Garmisch and before the summer spectacular in Berlin. In fourteen-year-old fashion, my friends and I particularly followed the summer games. The high point was the performance of Jesse Owens, whom we watched on the newsreels at least twice each time he was featured winning one of his four gold medals, highlighted by his world record broad jump. There were some things in which Hitler could not claim Nordic superiority!

By the Christmas holidays of 1936-37 I had finished three semesters at Eastside and was developing a feeling of frustration about which I was somewhat baffled. My grades at school were neither bad nor good; but considering that I rarely did homework except when it interested me, I had nothing to complain about. I did a great deal of outside reading, mainly of a historical nature, but the commercial subjects I was studying held little interest for me outside of class—undoubtedly part of my frustration.

By the fall of 1936 my friends were discussing girls, and some began dating occasionally. Although there was a girl in my English class, Mildred Van Dine, that I would have liked to date, I did not feel that I had the home support structure in which to introduce dates. On New Year's Eve 1936-37 I went along as an extra with two of my former St. Joe's classmates and their dates. Since all five of us were from St. Joe's class of 1935 and knew one another well, I did not feel as awkward about this as I would with newer friends; still, it was a bit embarrassing. Probably such matters were another cause of my feeling thwarted.

I took out this frustration in other ways. in the spring of 1936 I published my first piece of writing in the *Paterson Evening News* on the once-a-week page dedicated to the young writer. Entitled "Uncle Ezra's Ghost," this epic had the setting, not identified, of Sperry

Springs, in particular the house that Aunt Fanny rented there in the late 1920s.

Mainly, though, my energies were increasingly directed toward the Boy Scouts, possibly because my accomplishments there were tangible to me and to others. By the fall of 1935 I was a First Class scout and an assistant patrol leader. A year later I was a Star Scout with my own patrol. All this helped temporarily, but I still lacked a real goal or true self-confidence—whatever the outside appearance. It was to be over a year before I was to come up with the answer to the question in one of Lenin's book titles, "What is to be done?"

Some sophomore traits appeared in our class of 1939. Almost overnight in the spring of 1937 all the boys at Eastside High who were "with it" appeared in saddle shoes and beer jackets. In self-defense I joined the crowd, much to the amusement of Toots, Aunt Fanny, and my St. Joe's friends. I was trying hard to be one of the BMOC who seemed to have taken over my history class, which also seemed to have the prettiest girls. One especially capturing my attention was blonde Milly Roeder, who sat next to me. Although she had a ready smile and responded to my sense of humor, she seemed out of my reach for anything more than our daily conversations. When I discussed my feelings with a friend—who subsequently reported them to Milly—word came back, "Tell him to come around when he grows up." We remained friends, though, and the pain gradually subsided.

My home room that spring was my Commercial Geography class, in which I did well and established a rapport with the teacher, a Mr. Motola. Representing the group at Student Council meetings, I met an interesting teacher named Kathleen Westman, faculty advisor to the Council and head of the English department. In a couple of years she was to be a major influence, but at the moment her relationship consisted of explaining Robert's Rules of Order to me after the first meeting I attended. Apparently, I had been in violation—not unusual since I did not know of the existence of the rules and had not attended the first meetings.

From time to time the school assemblies were given over completely to outside groups, although I do not recall ever being aware of what was coming until I sat down. One day that spring we entered to find a large orchestra. It turned out to be the WPA orchestra for Passaic County, part of Roosevelt's Federal Music Project that had put around fifteen thousand musicians to work. Studying the group as they prepared for the opening number, I thought I saw my father. After further scrutiny I was certain that it was he in the woodwinds section.

I knew, of course, that he had been a musician for many years off and on. As a young man enlisted in the Spanish-American War he had played in an army band, and had kept up his performing later even while in the insurance business. I had heard that since his divorce from my mother he had played in a theater orchestra in Hackensack. For a while he and his wife had even owned a music store in New York. In any event, here he was at Eastside, a member of a good orchestra that the students appreciated. In one number, "Peter and the Wolf," my father, as flutist, played the solo part. An interesting but detached way to come across one's parent.

During my first two years in high school several changes occurred within my adopted family. Toots took over Aunt Rosie's establishment, which I visited almost as often as I had in Aunt Rosie's time; but for a long time I was sad at not seeing that large frame in her rocking chair and not hearing "Hello, Doug." Johnny Bustard meanwhile rejoined Aunt Annie, reestablishing in South Paterson some distance from my location. Georgie Bustard died of leukemia in the spring of 1937; and Mrs. Pettigrew, Aunt Fanny's boarder, passed on a couple of months later. With the nurse, Marie Riley, also gone, Aunt Fanny was left in a shaky financial condition. At this point Annie reentered the scene with both financial help and a promise to secure a new boarder for Fanny.

By that spring I was a Life Scout and beginning to think seriously about another objective. Though St. Joe's Troop had been established before the Great War, it had never produced an Eagle Scout. Why not be the first? An obstacle was that some of the merit badges could not be accomplished in Paterson; for example, Bird Study, requiring the identification of sixty species of birds, could be accomplished only if I were able to spend an entire summer at Camp Altaha—and that would require financial support not available to Aunt Fanny.

In April came the annual Boy Scout rally of the Paterson Council at the Armory. It was the usual large affair: all troops marching in one by one and passing in review for Chief Lotee and visitors from the New York headquarters of the Boy Scouts of America. Then came the competition in various events, with each troop allowed one scout to compete in the individual events. That year Gus Rauchenbach, the scoutmaster, chose me to compete in receiving semaphore signaling. I was comfortable in this event, but my luck that day exceeded all my expectations. I won first prize for the troop! Gus and all the troop were as excited as I was and, I suspect, equally surprised.

One evening in early May my patrol was meeting in the yard of one of the members' homes. About 7:30 his father came excitedly out of the house to announce that the German dirigible *Hindenburg* had just exploded and burned while trying to land at its mooring, the Lakehurst, New Jersey, Naval Air Station. A little earlier two scouts had mentioned seeing the giant airship, with huge red, white, and black swastikas painted on its tail, as it passed over New York City that afternoon. The first page of next day's *New York Times* gave the crash Titanic-like coverage. The zeppelin, which carried fifty passengers and a crew of about the same size, had made ten round trips the previous summer. On this trip, the first of the 1937 season, thirty-six people were killed. There would be no more trans-Atlantic dirigibles. The cause of the fire and explosion, taking only thirty-two seconds, was attributed at the time to the chance igniting of the hydrogen lifting gas.

June of that year brought with it the closest thing to a reunion of my own family that I ever attended. Only my father was missing. The occasion was the marriage of my sister Ruth (like me a "graduate" of the Home) to Andy Parinello, a gregarious and energetic mailman. A telephone operator, Ruth lived with a family named Shapiro, who hosted the reception in their home in Far Rockaway, Long Island.

My family came from all different directions. Jim and Harry picked me up, noting with slight smiles my outfit of blue jacket and white ducks. Jim drove, and I occupied the rumble seat. On arrival we joined Lil, my oldest sister, with her husband Mel, who was by then a partner in a New York liquor store; my mother, without Tom, her second husband; and my sister Helen, who came with Daisy and Steve.

Everyone got along fine and seemed to enjoy the day. I wondered as I observed Andy, whom I liked, whether he thought he was marrying into a real family. At dusk we all headed back. Harry took over the driving from Jim, who apparently had consumed my share of the wine as well as his. From my perch in the rumble seat I took in the sidewalk scene and lights of New York as we crossed Manhattan toward the Holland Tunnel and the Jersey meadows.

The summer of 1937 was the most memorable of those I spent at Lake Hopatcong—it also was the last. With support from Walt and Irene and Aunt Annie, I was at Camp Altaha from the opening day to the closing. About half a dozen of us were in that fortunate category, riding up in the bus together with the first week campers and meeting with Chief Lotee later that morning.

The Chief had been head of the Paterson Council for eighteen years and was only a couple of years from retirement. A big, strong man who spent the summer days walking around in shorts and moccasins, he missed nothing in his daily rounds. Every noon he stood up in our dining room, an open L-shaped veranda overlooking the lake, to make announcements in a voice with remarkable carrying power. The only announcement I now recall was one praising the value of sour milk to the human body. This announcement just happened to come on a weekend when all our milk supply had turned sour. The Paterson scouts at my table simply looked at one another and reached for the water pitcher.

On the day we arrived, Lotee's talk to the six of us pointed out that as campers for the entire summer we had certain responsibilities. Each of us would be in charge of one of the eight-man tents since there were not enough counselors to cover all of the twenty or so tents. In addition he had a "suggested" task for each. In my case on days I was not on a hike or canoe trip he wanted me to be one of the lifeguards at the morning and afternoon swimming sessions. This seemed logical since I had qualified as a senior lifesaver the previous summer.

Most of the all-summer campers were working on merit badges for Eagle Scout. Two of us—a boy named Ted and myself—were particularly interested in bird study. For this we were to work with a senior counselor, Eugene Vivian, a science teacher at Paterson Central High. I remembered him from the previous year, and how he moved oddly, approaching a modified version of an orangutan. He was a great mentor, though, for Ted and me. Every morning before reveille the three of us went out on a short hike to work on identifying birds. On occasion we spent the night at some remote location where he guessed different birds would appear at first light; this included a mosquito-infested swamp area. By the end of August we each had our sixty birds.

I was also working that summer on another merit badge that demanded time and effort—Camping. This involved many nights away from Altaha, including preparing our own meals. Fortunately, I found a kindred spirit—Don Fegley from Clifton, New Jersey. Don was a handsome, clean-cut boy who was there for three weeks. Together we spent many nights in locations remote to Altaha working on the requirements. At first this meant long hikes carrying our equipment, but soon one of us thought of substituting canoe hikes, which with little effort took us to equally remote places. Hopatcong was a big lake, and we often spent the night on one of its many islands. Once the owner of the island we were on appeared just as we were cooking dinner. Happily, Don was such a born diplomat that by the time the owner left us, he had invited us to come back any time.

Our discussions ranged on many topics of interest to fifteen-to-sixteen-year-old boys, including, of course, girls. Don also talked about the YMCA, extolling its virtues. He was a member of the Paterson Y, a striking building I had walked past many times. Though I did not raise the issue, I recalled that there had been some talking down of the Y on semireligious grounds in the St. Joe's environment. This had snuffed out any potential interest I may have had in the past. Don, however, made me promise to look into membership when I returned home. On the Monday when his three weeks were up and I saw him off at the bus, we swore our eternal friendship. We did, in fact, exchange a couple of letters during the remainder of that summer.

A daily highlight at Altaha was the hour-long campfire each evening starting at eight o'clock. It took place in a large room with a great fireplace, part of the same building containing the kitchen, dining veranda, game room, stove, and upstairs craft shop. Chief Lotee usually presided, but many were called upon to participate; at times we had visiting speakers. In residence that summer was a senior counselor, Bruce Barton, an Englishman who had recently lived in one of the British African colonies. He often gave us short talks on international matters including the Spanish Civil War, then at its height, a subject that always ignited conflict from the floor among those for and against Franco; the current Japanese invasion of China, about which everyone seemed more passive than they did on European matters; and, of course, the German question.

Bruce was also a lot of fun and seemed to know all of us. Toward the end of the summer he organized a large aquacade held on a Saturday evening at the camp waterfront, but open to the public. All the experienced swimmers took part after a week of rehearsals. Part of the performance required a chorus on the pier while the remainder put on a version of an Esther Williams show with the lake lit up by spotlights. Some of the songs were parodies such as "Toreadora—don't spit on the floora—use the cuspidora—that's what it's fora." (I do not think Bizet would have recognized our version of the Toreador song from *Carmen*.)

At the end of the program as the Chief was thanking Bruce, Eugene Vivian (or Avivliano, as Ted and I called him by then) by prearrangement stepped in front to lead us in Gilbert and Sullivan's "For He Is an Englishman." When we came to the other nationalities that Bruce might have been, we acted out en masse some humorous characterizations that today would probably be labeled racist. It was all great fun and Bruce enjoyed it. I often wondered what happened to him after he returned to England in that fall of 1937.

The summer ended all too soon. Though I had finished all my merit badge work, I was cautioned that the acid test still lay ahead—whatever that meant. On the last day of camp after the others had left, the Chief kept four or five of the all-summer group behind to help him and a counselor with the final closing. Before we left, he thanked us for our efforts that summer and asked that we think about returning next year as junior counselors. It sounded exciting, but in my case was never to be.

Junior year at Eastside "was the best of times and the worst of times." In addition to English and history I now faced three commercial subjects: bookkeeping, typing, and stenography. Some of my classmates seemed to have a natural facility for stenography, but to me it was a horror and as relevant as learning to bark. An understanding and sympathetic teacher prevented a complete disaster.

More interesting to me that semester was joining a newly formed group at school—the International Relations Club. At our weekly meeting we listened to a short talk by a student or visitor; then for the remainder of the hour we discussed the issue. Topics ranged widely—the Spanish Civil War, especially the role of the Abraham Lincoln Brigade, was always good for some fireworks, as was the German and later the Italian role in that war. Since we had some members recently arrived from Germany and Austria, the Nazi regime and its goals made for a heated topic. One of this group, Bella Finer, particularly impressed me, though she was usually my opponent in the debate about U.S. isolationism. I was at that point very much an isolationist—not unusual in 1937.

We had a very effective faculty sponsor, a Ruth Tierney who insisted on advance preparation so that we did not talk off the top of our heads. Through her we had literature from the Carnegie Endowment and, of course, from our own school library. The *New York Times* had started "The News of the Week in Review," a couple of years before; most of us were at least at that level for our discussion background preparation.

Scouting activities peaked for me that year. At the first meeting in September the scoutmaster, Gus Rauchenbach, announced that I would be senior patrol leader that year. This was a kind of first-sergeant type role: assembling the scouts, passing on instructions, supervising activities, and so on. All in all, it was a good experience for one just turning sixteen.

The so-called "acid test" for Eagle Scout turned out to be a meeting in late September with the scoutmaster and scout committee of fathers. Primarily, they had to ascertain that I understood my responsibilities as Troop 35's first Eagle Scout. At the end of the session Mr. Hodgson, the chairman, said that he would discuss the matter with Chief Lotee, who had the final decision. About six weeks later I received a long letter of congratulations from James E. West, the Chief Executive of the Boy Scouts of America. He pointed out that only one-half of 1 percent of scouts had Eagle rank, and that big things were expected of me. Something to think about. I was told that the ceremonial award would come later.

Following up on my discussion with Don Fegley, by November I got around to visiting the YMCA and inquiring about membership. I ended up talking to one of the managers, who said that I could earn my membership by working at the desk on Saturday mornings. Also, since I was sixteen, I was free to come and go, using the facilities as I wished. The setup was impressive—a large gym and track as well as a swimming pool, showers, and barber shop. After quickly accepting, I soon began to use the facility about three times a week. Don, still fifteen, was in a group that met together under supervision, so I saw him only occasionally.

Early fall of that year marked the beginning of the 1937-38 recession; in a matter of months the gains made over the years by Roosevelt's New Deal seemed to be slipping away. It was in this environment that Aunt Annie kept her promise to Fanny and procured a boarder, one safely ensconced with the WPA, a Mr. McDougal. He was a slow-moving Scot who was in some way affiliated with the project to rehabilitate the Dey Mansion, a relic of the Revolutionary War in the countryside near Paterson. One boarder, though, was not enough to solve Fanny's financial problems, as her resources had about run out; to further complicate matters, her health began a slow deterioration.

Annie relocated that fall from South Paterson to an apartment at 291 Market Street on the corner of Straight Street. At the end of the fall the apartment beneath her was coming open. Annie's plan was to move Fanny in there, get additional boarders for her, and help with the work entailed. Though reluctant, Fanny had little choice. Action followed plan and by December I was for all practical purposes back again with Aunt Annie and Johnny Bustard after almost nine years, though technically I lived still with Aunt Fanny. I had no way of knowing this in December 1937, but this was to be the last of the nine moves made during my Paterson years.

Because things were in turmoil from the move, I took Andy and Ruth up on an earlier invitation, spending a brief Christmas holiday with them in their new apartment in Far Rockaway. En route home I stopped with Aunt Dick in her Forest Hills apartment from which her second husband, Sid Babcock, commuted to an office job in Manhattan. A good hostess, she gave me a walking tour of the area, including the old tennis club where the U.S. Open took place. We ate lunch in a delicatessen, typical of that area, that had a rack full of newspapers. There were still news stories on the aftermath of Japan's bombing of the U.S. gunboat *Panay* in China's Yangtze River earlier that month. These accounts triggered a luncheon discussion that brought out my isolationist outlook. Aunt Dick was a real Anglophile who countered my views with some pretty good arguments.

When the spring of 1938 semester began, I felt my lack of direction even more intensely than before, and I still had a general feeling of frustration. When the semester ended five months later, though, both of these feelings would be gone, and the direction of my life would completely change.

Life at 291 Market Street was different. By that winter Aunt Fanny had two boarders besides Mr. McDougal—a Mr. Ross and a Mr. McLain. Both were retired and had been deposited by their families, in Ross's case by his son, a schoolteacher from northern New

Jersey. Mr. Ross was a good storyteller and I suspect never tarnished a good story with fact. Mr. McLain was a bit more taciturn. Fortunately, both liked to play cribbage, as did Mr. McDougal, so in the evenings all three kept one another engaged.

Despite failing health Fanny ran her own show with increasing help from Annie. I moved freely from floor to floor; it was all one house to me. Annie, by then a teetotaler, allowed no alcoholic beverages in her apartment and had become a big radio fan since our earlier days together. In the 1930s radio had become a craze in America and was still something of a novelty. Annie's tastes were eclectic. For soap operas her favorites were "Helen Trent," "Myrt and Marge," and "Just Plain Bill." For adventure she tuned in to the Lone Ranger, who was helped by his companion Tonto and, of course, his faithful steed Silver. I never broke her spell with the news that Silver was a couple of coconut shells on a soundboard. By far her favorite singer was Kate Smith with her signature "When the Moon Comes Over the Mountain."

Sunday evenings two shows took priority over all others. First, there was Major Bowes Amateur Hour in which the unctuous major brought on an assorted array of singers, musicians, tap dancers, etc. Occasionally a performance was terminated in midstream with the major's gong. The other Sunday evening regular was Jack Benny, who always remained thirty-nine, and his sidekick Rochester. I never listened to any of her shows, except for Jack Benny. My own favorites were the orchestras, such as Guy Lombardo and Tommy Dorsey and the Lucky Strike "Hit Parade."

Each year in February St. Joseph's Church sponsored a Communion Breakfast for Troop 35. The boys and their fathers went together to eight o'clock Mass and afterward to the school hall for a large breakfast. Toward the end of breakfast one or two members of the scout committee, followed by the scoutmaster, made remarks. In 1938 when Gus Rauchenbach's turn came, he concluded his remarks by announcing that he was convening a Court of Honor. He called me forward to receive the Eagle Scout badge officially. As I started back to my seat, he grabbed me and, to my surprise, said that he had another award. He began by telling how almost four years ago he had helped me through my Tenderfoot tests; today, he said, with a slight tear in his eye, he was inducting me into the Flaming Arrow Patrol, the highest honor the troop could award. I was really surprised, since that award required a unanimous vote by the relatively few members in this honorary group and all were at the Junior Assistant Scoutmaster level or higher. It was a grand day for me, but I was brought down to earth by being placed in charge of the cleanup detail.

In the winter of 1938 the Columbian Squires were assisting the Knights of Columbus with their Sunday night bingo games—our task being to sell the "special" cards to members of the audience when those games were announced. The locale was in the main ballroom of the Alexander Hamilton Hotel, in those days North Jersey's finest. This eight-floor hotel, built in 1930 next door to the Fabian Theater, had elegant appointments; and its lobby included a number of stores featuring such items as cigars and Fedora hats.

One Sunday in March it was announced that there would be no bingo the following week. Since I was free that next Sunday, March 27, I decided to see the first evening movie then playing at the Fabian. The program began with a "March of Time" on the United States Coast Guard. It featured the various activities of that service: breaking up ice in the Great Lakes, international iceberg patrol, the lighthouses, and more. The end of the film focused for a few minutes on a small but attractive campus showing cadets on parade and in other activities, then a class of cadets graduating and being commissioned in the Coast Guard. The school was the United States Coast Guard Academy in New London, Connecticut, the smallest of the three government academies. I had been unaware of its existence, but now I wondered how one could become a Coast Guard cadet. Since the film was at the beginning of the program, I stayed over to see it a second time, meanwhile thinking about it off and on while trying to concentrate on the feature.

The next afternoon after school, having determined that there was no Coast Guard facility in town, I went to Navy recruiting to ask how I could get information on the Coast Guard Academy. The petty officer I talked to wrote out the address of the Commandant, U.S. Coast Guard in Washington. That same afternoon I mailed a letter requesting information on the academy.

About ten days later the mail brought a copy of regulations for appointments to the Coast Guard Academy. It had all the appeal of a booklet on fire drills. Fortunately, it was accompanied by a public-relations type booklet explaining the regulations in more appealing terms and containing pictures of cadets in various activities. After several readings of both I deduced the following: appointments were based on a nationwide competitive exam held in May of each year; about two thousand boys competed for some one hundred appointments; to qualify for competition one must have taken inter alia four years of math, two years of science, and two years of a foreign language. My commercial course contained none of these and I had only one year of high school remaining. A Coast Guard appointment sounded like an impossible dream, but why not look into it? I had nothing to lose and "a world to gain."

On the day that school resumed I found the academic counseling office (I was previously unaware of its existence) and paid a visit. The counselor listened to what I had to say, perhaps a bit incredulously. She asked to borrow the regulations, told me she would look at my record, and asked me to come back in two days. When I started explaining my modest record to date, she stopped me and repeated, "Come back in two days." By the next day I began to have doubts but kept the appointment.

When I returned, she seemed upbeat. Though my record was not outstanding, she said, my average did meet Eastside's college certification level. My "other" test scores indicated that I had the ability to meet higher standards. In addition she had talked to my home room teachers for the past three semesters, and they had confirmed this, especially Mr. Motola. The question was, did I have the desire and willingness to begin to use my ability? That, she said, only I could answer.

Before I could respond to her challenge, she laid out a paper outlining a two-year program. I would graduate on schedule, but then return for a year of postgraduate work. The PG year would require second, third, and fourth year math to be taken simultaneously, along with science and a foreign language. By May of that year I could be ready to compete in the Coast Guard exam. It was, she said, a big gamble and required "a borrowed year," as she put it. "Think about it, talk to your guardian and come back to see me Monday." Wow!

For the next couple of days I thought of nothing else. I might be pursuing an impossible dream, but so was attaining Eagle Scout when I first thought about it. What did I have to lose, really? Aunt Fanny's health was such that I did not bring it up to her; because Annie was again the boss, it was to her I described the change in direction. I emphasized what the counselor called my borrowed year. She listened and her reply was, "Doug, I think you should try, and don't worry about the extra year." Now it was up to me. On Monday when I conveyed my decision, the counselor smiled and said, "You made a good decision. Go for it and don't look back."

Evaluating my situation in the next few weeks, I realized that I was embarked on a very competitive venture. The Great Depression had taken its toll even on the relatively small number of youths who attended college in those days. Because families could not afford other forms of higher education, the government academies became very attractive to many boys. To meet this competition and at the same time embark on a new direction in school would require complete dedication on my part. Obviously, my lifestyle had to change a great deal even before September. I could not, for example, spend the summer at Camp Altaha because of the opportunity costs involved. No more Lake Hopatcong!

While all this was occupying my thoughts that spring, I chanced on a most fortuitous contact. One day as I exited the Danforth public library one of my holdover friends from the St. Joe's days, Walter Kennedy, was heading up the steps with a boy I had never seen before. He was introduced as Harry Hionides just arrived from Canton, Ohio (where he had lived with his father), to move in with his mother and siblings already in Paterson. His purpose, Walt said, was to qualify as a resident and eventually to compete for the West Point appointment in the local congressional district. Meanwhile, he would be taking some postgraduate courses at Eastside. I could scarcely believe my ears and quickly suggested that we three go for coffee across the street. After normal pleasantries I made arrangements to visit Harry at his home over the next weekend.

As it turned out, I could not have chanced on a better mentor. Though his mother's flat was modest, Harry had already carved out a study complete with blackboard, desk, books, and files. He even had all West Point entrance exams going back to 1920. When Harry looked over my new school program, he had some practical ideas that I adopted. The three years of math in one troubled him, he suggested auditing geometry in advance during my senior year and getting tutored in second-year algebra the following summer.

Harry was an interesting guy and we became good friends. Eccentric both in dress and habit, he looked older than his age—a Greek version of Mr. Chips in the vest and coat that he always wore except in hot weather. It turned out that his uncle owned two counter restaurants on Paterson Street that featured "hot Texas wieners." Back in my newspaper delivery days, I had spent some earnings there each Saturday after the week's collections.

During many long walks that spring and summer he expounded on many topics, including girls. His favorite topic, though, was West Point, about which he knew a great deal. In time my own interest grew, but in those days I did not connect West Point with my own future. All the while, though, Harry was making my conversion from an uninspired commercial student to a competitive college prep student much less difficult—indeed maybe the word is *possible*.

Sometime early that summer Harry began to work part time serving up hot Texas wieners and by then Walt Kennedy had an ushering job at the Fabian Theater. I realized that I, too, should earn at least my own spending money. Again, Walt came to my rescue, arranging for me to be interviewed at the Regent Theater by the assistant manager, a Mr. Plowman. I was hired at the going rate of twenty-five cents per hour. The minimum wage in 1938 was forty cents, but that applied only to firms involved in interstate commerce. Apparently, shipping films from Hollywood to Paterson was not considered interstate commerce—at least by Mr. Plowman and his superiors.

Because I now had little free time, I had to give up, painfully, one important activity—scouting. In August the Troop 35 leadership had a preliminary meeting to discuss the coming year's agenda. My invitation to attend meant that I was to be designated as a Junior Assistant Scoutmaster. I attended but only to explain why I could no longer participate actively. Everyone understood but that did not lessen the pain accompanying this necessary decision of passage.

September 1938 marked the launching of my new academic program. I began by stopping by each teacher's office to explain what I was up to. Kathleen Westman, a Wellesley graduate and head of the English department, immediately asked me to write a theme for her. After she read it, her critique was merciless. My essays and her constructive criticism went on all semester, and I did emerge with a passable writing style.

Hallie Turner, my physics teacher and head of science, was most friendly and suggested I come by to see her anytime I felt I needed help. Mrs. Gibson in American history suggested that I volunteer for oral reports, and I did so, even for a couple of debates. At Harry's suggestion I joined the math and Spanish clubs but did not visit the teachers since the classes were lower level. The math club turned out to be very useful; the Spanish club was *nada* in my case.

That month of September brought the famous hurricane. (Stories about it lasted for years in Long Island and New England.) The storm began with a rainy period about the 16th and by the 19th became torrential. On Wednesday the 21st the storm hit Long Island and then New England; in Paterson it was mainly torrential rains. For days we read in the papers about the destruction along the coast and New England.

In Europe there was another storm that month—a mortal one that would change all our lives and reshape world society. At the time, though, it seemed distant, dealing with increasingly strident

German demands on Czechoslovakia. The question was, What would Britain and France do if Hitler seized that part of Czechoslovakia known as the Sudetenland with its heavily German population? Events were intensified by the Nürenberg party rally of September 12. For the next eighteen days radio and press took us on the three trips to Germany made by British Prime Minister Neville Chamberlain. With his umbrella, high collar, and mustache, he looked remarkably like an actor playing someone from the Victorian period.

The culmination came at Munich early on September 30 at a meeting between Chamberlain, Daladier of France, Hitler, and Mussolini (we called him Musso). The meeting ended in a sellout of Czechoslovakia—the Sudetenland now and more to come. Ed Murrow was on the air from London reporting the prime minister's return—that of a returning hero, except to the Cassandra of 1938, Winston Chuchill. Who of us who were around then could ever forget Chamberlain's unfortunate statement as he leaned from the window of 10 Downing Street? "It is peace with honor. I believe it is peace for our time." That fall my schedule did not permit me to attend many meetings of the International Relations Club, but when I did, my views had become ambivalent; I no longer took a strong position for United States isolationism. Still, along with most Americans, I felt relief after the Munich "settlement." The general feeling was that the issues involved were not our problem.

With school underway my ushering at the Regent was now confined to weekends, including Sunday evenings, our busiest time. I was thus not listening to the radio on Sunday, October 30, 1938, when Orson Welles dramatized, a bit too realistically, H.G. Wells's *The War of the Worlds*. When his Martians landed in huge cylinders near Princeton, I was in the Regent fighting the German air force of 1917 with Errol Flynn in the *Dawn Patrol*; hence I missed the ensuing panic that the Welles broadcast had set in motion.

The Regent Theater had been built before the Great War. Its lobby, though small, was very ornate with an elaborate decorative frieze and attractive paneling. It was previously used as a combination vaudeville theater and cinema. Bill, in charge of the elaborate stage, frequently regaled me with tales of past performers. It turned out that he knew my father, who had played there for a time in the orchestra.

As the fall wore on and I became more deeply involved in school work, I began to model my study after that of Harry Hionides. Since Aunt Fanny no longer used her kitchen, I inherited it; the table became my desk. Between the study, school, ushering, and the YMCA, I had time for little else except trying to make Fanny's life a bit more comfortable by bringing her meals and other small items. My attentions were important to her, but her time at home was not destined to last long.

Aunt Fanny's doctor, who occasionally made house calls, was Andrew McBride, a rather remarkable individual. A staunch and influential Democrat, he had been mayor of Paterson in 1913, later serving in the Great War. His party affiliation had long before tied him in with Fanny's family, the McCues. Always taking some of his visiting time for me, he seemed interested in my future plans and, in fact, later proved very helpful. A decade later, after his death, the great Paterson sculptor Gaetano Federici created a statue of him. It was placed in City Hall Square near those of Patersonian Garret Hobart (McKinley's first vice president) and Alexander Hamilton, founder of the city.

By the end of 1938 it was evident that I had adjusted to my new school program and busy schedule; my grade average had jumped many points. I had begun to feel as if I had goals at last. There was a price, though. I had become more of a social drone than ever. Maybe, I reflected, I could remedy that situation later, when time permitted.

It was not an easy time. Aunt Fanny, with whom I had lived for almost ten years, was now seriously ill. I did all I could to help and comfort her, but by the turn of the year she was back in St. Joseph's Hospital. She had been in and out, but now her condition was terminal with some kind of abdominal cancer. On Monday, February 6, 1939, she died.

As was the custom still observed by some in those days, the viewing and wake were at home. Besides the family, many old friends and acquaintances appeared. The mourners included Mrs. Lappin, the scout in my 1929 rescue, and the Gallaghers. Georgie, my old buddy, threw his arms around Annie and said, "Cheer up, the worst is yet to come." This was greeted with a silent derision by those who heard, including a perplexed Aunt Annie. In later years, though, I realized that whatever it was he intended to say, he was eminently correct. The funeral the next day followed the same general pattern as Aunt Rosie's had three-and-a-half years before; Fanny was laid to rest next to her in the family plot. Gone were two of the three sisters to whom I would always be indebted; now I was back with Annie, as I had been a decade before.

That winter Harry Hionides decided that all work made Doug a dull boy—and he was right. He insisted that I join him Friday evenings at a jitterbug-type hangout that was flourishing on Park Avenue opposite Eastside High. It was not my style, but why not. Endless records featured Benny Goodman, Artie Shaw, Tommy Dorsey, and others. The songs I now recall: "A-Tisket A-Tasket," "Ti-Pi-Tin," "Three Little Fishes"; and for those of my speed "Harbor Lights" and "Thanks for the Memories." Always present were friends of Harry's and seemingly plenty of girls; occasionally there was a car available to all. I began my on-the-job training in necking and related wrestling activities with one of the dates I found attractive, though to Harry's amusement I avoided "going all the way," thanks to inhibitions planted at St. Joe's. Still, the Friday evenings were fun as long as they lasted.

During this period I occasionally saw my father in his apartment, always in the daytime when his wife, who worked in New York, was not present. On one occasion he mentioned that he would be taking a trip to West Point in early April for some business with the band and asked if I was interested in the trip. Since I had never been there, I accepted on condition that Harry could come with us. We headed up the Hudson on old 9W, and I was really struck by the beauty of the Hudson Valley.

As my father conducted his business, Harry, who had been there before, acted as my guide. I was especially interested in the cadet library with its medieval-like construction. One corridor contained a white marble memorial to Edgar Allan Poe, who had been a cadet for less than a year before being court-martialed and dismissed as unfit in 1831. On the memorial was a most appropriate quotation from Francis Bacon: "There is no exquisite beauty without some strangeness in proportion."

By the time the tour was over, I was completely taken with the academy; but I knew realistically that there was no chance of my getting an appointment. The competitive exam Harry was pointing toward would be given in November. By then I would be only a few months into sophomore, junior, and senior math—a key part of the exam. Still, from that April day on, West Point as a school interested me.

There were dramatic developments in Europe all during that spring of 1939. Not content with grabbing the Sudetenland the previous year, Germany now occupied Prague and swallowed up large parts of Czechoslovakia (the other parts were in course overrun by other jackal nations). That model democracy established by the Treaty of Versailles had ceased to exist, but there was not yet a general European war. In the same month, March, Franco's troops reached Madrid and ended the thirty-two-month Spanish Civil War. The following month Mussolini occupied Albania, ending the rule of King Zog, a name that had intrigued me since my grammar school geography classes. The lights had not yet gone out in Europe, but they were flickering and dim.

Soon it was time for Eastside High's class of June 1939—the largest in its thirteen-year history—to start thinking about graduation. In my case, though I would be receiving my commercial diploma, I would not actually be leaving Eastside, just saying goodbye to my classmates. When our yearbook, the *Senior Mirror*, was published, it was interesting and fun to visit briefly with those I knew best as we exchanged signatures and wishes. Many years later in reading over their messages to me, I could find no pattern except that my colleagues considered me a good American history student. The comment along those lines I treasured most came from my debating opponent of the International Relations Club, Bella Finer, who also happened to be in history class with me.

Rehearsals began a week before, supervised by the music director, Mabel Wood, a live wire with boundless energy. On the big night, Tuesday, June 27, we entered to Elgar's "Pomp and Circumstance." The remarks of Harvey Asher, class valedictorian, were oddly prescient about what our own role might be in the mortal storm breaking over Europe. Of course, no one there that night could realize that the males in this class of June 1939 would provide some of the "Boys of D-Day." We exited to Verdi's "Grand March" from *Aida*. As we turned in our caps and gowns, a teacher handed each of us an envelope containing our class standing. I opened mine somewhat apprehensively but was pleasantly surprised, given my mediocre efforts of the first three years. Afterward, I talked with Walt and Irene, who had attended the ceremony, but this time there was no Aunt Rosie, no party. Later, I did join some classmates in party-hopping; at one I ran into Milly Roeder and had a long chat. As I left her, I said in mock straight-face, "When I grow up I'll be back to see you." After looking perplexed for a moment, she then broke into her box-office smile. I never saw her again.

The summer of 1939 was all work for me. Each morning I was tutored in second-year algebra. To pay for it, I ushered from midafternoon to early evening. My ushering was now in the elegant Fabian, which offered many opportunities for work that summer. Coincidentally, that year of 1939 was probably Hollywood's best year of film-making; and, balanced as we were between the Depression and the war, attendance was high. Two great movies I remember particularly, not only because I saw each about a dozen times as an usher but also because they were most impressive in their own way: *Goodbye Mr. Chips* and *The Wizard of Oz*. It would be hard to forget Robert Donat's remarkable performance as Mr. Chips, and almost everyone's, particularly Judy Garland's, in the other.

Harry Hionides, whom I saw occasionally when neither of us was otherwise engaged, was busy getting ready for both Senatorial and Representative West Point competitions in the fall. He convinced me that I too should take the exams, not in expectation of winning anything, but as preparation for my own big effort the following May.

Early in the summer there seemed to be a lull in the European crisis; but, as July progressed, news reports made it clear that Hitler had intentions of absorbing two creations of the Treaty of Versailles: the "free" city of Danzig and the Polish corridor separating Prussia from greater Germany. Then on August 21 came the bombshell: Germany and the Soviet Union had signed a nonaggression treaty, which effectively isolated Poland between two enemies. What would Britain and France do about their treaties with Poland? Would there be another cop-out—even though Western Europe was mobilizing—as in the case of Czechoslovakia?

The answer came fairly rapidly. Early on the morning of Friday, September 1, Hitler's armies marched into Poland. During that Labor Day weekend we listened to the radio whenever we could, especially to H.V. Kaltenborn and Edward R. Murrow. Early Sunday, September 3, came the tired voice of Neville Chamberlain in words that none of us who heard it would ever forget:

> This morning the British Ambassador in Berlin handed to the German government a final note stating that unless we heard from them by eleven o'clock that they were preparing at once to withdraw their troops from Poland, a state of war would exist between us. I have to tell you now that no such understanding was received and consequently this country is at war with Germany.

The interwar years were over.

Two days later I began my final year at Eastside as a postgraduate student and as the object of some curiosity on the part of the math department. Mr. Daugherty, the head, called me into his office, presumably to look me over. He began by telling me that no one had ever attempted three years of high school math in one year and that he would be watching my progress. At the end of our meeting he offered me a part-time job in his office, answering phones and other clerical work. Apparently he had some money for this, and I readily accepted. He was a strange fellow, but once I got used to his abrupt manner, he was easy to work for.

When I was at home, I was naturally working on lessons. The lower floor was quiet, for the eating and congregating occurred in Annie's upstairs apartment and I pretty much had my kitchen-study to myself. Ushering in the Fabian continued but for weekends only. Trips to the YMCA for exercise were all the more important since my gym days at Eastside were over. Friends usually visited a couple of times a week. Jim Farrell from St. Joe's days was a regular en route home from his evening classes at a downtown business school. Others included Walt Kennedy, temporarily in a local teachers college; Harry Hionides, when his schedule permitted; and occasionally some of my scouting friends.

That pretty much was my dull but academically productive life in the fall of 1939 as Europe unraveled. Aunt Annie, Johnny Bustard, and Toots remained supportive as did Walt and Irene. I am afraid that, preoccupied with trying to escape from a future in Walt's office, I took my adopted family for granted. I suspect, though, that they understood.

In Europe the month of September ended with a bang whatever was left of the long armistice. By the 10th, Britain had its small expeditionary force in France. By the 17th the USSR had attacked Poland, and by the 27th Warsaw had capitulated to the German blitzkrieg. Notwithstanding, a substantial majority of American citizens were against any form of U.S. involvement, and FDR had proclaimed both a state of limited emergency and neutrality.

After Poland the Germans did not move westward. The war then entered a strange phase that the isolationist senator from Idaho, William Borah, called the phony war; the Germans called it the sitzkrieg. The only action that fall was the Soviet invasion of Finland at the end of November. During what became a winter war with Soviet setbacks, American citizens rooted for the Finnish underdog, realizing, of course, that in the end there was no hope.

In October and November came the West Point competitive exams Harry had been preparing for. I took both as part of my learning process. The first, given by New Jersey Senator W. Warren Barbour, was statewide with around two hundred boys competing. I managed to overlook one page of the English exam to seal my disaster that day. In a couple of months we got the results: Harry did well but was not high enough for the appointment. I ended up as number forty, but the experience was worth the "also ran."

The local exam, sponsored by Congressman George Seger, attracted about sixty boys to Paterson Central High the day after Thanksgiving. I can now remember only one event connected with that day. During the geometry portion of the exam I happened to glance up briefly and saw a competitor struggling madly with his broken compass as he tried to set up a geometric construction. I had a perfectly fine compass lying on my desk. As I was looking, I caught the eye of another competitor nearer him who also observed the frantic fellow about to give up trying to prove that S, B, and R lay in a straight line. We both turned back to our own work and our resting compasses. Ah, competition. Harry won the appointment that day, and a friend from the Eastside Math Club, Saul "Curley" Jackson, was one of the two alternates. I ended up ninth, but before the results were announced had a few dreams of glory. Now West Point was beginning to interest me as a place, not just as a practice competition.

With the turn of the year in 1940 I was now in the second half of my borrowed year and could begin the Coast Guard Academy application process. Unlike the military and naval academy admissions, no members of Congress were involved. All aspirants began and ended the process with Coast Guard headquarters. Normally, about two thousand boys qualified nationally to compete after the headquarters evaluation. I began the procedure in early January; but since I was still taking so many required courses, Eastside was required to submit intermediate grades in mid-semester before I could receive approval to compete. Candidates also needed letters of recommendation; mine were from Chief Lotee, recently retired, and my teachers Hallie Turner, head of the science department, and Kathleen Westman, head of English. On April 5 I received approval to compete on May 15 and 16 for a July 1940 appointment.

At this point I was fully at home with my school situation and knew that I was about to achieve what I had set out to do. Mr. Daugherty had actually used me several times as a substitute teacher with lower-level math classes while waiting for a regular substitute to appear. Though I was uncomfortable with this position, it worked out fine, thanks more to my experience as a Senior Patrol Leader and theater usher than to my math background. I was thankful, however, when my Spanish teacher, who correctly considered me marginal to meet the college-level 80 percent for foreign language, went to Daugherty and put an end to my teaching.

In early March, a few days after he had taken the West Point entrance exam, Harry called to say that he had some things for me. He appeared with a box of old exams and his copy of *West Point Today*; then came a surprising announcement. He had flunked the entrance physical because of albumin in his kidneys. The rejection seemed final, as there was little chance of the condition improving. Apparently, he had been aware of the defect but was hoping that it would clear. He announced that within twenty-four hours he was leaving for Canada to join their Air Force if possible. I tried the best I could to make him feel better, but he did the talking. He hoped that someday I would go to West Point; that was why he was giving me the materials. He said he must leave now to prepare for his trip. I thanked him profusely as we said our goodbyes. After he left, I sat thinking for a long time, then read over the West Point physical requirements. They were the same as for the Coast Guard with one exception: one could fail the West Point physical for "extreme ugliness." I surmised that I could get by that one in the unlikely event that I ever received an appointment to West Point.

That spring both Kathleen Westman and Hallie Turner pointed out the risk in counting on a Coast Guard appointment based on an exam. Both suggested that I have a fallback position. When I brought up the financial problem, each independently suggested Montclair State Teachers, the flagship of the vast state teachers college system. Entry was based on their own test given at the end of May, and scholarship possibilities might cover residence dorms as well. I applied.

During my overpreoccupation with myself that spring, Western Europe had its final unraveling. In mid-March Finland collapsed in its one-sided war after a good blooding of the Soviets. Hitler began his spring activities by invading and occupying Denmark and Norway with remarkable precision and speed beginning on April 9. This was merely preliminary, though, to the major event that he was about to launch, transforming the face of Western Europe for years to come.

Hitler's campaign in the West, which opened on May 10, was one of the world's great military masterpieces. By early morning of that day the Germans were moving forward all along the Dutch and Belgian frontiers. The whole campaign in Holland took the Germans only four days, and about the same in Belgium. The big surprise came, though, on the supposedly impassable Ardennes Forest farther south. Pouring in three armies, the Germans moved ahead virtually unopposed, arriving on the Meuse, the main French defense position, by the night of the 12th. The next day the Germans surged on virtually unopposed—armor racing ahead supported in their new blitzkrieg tactics by the Stuka dive bombers. It was a strategic breakthrough of staggering proportions. On the day Hitler launched his attack, Winston Churchill became British prime minister and announced that he had nothing to offer "but blood, toil, tears, and sweat." He was right.

Such was the situation when I sat for my Coast Guard Academy exam on May 15, 1940. The exam was given in many places around the country, but surely the greatest gathering was in that huge room in the old Post Office building on Manhattan's Christopher Street. As advised in the letter of instructions I handed to the Coast Guard petty officer at the door my entrance pass and my photograph with name written on the bottom. The laughing photograph taken and developed hastily by the father of a friend the week before made me look more like a raconteur than a serous applicant, but it served the purpose.

Since I had never met anyone who had taken this examination, I had no idea what to expect. The morning was devoted to math and consisted of a dozen tough questions covering all aspects of high school math. The afternoon was the English exam, and to my surprise the final question required a book review on a book of one's choice. The only book I had read that academic year was the one Harry left me, *West Point Today* by Banning—not very politic, but the best I could come up with.

As the day ended, I felt uncertain about how well I had done. The next day was the aptitude exam, a personal interview with a Coast Guard captain during which he looked you over in terms of appearance, conversational ability, bearing, and so on. Scuttlebutt during the break between math and English the first day was that one had better be up on Coast Guard history. That night in lieu of dinner I was in Paterson's Danforth library, until it closed, reading anything I could get my hands on about the Coast Guard. Back in New York the next day I waited in line for my turn, which lasted exactly five minutes. There was time in the conversation, though, for Captain Farwell to toss me a teaser on the Lighthouse Service, and I was able to fill the minute or so allowed by disgorging some of the material read the evening before. I expect that Farwell sensed the source of my knowledge, but he seemed satisfied. That was it for the exam.

On returning to Paterson I ran into Walt Kennedy, and we talked not about my exam but about the German breakthrough. Almost everyone that spring watched the news in papers and listened to the European correspondents' analyses and constant bulletins. I even bought myself a small hand radio, something fairly new on the market. It was hard to keep up with the speed of events. In late May the British and some Allies were evacuated at Dunkirk, an amazing operation for two reasons: Hitler letting it happen, and the British being able to pull it off. Italy entered the war on June 10; on that same night I heard on my radio Roosevelt speaking at the Charlottesville commencement: "The hand that held the dagger has struck it into the back of its neighbor."

Now the end was near for France. On June 14 the Germans entered Paris; on the 22nd France surrendered. The lights had gone out in Western Europe. The pictures of German troops parading past the Arc de Triomphe in Paris brought it all home to me in a way that nothing else had. Though I had never traveled farther than New Jersey and New York, I always considered Paris the first city of the world—one that in a spiritual sense belonged to all of us. Seeing that picture I knew for the first time, at least in my own mind, that someday our country would be in the war and that my generation would be fighting in it.

In the period after the exam I was mainly concerned with tidying up my last semester at Eastside and taking the Montclair State entrance exam, a two-day affair that included a tour of the impressive campus. As math would be my major, I met with the department head, who had my high school and exam grades by then. After a rather long conversation he offered me a full scholarship, including residence. Surprised and pleased, I did not tell him about the Coast Guard Academy; after all, I might not get that appointment. In any case, the college seemed a nice place to spend a year while taking the West Point exam in the fall.

About the middle of June a letter with my exam grades arrived from Coast Guard Headquarters. While I was not in the top one hundred, I was high enough to take the physical. Some of the initial winners would be eliminated by the physical, and some would change their minds, thus advancing those, like me, who scored lower. After the physical, held at a public health service hospital in New York City, I was at loose ends for a while; but now at least I had a fallback. The borrowed year was paying off.

For the first time in two years I could put aside studying in favor of a social life. One such event was a trip to the New York World's Fair with a couple of my sisters and their husbands. The fair had opened in 1939 on over four thousand acres in Flushing Meadow, Queens. Under development since 1935, this international exposition was the biggest and most ambitious ever and included exhibits from over thirty states, almost sixty foreign countries, and about thirteen hundred firms, ranging from vulgar to inspirational. At the fair's center was a 700-foot needlelike tower called the Trylon, and a

200-foot globe called the Perisphere. This combination symbolized the fair in media and literature.

In the one day available to us we could hardly do more than scratch the surface. At this remove I remember being impressed by the General Electric exhibit with its manmade lightning and thunder. Especially fascinating to me was the 250-foot parachute jump. Strapped in your seat, you were slowly hoisted up and got a bird's-eye view of the whole fair; then at the top you were released and had a wild moment until the chute filled with air and slowly floated down.

Since the fair opened in April 1939, what turned out to be the greatest war in human history was already underway. Understandably by 1940 many exhibits were missing, such as that of the Soviets, whose building had been razed. Still, it was great fun, even though its theme, "The World of Tomorrow," turned out to be only a PR christening after all.

As July went on, I was uneasy. I had heard nothing more from Coast Guard headquarters, and their last letter had advised all candidates not to contact them. Surmising that they had filled their quota, I began to think about how to spend the summer and where to look for a job.

On Friday, July 12 in the second mail came a letter from Coast Guard headquarters. I opened it very nervously. The opening paragraph told the story: "You are hereby tendered an appointment as a cadet in the United States Coast Guard." The letter directed me to report on Wednesday, July 17, to execute the oath of office at the academy in New London. I sat in my kitchen-study, where I had opened the letter, for a full ten minutes, trying to regain my composure before passing on the news to a delighted Aunt Annie.

Since I was leaving home permanently, there were many things to do in the few days remaining—packing, disposing of things; and making many telephone calls. I received more calls after Saturday's *Evening News* ran an article, complete with my picture, announcing that Leo Douglas Kinnard was the first Eastside High graduate to be appointed to the Coast Guard Academy. I decided to leave from the

Paterson station on the Erie Railroad early on the day I was due in New London. As I would be changing trains in Grand Central, Annie insisted that Johnny Bustard accompany me that far. I knew a lot more about New York than he did, but I guess that the symbolism was important to her.

On the Erie part of the trip Johnny and I talked about various things, but mainly I read through the *New York Times*, a luxury I would not have time for soon again. The *Times* that morning was filled with stories of the wrangling going on at the Democratic National Convention in Chicago. At the end of June the Republicans had nominated Wendell Willkie of Indiana, a former Democrat and Wall Street lawyer. Now FDR was about to be nominated for a precedent-breaking third term.

Boarding the second train, I left a somewhat emotional Johnny, my friend since the day fourteen years ago when I left the Paterson orphan asylum. On this hot, muggy day I was delighted to find that the New York New Haven and Hartford coaches were air-conditioned, my first experience with such. I found a comfortable seat and though interested in the passing scenery, which was new to me, spent much of the two-and-a-half-hour trip in reminiscense.

Mostly, I thought of the people who had accepted the little boy from the orphanage and helped him all the way to his modest accomplishment of that day: my "adopted" family, many now dead, and especially Aunt Annie, who—whatever her earlier faults—had caused me to believe in myself; the nuns who somehow tolerated my constant talking in class; the scout leaders, especially Chief Lotee and Gus, my scoutmaster; many friends, early and late, with whom I shared those uncertain years of the Great Depression and the now-gathering storm that would probably break soon over all of us; and finally, the high school teachers who helped make my impossible dream of two years earlier happen. Overall, I reflected, it had been a lot of fun, and I had been damn lucky.

The commanding voice of the conductor broke the reverie with a start. "New London! New London!"

PART II

RENDEZVOUS WITH DESTINY (1940-1947)

"There is a mysterious cycle in human events.
To some generations much is given. Of others much is expected.
This generation of Americans has a rendezvous with destiny."

Franklin Roosevelt's Acceptance Speech
Democratic Convention, Philadelphia
June 27, 1936

6. New London Swab

As I stepped off the train into a hot muggy New London, straight ahead was a neatly dressed individual who immediately came toward me. "I'm Joe Steele. Are you headed out to the academy?" After I said yes and introduced myself, he steered me toward a cab that we shared. I had little chance to look around the town, as Joe launched at once into a brief bio. He had recently graduated from the University of Alabama and at some point had also been in the Marine reserves. I wondered uneasily how many more of my new classmates had comparable college backgrounds. All I could claim was Eastside High.

Arriving at the academy Joe and I were directed into Chase Hall, the cadet barracks, to drop our bags and to form a small group with some other newcomers. We then proceeded to the administration building, Hamilton Hall, centered on the parade field in the front part of the academy grounds. On the walk over, I was struck by the beauty and neatness of the small campus with its Georgian architecture. About eight of us gathered in the office of Captain James Pine, Superintendent, who without fanfare swore us in. Pine, who had graduated from the academy in 1908, was newly assigned to his position. Calm and personable, he was destined to be the academy's first superintendent to hold the rank of flag officer.

The oath he administered which we signed on leaving his office was standard for government officials, but with one rather specialized Coast Guard addition: "I will use my best endeavors to prevent and detect frauds against the laws of the United States imposing duties upon imports." I wondered what event had triggered that addition.

In any case we were now fourth-class cadets, U.S. Coast Guard, or, as fourth classmen were known, Swabs. From swearing in, we newcomers were directed to the Cadet Mess Hall already in operation for the noon meal. I had never seen so much food served at a midday meal, but my own appetite was nonexistent that day. This was also my first chance to see my classmates in any large number. Most looked a bit older than I had expected, and a substantial number seemed to be built like athletes, a contrast to my own "asthenic" build (as described on the physical exam report of the previous month). The classmate next to me at lunch solved one mystery that had been bothering me: where were the upperclassmen, those terrors I had read about in Harry's book about West Point? They were away for the summer on cruises and leave, and none would be in residence during Swab Summer, as it was called. What good news!

After lunch we had more paperwork. I can recall only one form, probably from the athletic department: What were my varsity sports and my physical dimensions? Answers: *None*; weight *137 lbs.*; height *5'11½"*; waist *29 inches*. I surmised that measurements such as mine were the stuff of water boys or assistant managers. What I did not know was that in a corps of roughly three hundred, each cadet was required to be on a varsity squad for at least two of the three seasons.

Next, we boarded busses to Fort Trumbull, which turned out to be a former Army coast artillery post. It had been one of a chain of such installations built in the nineteenth century to "protect" our East coast—but from whom or what I was never able to find out. Those were the days when the American fleet was based in Newport harbor, just down the Long Island Sound from New London. By 1910 the installation was no longer needed to protect anything; it became in that year the home of the Coast Guard Academy. With much help and great interest from locals the land was procured for the site of a permanent academy in New London—the scene of my arrival that day. The purpose of our visit to Trumbull was not to visit history but to procure our sailor-type uniforms, which we were expected to be wearing by the evening meal formation.

Back at the academy we were assigned our rooms in Chase Hall, where we could get organized, shed our civvies, and meet our roommates. My room faced the parade ground in front of the academy and, like all the others, was sparsely furnished: cotlike beds; and, for each occupant, a chest of drawers, bookcase, and well-beaten desk. My roommate for the early part of Swab Summer was Lilbourn Pharris from Medford, Massachusetts. Like me, L.A., as he called himself, had just finished high school. A good football player in high school, he now looked forward to playing for Coast Guard. My first reaction to this nice guy was that he bore a remarkable resemblance to movie star Jack Oakie, who had made many films in the 1930s and was famous for his "double takes." As a former theater usher I was tuned to such comparisons when I met new people.

When we assembled for the evening meal formation, the mystery of who would lead during Swab Summer was solved. I had half-expected the argus-eyed Joe Steele to be out in front, but it turned out to be Bob Adams, a turnback from the class ahead of us. There were enough other turnbacks as well to lead our four platoons. From the evening meal we went to a lecture by Lieutenant Commander Richards, Commandant of Cadets. He told us that our next two days would be for orientation and that on Saturday the 20th we would begin our summer academic semester. The Commandant then gave us a detailed but interesting lecture on the history of the academy, which Congress had established in 1876.

From its opening location in New Bedford it became a transient for many years until 1910 when it was located in Fort Trumbull. In 1929 Congress appropriated funds for the new academy, which was open for the beginning of academics in September 1932. Since the construction took place during the worst days of the Great Depression, the appropriations went a long way; the attractive red brick Georgian-style buildings I found myself in were the result.

The "new" academy, with a corps under two hundred, did not even come close to filling Chase Hall. The course expanded from three to four years, and during the 1930s the student body gradually increased from two to three hundred. At the 1932 opening, representatives from Columbia, Harvard, Yale, and MIT served as an advisory committee to help guide the school into a new curriculum. This turned out to be heavy in math, science, and engineering, with a touch of liberal arts education. In concluding his lecture, Richards indicated that he expected the academy to receive degree-granting authority within a year.

En route to my room I wondered, Was it possible I had left Paterson just that morning? I had no difficulty sleeping that night.

At six o'clock next morning, orientation began with my first reveille since Camp Altaha. This time, though, instead of strolling to the mess hall, we formed platoons and double-timed down to the academy waterfront, which ended on a huge pier jutting out into the Thames River. Across the wide river upstream about a mile was the U.S. Navy's submarine base; downriver a shorter distance, still on the opposite side, was the Electric Boat Company's facility for manufacturing submarines.

That morning exercise was to show us what we would be doing, starting the next day, six mornings a week, except during the winter. Attached to the pier was a structure with an overhead cover; below were a large number of whaleboats that could be lowered into the river. With a crew of ten—both turnbacks and some seamen—a lieutenant demonstrated the launching and raising of a boat, and in the adjacent water the proper handling of the oars when the crew received various commands. Each day at this hour cadets rowed the boats across the Thames, and then lined up to race back. The entire academy participated, but as Swabs we would raise the boats (while the upper classes marched up the hill) and then alternately march and double-time ourselves up to barracks. On returning to barracks we had a brief period to prepare ourselves and our rooms for inspection, and at 7:00 a.m. we met the breakfast formation. We were reminded that for the summer we had much more time to accomplish all this than we would when the upper classes returned and had priority in the washrooms. Something to look forward to!

The two orientation days consisted of group visits to all the buildings and activities—academic, athletic, and waterfront—and attending lectures on Swab "customs" and Coast Guard history. Fitted in were individual measuring sessions with representatives of Goodman's tailors, a New London firm that would be making our uniforms. The only bit of relief came with the chaplain's lecture. He explained that since there was no Catholic chapel service at the academy, those of us who were of that persuasion were free to attend the nine o'clock Mass in town on Sundays. With tongue in cheek he explained that most of the Catholic Swabs took communion (with fasting beforehand) and therefore had breakfast in town. This extended their absence (read liberty) until late morning.

The orientation period ended on Friday evening with a band concert. Since the bandstand was adjacent to the barracks, we could listen through our open windows, but most of us preferred to sit on the parade ground. Heading this band of about thirty-five musicians was Chief Petty Officer Charlie Messer, who had been with it since its establishment in 1925. In the future they would play at our dances (called hops) and especially at parades. Their program that evening began with the Coast Guard song "Semper Paratus" and ended with the Academy alma mater. For the latter we all stood and sang from the printed program: "Men, we are Kaydets, proud of our Corps, Proud of our heroes brave who guard every shore . . . ." The bonding had begun.

Getting to know one's classmates was among the more rewarding aspects of Swab Summer. Without upperclassmen around, we could use the facilities in leisurely fashion, and there was ample opportunity to get acquainted. I was struck by the great diversity in backgrounds. Thirty-nine states and many colleges were represented. There was a Yale man (who wouldn't let you forget it), a cowboy from Texas, a California mountain climber, a New Englander who was tutored through grammar school on his father's schooner, and so forth.

One classmate, Bill Banks, whose room was next to mine, seemed particularly compatible—perhaps because in our early days as cadets he gave the impression of being as confused by the system as I was. Bill came from Winchester, Tennessee, though in the previous academic year he had prepped at a small school in New Haven, run by his uncle. With his personable manner and natural antipathy to worry, he became in time my closest friend at the academy.

A couple of weeks into the summer session the class was relocated into new room arrangements with three per room in anticipation of the eventual return of the upper classes. One of my roommates was already there when I arrived with my belongings, and to my great relief he had assigned himself to the upper bunk. His hand shot out—"I'm Hancox F.J. from Reading PA"—followed by a big smile. I had seen Fred around but never to converse with. He had, he said, attended one of the Army prep schools, which prepared candidates competing for regular Army appointments to West Point, during the previous year. Like me, he had not received that appointment and had gone on to take the Coast Guard exam. At some point he had also attended the University of Michigan, stressing, I gathered, liberal arts.

The other roommate who soon appeared was Norm Barlow from Tiverton, Rhode Island. He was personable, and to me seemed New Englandish in speech and manner. I had noticed Norm before, as he blew the bugle for our class formations, apparently with experience as a trumpeter in various bands. Norm struck me as having a quick mind, and he was well prepared, having spent some time at Brown.

The six-week summer session turned out to be about 60 percent academic, covering what in those days was first-year college math. While I was able to handle it, I was rather uneasy about the future. The instructor did not seem to be particularly effective and certainly not of the quality I had encountered in my last two years at Eastside. As I reflected on this, I had an anxious premonition about calculus, which we were to begin in September. In talking to my roommates I discovered they both had previously taken the subject. I did not bother to explain to them that just two years before I had not had a single high school math course.

The other 40 percent of the summer session was in practical subjects: seamanship, ordnance, shop work, and signals. In the latter I secured my only high grade in New London, a 98. This proficiency in signaling came from my Boy Scout experience a few years earlier. In the other subjects I did passably but again was uneasy, this time for a different reason. I realized that the subjects did not really interest me for the long run. It was the way I had felt when a commercial student at Eastside.

Once the summer session was underway, we were free on Saturday afternoons and Sundays to explore New London and nearby Ocean Beach Park with its own boardwalk on Long Island Sound. Fred and I usually made these forays together. We found New London a quaint town, dating back to the middle of the seventeenth century and for two hundred years a principal whaling town. Car ferries plied back and forth from there to Orient Point, the northern tip of Long Island. I thought of the miles of driving that the trip over water could save. What struck me most about the town, though, was that it looked old as a piece—not in a sense of coming apart or in any contrived way, but in a genuine sense. I had the feeling of being transported back to one of those Fabian Theater movies set in the early part of the century. My judgment was confirmed when, later that year, Henry Luce's company picked the town to film a "March of Time" that was a World War I retrospective.

Once we had seen the town, Fred and I hoped that in future forays we would meet some girls. Wearing a uniform somehow gave me a certain degree of external confidence, though deep down I assumed I'd still be the same bumbler. In any case that problem was solved for us, not on the streets of New London, but by the academy. About seven times during the academic year the academy held for all classes a formal dance, known as a hop. A couple of weeks or so before, notices were posted saying, "Cadets are invited and will attend a formal dance to be held at Billard Gym on the evening of———." The primary source of dates for these events (for those whose regular dates were at a distance or nonexistent) was nearby Connecticut College for Women—a fairly selective school in those days.

Toward the end of August the academy authorities had arranged a "rehearsal" for us of an informal nature. The new freshmen of Connecticut College arrived after the middle of August, and the first Saturday afternoon thereafter a group of them about the size of our class were invited down to the academy for an informal dance and social to meet the Coast Guard Academy class of 1944. Before the event those of us who checked "no dancing experience" on one of our entrance-day forms were summoned to the gym for lessons from a dance instructor and her husband. Dancing with another Swab was a bit awkward, as both wanted to lead, but after a couple of sessions we were all declared qualified.

At the appointed time our class was lined up in sailor suits on one side of the gym. Opposite us across a newly waxed floor were the coeds. When the band leader, Charlie Messer, gave the signal, the band struck up a lively tune and we began racing across the floor. Two-thirds of the way over, my feet went out from under me, and I slid on my rear end into the giggling coeds. Despite or because of my pratfall, a comely coed reached down to help me up; she became my date. Her name was Nancy Troland, one of the more attractive of the freshmen. Naturally, my classmates later accused me of staging the slide, like someone stealing second base. Nancy was very young, even by freshman standards, full of life, and had an Army brat background. We had several more dates in the months ahead, to academy hops and dances at her college as well as a couple into town for movies. My preposterous entrance into the academy social scene turned out just fine.

At the very end of August I had my first visitors. Daisy and Steve drove Aunt Annie up from Paterson for an enjoyable afternoon: visiting the grounds, a quick turn around town, and a long stop at the Martom, a restaurant and dairy bar near the academy and a cadet favorite. I was able to fill up on goodies, to listen to a new favorite song of mine, "Blueberry Hill," several times, and to get caught up with home events—one of which was the recent sudden death of

Tom Ruddy, my mother's husband. Aunt Annie promised to start sending occasional copies of the Paterson papers. I did not disclose my uneasy feelings about the academy for two reasons. First, I was not yet certain about them; second, that was now my problem. Annie had done more for me than anyone could expect; any future initiatives would be up to me to ponder and to decide on. It was a good visit, and they were all proud of me in my new blue uniform.

During the course of that very busy summer it was difficult, but not impossible, to keep up with the world news. The New London paper was not much help; but, as time permitted, I was able to slip over to the library, an extension on the rear of the administration building. It was a lovely, high-ceilinged, paneled room with historical murals of a nautical nature on the walls. The murals were painted by Aldis Browne, a graduate of the Yale School of Fine Arts. Legend had it that Browne and the then-superintendent, a Captain Jones, had their differences over the murals. On one occasion Browne, who happened to be a dwarf, rose to his full four feet and threatened to paint Jones's face on the figure of a smuggler in one of the murals.

The library had a fair selection of papers, but I concentrated on the *New York Times*, as I had since my days in the Eastside High International Relations Club. In that summer of 1940 the European war was being waged in the air between Great Britain and Germany. About the time I had left Paterson the battle for control of the air, later known as the Battle of Britain, had begun. The German goal at that point was to neutralize the Royal Air Force (RAF) so that the invasion of England (Operation Sea Lion) could begin. A frequent song on German radios in those days was "We Sail Against England."

All through August the battle continued, bringing forth on the 20th Churchill's famous tribute to the RAF, "Never in the field of human conflict was so much owed by so many to so few." Then came that great morale builder for Britain and great shock to Germany from Hitler on down. On August 26 the RAF flew a bombing raid to Berlin in retaliation for the first major raid on London. Not to be deterred, on September 7 the Germans began their aerial "blitz" against London. At the height of the raids on the 15th, London was terrorized by waves of Luftwaffe bombers. The German aerial losses, though, were staggering (fifty-six planes downed in one forty-five-minute period alone); Sea Lion was postponed indefinitely, as it turned out, forever. This phase of the Battle of Britain was over.

With the upper classes returning on Labor Day weekend, that Monday evening ended Swab Summer with a bang—or, more accurately, a roar: "Swabs out!" As we flattened against the walls—"Sorry, sir, bulkheads"—outside our rooms the upper classes came by to view and intimidate the newcomers assigned to their platoons. Along with the inevitable questions: "Where from" and "What was your 'pcs?'" (previous condition of servitude) came the corrections. "Mr. Kinnard, take on a brace; you look like a question mark," and "Hasn't anyone shown you how to tie your kerchief?" Then, to be certain the message was driven home, "How about twenty-five pushups as a starter?" Farewell the tranquil mind!

In the morning we got to meet, or more accurately see, the upperclassman directly connected with us. Bob McLendon from North Carolina, our platoon leader, was like most of the first classmen—somewhat detached from Swab indoctrination or depending on one's perspective, hazing. Norm Horton, a second classman from Phoenix, was my table commandant in the mess, where much of the routine indoctrination often took place. Horton, though involved, seemed calm about it all. Not so a couple of third classmen, recent graduates of the Swab system: "Muddy" Waters, also from North Carolina, and George Breitweiser from East St. Louis. George was a self-styled wit, and I gathered that the Swabs were supposed to be his silent claque. Waters, on the other hand, was an activist. "Mr. Kinnard, you do not sit erect enough when you eat—shove off." (Translation: sit at attention without a chair and continue to eat. Rather hard on the thighs.) I was not being singled out, though, as all of my classmates sooner or later received the same treatment. Thanks to the subtle interventions of Norm Horton, we all got plenty to eat. My first indoctrination in the bad guy-good guy technique of management.

On certain afternoons the entire corps assembled on the parade ground for close-order drill, initially designed to lead up to our first full dress parade. This would mean a nightmarish five minutes to get into leggings, put on sidearms, and grab our Springfield model 1903 rifles before heading for the parade ground. In the first few weeks the drill proceeded from individual manual of arms, through squad, platoon, and company, finally reaching massed battalion. The battalion commander that year was a tall Texan, Chet Richmond. I had observed him strolling through barracks humming and sometimes singing a current popular tune like "All the Things You Are" or "I Hear a Rhapsody." Chet played the role of the good guy; the bad guy was his executive officer, Chris Bruskevich from Pittsfield, Massachusetts, who gave everyone hell at close-order drill. He always reminded me of Victor McLaglen playing a tough British sergeant in *Gunga Din*.

About the third Saturday in September the entire corps was invited to a large dance at Connecticut College up the road from the academy. On this cool evening our uniforms included topcoats, which we placed in a small, very crowded cloakroom. That caused confusion when we departed, since all cadet coats looked the same. I thought nothing more of it until the next morning when, returning from church and breakfast in town, I found my roommates sprawled across their beds. I gathered that they had just completed a rough workout organized by upperclassmen for all Swabs. Apparently, we had failed to make way for the upper classes at the cloakrooms the previous evening. No sooner had I heard this, than the loud voice of Francis X. Riley a third classman down the hall, boomed, "All Catholic squad Swabs turn out in work uniform and rifles in five minutes."

What a workout: duck waddling with rifles held out in front; clean sweeps with our rifles; pushups—then start over again. Riley, who led the formation, seemed to relish it. After about twenty minutes, when I was beginning to wobble, one of my classmates fell on the floor; soon a second could not continue. About that time Bob McLendon appeared, ending the workout with a brief lecture on Swabs' place in the order of things on or off the academy grounds. "When you pass an upperclassman in New London, salute and say, 'By your leave, sir.'" With that, school was out. I staggered to my room and collapsed on my bunk. Later I found out that this was a yearly event based on some actual or contrived offense committed by the Swab class.

Of course, the Swab system was only a backdrop for the fall academic program, which was heavily technical—math, chemistry, and descriptive geometry—with a dose of liberal arts in the form of Spanish and English. The math accelerated rapidly from analytical geometry to differential calculus. By the end of September, I was on what was known as a tree in the calculus: I was flunking. My weekend liberty was thus somewhat restricted, presumably so that I could sit in my room and study.

My one bit of relief in the academic program that fall was the English course taught by a civilian professor, Ernie Espelie, who was also the librarian. He built his course around a recently published thousand-page text, *This Generation*, a survey of British and American literature since the beginning of the Great War, interspersed with historical and critical essays to which Espelie added his own commentary. He was fascinating when discussing the British generation of 1914, Siegfried Sassoon, Wilfred Owen, and Robert Graves, forever connected with Ypres, the Somme, or Passchendaele. American writers like F. Scott Fitzgerald and Hemingway were also among his favorites. It was hard, sometimes impossible, during evening study to put the English book down and pick up one on descriptive geometry.

Being on at least one academic tree that fall took up several hours each weekend but did not eliminate other activities. One, coming during so-called free time, was the "Bull Gang." Each Saturday afternoon those Swabs who needed additional attention for one offense or another (in the eyes of some upperclassmen) reported to the quadrangle behind Chase Hall for a thirty-to forty-minute session of physical exercises with their rifles, such as clean sweeps: rifles held over head, then lowered to foot level, then returned over head, all the while keeping one's legs straight. The exercises were interrupted with lectures on the proper conduct of Swabs. About 20 percent of the class made this "elite" group, and I was more often than not included.

As the semester moved along, I sensed that I was not fully prepared for mathematics, though I estimated that I could probably get by marginally. At times I wished I had taken the Montclair scholarship and then the West Point exam in my district. About that time Annie sent me a Paterson paper containing a long article on the death of Congressman George Seger of my district. After musing over this, I started plotting a course of action. I had once or twice met Seger's secretary (today called administrative assistant), Gordon Canfield, at scouting events in Paterson. At one of those, a Boy Scout rally, I had won first prize in the signaling competition. Yes, it was indeed a small world. Following an exchange of letters of condolence, I inquired about West Point appointment plans. He said that we must await Seger's successor as congressman. My guess that it would be Canfield himself was confirmed by the electorate on November 5. In responding to my congratulatory letter, the congressman-elect enclosed a list of matters that he would announce after assuming office in January. One was the details of competitions in his district for West Point appointments. Swab Kinnard now had a hidden agenda.

For now, though, Coast Guard life must go on. The academy had a surprisingly good football team that fall, thanks to a generous input from my class, including two breakaway backs, Mario Cataffo and Rufus Drury. The opponents were mainly small colleges from New England such as Wesleyan, Trinity, Worcester Tech, and our big rival, Norwich, a military school in Northfield, Vermont. As Coast Guard was host for the game that year, the entire Norwich cadet corps came to New London.

The night before the game, known as Norwich Night, was traditionally the scene of some Swab high jinks. My contribution after everyone turned in for the night was a wet washcloth tossed on the face of the sleeping Francis X. Riley, the Swabs' nemesis in our wing of barracks. By the time he stormed out into the hall looking for the culprit, I was "asleep" in my bunk.

For nonathletes like myself, choosing a fall varsity sport was a real challenge. After looking over the options I chose cross-country. The three and one-half mile course along the Thames River, though painful at first, proved both challenging and interesting as the season moved along. Eventually, I could finish almost in the middle of the pack. One day on the course I passed a third classman, Charlie Johnson, and muttered a challenge, "Get a horse." That evening he shoved me off at dinner on my already tired legs. When, I wondered, as I struggled to eat, would I ever learn to be a proper Swab?

I was fortunate with my assigned roommates; despite our diverse backgrounds we were quite compatible. Fred Hancox, the anglophile, saw every aerial battle in the Battle of Britain that fall as a great victory for the British no matter what. He also had a running dialogue of self-defined humor, ending his stories with a facial expression signifying, "I am very funny." (He could be when I understood the punch line.) Norm Barlow, who was academically very sharp, liked to talk about girls from Connecticut College or elsewhere. Some of his stories could have appeared in *True Confessions*.

Fred served as our not-always-successful mentor for our constant inspections—every day but Sunday for both uniforms and rooms, with Saturday's inspection more than making up for the next day off. Though the inspector was usually a first classman, occasionally, especially Saturdays, a commissioned officer came instead. Most of my demerits as a cadet came one at a time from these inspections described in the reports as untidy in dress; room in disorder; article adrift in room. Once I received ten demerits for unauthorized burning of lights after taps—I was caught studying under a blanket—and wondered in how many colleges studying late at night was considered an offense.

The social schedule that fall included three formal dances in cadet full dress. The coats, known in cadet slang as monkey jackets, had all the leeway of a strait jacket. Dates usually came from Connecticut College. (What would we have done without them in those days of single-sex government academies?) The dances were a cohesive force for the academy, since all classes attended on an equal basis—that is, if the Swabs stayed away from the cloakrooms, something we did automatically after our September experience at the Connecticut College dance.

During that fall of 1940 events in the United States vied with the European war for attention. On September 16 the Selective Service Bill became law, requiring all males between twenty-one and thirty-five (some sixteen million) to register for the draft. The first numbers were drawn on October 29; those inducted as a result were obligated to serve for one year. Some in this group painted OHIO (over the hill in October—meaning in 1941) on the outside of their barracks. The country still had a strong isolationist sentiment encouraged by many well-known leaders such as the Lone Eagle of 1927, Charles Lindbergh. On the opposite side was Franklin Roosevelt, elected over Wendell Willkie on November 5 for an unprecedented third term.

Meanwhile, the German bombing offensive continued over Britain, now more to destroy British morale than as a prelude to invasion. On October 10 that landmark St. Paul's Cathedral, designed by Christopher Wren, had its high altar destroyed but the great dome remained; on November 14 it was Coventry's turn. All this was intensely interesting to my anglophile roommate, who kept me fully informed. Out came his maps when the Italians invaded Greece in late October, followed by a British countermove in that area. I began to appreciate Fred's briefings as time went on, since my chances to get to the library were few and far between.

My first autumn in New England happened to be a beautiful one, with November particularly appealing when it was no longer Indian summer and not yet Thanksgiving. Even with bare trees and a slight chill in the air, the pale sunshine kept away the cold of winter. During our morning rows I could see some of the Thames Valley details that the leaves had camouflaged earlier. Armistice Day was one of those invigorating November days when the clouds seemed to have the texture of steel wool. The cadet corps marched in a parade in downtown New London commemorating the end of that horror, the Great War.

Soon the colder weather brought an end to our early morning rows across the Thames and an additional duty for me in the mess. On mornings when it was below freezing, I was assigned the task of reporting the temperature after reciting the "Connecticut Poop":

> Christ but it's cold in Connecticut
> Colder than a hinge on a shithouse door
> Colder than a penguin's _ _ _ _ _
> Colder than a welldigger's _ _ _ _
> Christ but it's cold in Connecticut
> Sir the temperature this morning is _____ degrees.

With December upon us, fun and games were over for the moment—two weeks of classes, one week of exams, and then? Already in trouble in both calculus and descriptive geometry, I received no comfort from the finals. During the reading period before the exams I had taken breaks by walking down to the now-deserted academy pier and back. In my solos at the pier, I played *what if*, in the event I bilged out of the academy. Conclusion: No return to Paterson; seek work at the new expanding defense factories, say at New Britain, Connecticut, which also had a state college; and try for the West Point appointment just as I intended to do if I did not bilge.

At breakfast Friday, December 20, Muddy Waters turned to me and announced, "Today's the day they give babies away, Mr. Kinnard." A lousy analogy but I assumed he was talking about final grades. He was right; grades came about eleven o'clock, and at noon we were all off on Christmas leave. My babies included failures in calculus and descriptive geometry, meaning that I must return from leave early to retake two exams. Still, the return trip down to New York was fun, with all of us relaxed in a way we had not been since summer.

Aunt Annie had a grand Christmas planned and of course, showed me off in my blue uniform on trips to town and to midnight Mass. There was time to visit with all her family and, later on with my own at an affair arranged by my sister Daisy. I also saw many of my old friends. Annie was the only one to whom I confided that I was on an academic tree limb with two saws poised to cut. Early on, I managed a private talk with her, explaining in general why I could not stay for New Year's. I stressed the West Point option, which she liked but with reservations. Leaving Coast Guard might be tricky; so, too, might my getting an appointment to West Point. On December 30, along with about a dozen members of my class, I returned to New London, no longer feeling like one of the *wunderkinder* of the Eastside High math department.

It was a lonely time. As I was the only one in my wing of barracks, my studying was pretty much self-directed, even though I occasionally visited in other parts of Chase Hall to talk with fellow cadets who had to retake exams. My studying for descriptive geometry turned out to be lucky. I spent a lot of time working out a particularly difficult problem because I thought that it illustrated many principles of the subject. Apparently, the instructor did also, for there it was on the exam, worth 40 percent of the grade to boot. On calculus I was not so lucky, doing better than on the first exam but sensing that I failed. At that point, though I did not care much; I had started coming down with flu.

Worsening the next day, I ended up in the academy hospital. During the few days that I was a patient, Christmas leave ended for the corps. One day Bill Banks came to the hospital with my mail and academy notifications, including a note from Lieutenant Commander Richards, the commandant of cadets, on my academic status. I had passed descriptive geometry but failed differential calculus. I was being retained as a cadet on a probationary status for the next semester. To paraphrase Wellington the day after Waterloo, it was a near run thing.

When I left the hospital, we were already into the third day of academics. Two of the new semester's courses were a continuation of those that had floored me in the fall. This time things went better by following Bill Banks's advice ("Don't try to understand it, memorize it"), but I had a new bête noire—physics. A three-semester course at the academy, it underlay much of the curriculum. My immediate task was to understand such matters as the laws of motion and vector analysis. For me it was the intellectual equivalent of trying to get a sip of water from a gushing fire hose.

Again, the subject I was at home with, and enjoyed most, came from the limited liberal arts offerings: Scientific Thought was taught by the academy's best professor, A.A. Lawrence, who later became their first dean. His preliminary lectures on such topics as logic and dialectal stratagems were to me new and stimulating. The course was built around a text, *Architects of Ideas*, each chapter dedicated to a theorist. The most interesting, I thought, were Copernicus, Marx, Freud, and Darwin. When we discussed Darwin, my St. Joe's background made me rise to the bait, debating Lawrence in an informal way. My classmates were torn as to whether this was bravery or chutzpah, but Lawrence seemed to enjoy it. Inwardly, I felt that the Darwin hypotheses made a good deal of sense.

This course also had a few evening lectures by outside academics. One that made a lasting impression was titled "Non-Euclidean Geometry." Citing the theories of two of Einstein's predecessors—Lobachevsky and Riemann—the lecturer described some basic theorems of what he called "Pangeometry." The most startling to me was "two parallel lines approach each other continually." There went my world of Euclidean certainty, planted only one or two years before by Miss Duryea, my Eastside High geometry teacher. What could one be certain of after a course like this?

Meanwhile in afternoons our close-order drill periods, which had ended in November, were reactivated to prepare for an exciting event. We began practice marching in battalion mass formation as we would participate in Roosevelt's third inaugural parade on January 20. This would be my first trip to Washington and I could scarcely wait. On Sunday evening the 19th we boarded a special Pullman train at the New London station and awoke next morning on a siding on Fourteenth Street near the Potomac River.

Soon after breakfast in the dining car I was off with camera to the nearby Washington Monument. Many tourists were waiting for the elevator, so, along with a couple of classmates, I decided to walk up—all 137 pounds of me. We made it, but I knew that next time I would wait for the elevator. The day was sunny and cold with a biting wind. Visibility was good; from the monument's top I could focus my camera on all the major sites in Washington. Turning to Virginia, I saw a countrylike area. Eight months later, construction of the Pentagon would begin on what that day was nothing but swamps, dumps, and a rendering works.

Returning to our train we drew our weapons, put on full dress, and assembled in parade formation. One o'clock saw us in our starting position, third in line behind West Point and Annapolis. The Coast Guard band was not participating, as the Army would provide us one from the Washington area. When we arrived in position, there it was from Fort Myer—each musician mounted on a horse!

On moving forward, we soon discovered two problems that horse-mounted bands can cause in parades. One difficulty was trying to stay in step, but this was nothing compared to the other problem. We could solve that one only by violating marching protocol, that is, glancing down rather than looking straight ahead. For the horses this was just another day; their normal bodily functions were in order. For us it was a question of avoiding, if possible, or at least of not stepping in too deeply. The Fort Myer band was later known in New London as "Army's revenge."

On Pennsylvania Avenue we approached the White House and Roosevelt's reviewing stand. Being near the left side of the battalion formation, I got an excellent view of the Commander in Chief when, at Chet Richmond's command, we executed eyes left. Never having seen FDR in person, I was shocked. As I later wrote home, he looked as if he "was ready to be embalmed."

Roosevelt, of course, had much on his mind that day. The evening before returning to New London from my Christmas leave, I had listened to one of his fireside chats on the radio. I knew that when he used the phrase "arsenal of democracy," he was referring to our prospective role in supplying the British with guns, planes, ships, and, as he put it, "more of everything." While still in the hospital and with time to read newspapers I noted that his State of the Union address in early January had followed through on his plan. He requested Congress to support what he called a Lend-Lease program, the purpose being to supply war materials to the Allies.

When the parade ended and we could leave our weapons and full dress on the train, we were at liberty until 10 p.m. On my own I headed out to Capitol Hill. Because access to public buildings was easy in those days, I wandered around an empty congressional building until I found Gordon Canfield's office; but, as in the other offices, no one was there. En route to 14th Street, where I was to meet Bill Banks, I took in the other Washington sites, including a detour around Union Station. Understandably, everything but the congressional building was crowded, but for one who had a semi monastic existence in New London, that, too was fun, especially since Washington that day seemed to have more than its share of good-looking girls.

After an early meal Bill and I went to a theater on 14th Street that also had a few stage acts. The Alfred Hitchcock movie *Foreign Correspondent*, starring Joel McCrea and Laraine Day, was full of espionage and derring-do. It was also in tune with the British propaganda campaign against American neutrality. American reporter McCrea is sent to London, where he naturally falls for Day. As it turns out, though, her father heads a Nazi spy ring. That is all I recall, except that it worked out fine for the lovers. By ten we were back on our train; at seven the next morning came the return to New London and reality.

About a week after the inauguration the mail brought an announcement from Congressman Canfield's office. Instead of one appointment to West Point that year, there would be two, and the competition itself would have a new twist. The written examination would be given in the Clifton High School on Saturday morning, February 15 in English, algebra, geometry, and American history. This year, though, standing in that exam alone would not be the sole basis for winning an appointment. Candidates who made the top six on written work would appear at a later date before a three-member selection committee. This committee (whose names were not announced) would select the final order of merit of the six based on character, scholarship, and aptitude.

I could do nothing at this point to change those three qualities; moreover, I had a real problem: How, in the three weeks remaining to study for the written exam, could I still do all that was required of Swab Kinnard? Something had to go or at least be diluted; that had to be academy academics. I was really in a "Hail Mary" situation. It was during this period that I received the ten demerits for studying under a blanket after taps.

After academics on Valentine's Day afternoon I took the train to New Jersey and next morning the bus to Clifton High. (This school, incidentally, was across from a new apartment to which my sister Daisy and husband Steve had moved about a year before.) I counted about sixty boys in the examination room. The two, besides me, in uniform were from an Army prep school for West Point, aspirants competing for appointments allocated to the Army.

After a fairly straightforward exam, I returned that evening to New London, figuring out how to make up for my three-week neglect of academy courses. About ten days later came a call from Aunt Annie relaying a telegram from Gordon Canfield. He requested that I appear before his West Point selection committee on Friday evening, February 28, again at Clifton High School. The next day I sent another request for liberty to Lieutenant Commander Richards, this time spelling out the situation very carefully. Richards was a very understanding person, and I suspected that he viewed this as a form of damage control in the event that I bilged out.

On the train en route to New York I tried to "war game" my meeting with the committee. There was one question I sensed I would get and best be prepared for: "Mr. Kinnard, since you are already a cadet at one government academy, why do you want to start over at another?" I developed a pitch that, with a war probably coming on, I wanted to be an Army officer; in that way I would likely be more directly involved. Further, that in the long run I felt I was more suited to an Army career than to one based on ships and naval-type activities.

That evening the six of us, assembled in a Clifton High waiting room, eyed each other cautiously. I was the third called in. Since the first two had disappeared out of another exit from the committee room, there was no feedback. The committee members stood up, shook hands with me, and briefly introduced themselves. All three had been in Pershing's AEF. From Passaic was a retired and well-known businessman, Frederick Rohrbach; from Clifton, an attorney, William O'Brien; and from Paterson, a person whose picture I had seen in the paper many times, Henry Stam, president of the chamber of commerce. During a fairly direct discussion O'Brien asked the anticipated question. After seeming to pause for reflection I gave the answer I had rehearsed. In all, the session took about fifteen minutes and was very pleasant.

Back in New London by noon the next day, I suspected that I would know my fortune fairly soon. And indeed, late Tuesday afternoon when I returned to barracks from toiling over a drawing for descriptive geometry, I found a note in my box requesting that I call Aunt Annie. On answering, she told me in a trembling voice that I was one of the two principal appointees to West Point from the 8th New Jersey District that year. The other was Raymond Janeczek from Passaic. For the moment I kept the news to myself although at dinner Muddy Waters opined that Mr. Kinnard looked mighty happy. In fact, I was in a new ball game; just the same, I resolved to do the best I could academically and otherwise in the time left to me as a Coast Guard cadet.

Less than forty-eight hours later came Hundredth Day (meaning the time before graduation for the class of 1941), when traditionally the swabs reversed positions with the third class. As reveille blew, all hell broke loose in barracks as we started working out the third class. In anticipation most of them had shaved and cleaned their rooms before reveille; thus, we were able to give them a good quarter-hour of knee bends and clean sweeps. In the mess I beat my classmates to the draw: "Mr. Waters, Mr. Breitweiser, shove off." After breakfast a couple of third classmen failed to make way for us at the mailboxes only to have the wrath of God descend on them.

Lunch and supper produced even more antics in the mess hall. When I was working over Muddy Waters at supper, he reminded me that the odds against me were one hundred to one—which did not slow me, or any of the others, down. Between tattoo and taps we conducted an exercise session for the third classmen in our wing, including Francis X. Riley. Taps ended Hundredth Day. What happened the next day had best be left unsaid.

Before the end of March a plethora of forms descended from the

War Department: some to be made out by the academy, some by Eastside High, and some by me. The outcome was word from West Point for me to take a physical at some Army installation; then I should report at West Point on June 21 to take the validating examination in English and math. If all went well in these, I would enter West Point on July 1 as a member of the class of 1945.

Meanwhile, with the arrival of spring, morning rows across the Thames resumed, along with the need to choose a varsity sport for the new athletic season. Norm Barlow, a sailing whiz, had been talking for some time about my going out for the sailing team. He convinced me that I could probably find a spot as third man with some crew; as such, I could learn something about the sport. That worked out well when I was taken on by a couple of easygoing second classmen. Managing to stay out of their way, I actually learned a bit about sailing, a sport I had watched, but not joined, at Lake Hopatcong.

On Easter Sunday, a liberty day for all cadets, Bill Banks and I headed for New Haven, where he had spent the previous year at his uncle's tutoring school. After about an hour's train trip we debarked into a beautiful April day. Bill gave me a thorough tour of the Yale campus, my main interest. Except for the churches most of the buildings were closed that day, but Bill could still point out and describe such landmarks as the Sterling and Beinecke libraries. In 1940 town and gown areas in New Haven still merged nicely, and naturally for lunch and a drink we headed to Mory's. Bill knew Mory's, and I had learned of it when Ray Evans, our Yale classmate at New London, sang "The Whiffenpoof Song." The atmosphere was so congenial that a second drink seemed in order, and this led to an interesting return trip.

The late-afternoon New York to Boston train we boarded was crowded, but we reached our car in time to get a seat. Underway and glancing at the standing crowd, we simultaneously detected two attractive young ladies. Bill glanced at me, I nodded, and, in his best Tennessee gentleman manner, he offered them our seats; naturally, we stood directly in front of them, intent on obtaining the dating equivalent of name, rank, and serial number. Both were students at the Boston Conservatory of Music, heading back after a weekend in New Haven. Bill concentrated on Grace Landis, and I was busy with Jeannie Marie Carton, who, it turned out, was from Avon By The Sea, New Jersey, in the area of favorite summer shore locations of those days. By the time Bill and I left the train at New London, we had tentatively arranged for Grace and Jeannie to come to New London for our final hop that spring, two weeks hence.

The immediate challenge was the final week of academics followed by examination week. When it was over, I felt that I had made it through everything but physics, but I didn't want to find out. After the last examination I met with Lieutenant Commander Richards to say that I wished to submit my resignation that day. Naturally he asked why. My response: I was not sufficiently prepared academically to do well in the course work. Then the following: Q. Shouldn't the academy decide that, Mr. Kinnard? A. Yes, sir, but . . . Q. Is there another reason? A. Yes, sir, I did win the West Point appointment. Richards responded that he had heard my news. Yes, he would forward my resignation to the superintendent, but it had to go to Washington and would take a couple of weeks to work out all the details. For the first time I had mixed feelings about leaving, but I went to my room and typed out the resignation.

The next day began the weekend with the Boston coeds. We had arranged for them to stay at the Mohican Hotel, advertised as "New London's largest and best with rates from $2.50-$6.00 and luncheons and dinners from $.60 to $1.25." Looking spectacular in their formal gowns, they seemed to enjoy Charlie Messer's music and the general ambiance. Charlie, a great favorite with the cadets, was known to nip a bit; his music, invariably somber at first, always improved as the evening went on. Unfortunately, the academy rules allowed very little time from the end of the hop to signing in at Chase Hall; hence, we had no opportunity to see the upstairs decor of New London's best.

On Sunday after touring the academy, taking pictures, and having lunch at Peterson's in town, our guests were off to Boston. Jeannie and I discussed her visiting West Point, probably during Plebe Christmas when her school was out. Fourth classmen did not get leave at the Point but had the run of the academy while the upper classes were gone during the holidays. After hearing our descriptions of a swab's travails, Jeannie asked how I felt about going through another such indoctrination. I suggested that it was a subject best not to dwell on.

Spring term, starting the next day, took my classmates into practical subjects such as seamanship in preparation for their summer cruise shortly after graduation. Since I would be gone before the term ended, I did not attend classes. I did, though, meet all the other formations and remained a "practicing" swab.

Having spent the previous year at an Army-sponsored West Point prep, Fred Hancox provided guidance on the validating exam I was to take in late June. We agreed that I would probably pass the exam easily, but why risk it? I could use the six weeks between academies for fail-safe preparation. He suggested Stanton in Cornwall, New York, a small school that prepared candidates for nearby West Point. This seemed like a good idea in two ways: both as a form of insurance for passing the exam and a way of escaping six weeks in Paterson in a limbo situation. Fortunately, my escrow account coming from my $65 per month cadet salary contained enough to cover the costs. An exchange of letters with Stanton set May 15 as the date they expected me.

In the library while my colleagues were in class, I wrote letters and read journals and newspapers to catch up on the world beyond Chase Hall. Some of the most interesting events that spring had to do with Roosevelt's Lend-Lease program, signed into law on March 11, much to the dismay of the isolationist groups, still a strong political force in the spring of 1941. Michigan's Senator Arthur Vandenberg, for example, one of the thirty-one senators voting against Lend-Lease, opined privately, "We have torn up 150 years of traditional American foreign policy. We have tossed Washington's Farewell Address into the discard." The law he was regretting, of course, translated Roosevelt's arsenal of democracy idea into reality. It led directly into that first theater of operations for the United States in World War II: the not-so-secret but undeclared war in the Atlantic. Roosevelt had already greatly expanded the Navy's patrol force in the Atlantic—which he now renamed the Atlantic Fleet—with the mission of protecting American shipping. Both we and Hitler knew that for all practical purposes the United States was an undeclared enemy.

On the European front, though, and especially in the Mediterranean, Hitler seemed to be gaining victory after victory. General Erwin Rommel's newly established Afrika Korps launched an offensive that took him in a couple of months to the Egyptian frontier. Simultaneously, German forces overran Yugoslavia and Greece, gaining bases to harass the British lifeline in the eastern Mediterranean. Lots of interesting war news that spring for a future West Pointer.

Finally, word came that my resignation had been accepted in Washington and would be "effective at 1100 hours Saturday May 10." By 1030 that morning I had completed my final physical and changed into civilian clothes. With my roommates Fred and Norm, as well as Bill Banks, I had a final BS session, and a number of classmates came by to say their farewells. Also looking in to wish me luck at the Point were some upperclassmen in my platoon: Bob McLendon, my platoon leader; Norm Horton, and even Muddy Waters, who was all smiles. At 1100 hours citizen Kinnard headed for the academy gate, where a cab waited to take me to the New London station.

It had been a fast ten months. On this day I was like one-third of my former classmates who had entered that gate the previous July but for diverse reasons had gone many ways elsewhere. My feelings were mixed as we drove to the station; however, by the time the New York express had gone a few miles down the track I had feelings both of relief and of anticipation for what lay ahead.

On Monday morning I went to New York City to take my West Point physical at the Federal Building on 90 Church Street. All seemed to go well except for some discussion of my being very close to the minimum weight requirement. I remedied that at noon with a lunch of a half-dozen bananas and two quarts of water.

In the few days I spent in Paterson afterward, I could see that the depressed economy of only a year before was rapidly reviving, thanks to the beginnings of war production. Locally, Curtiss Wright set the pace, but smaller industries were also beginning to appear. Manpower remained readily available for industry, as the draft was still for a one-year term of service and restricted to the age group of twenty-one to thirty-five; hence, for example, my colleagues were not yet affected.

On Thursday, May 15, I headed to Weehawken, New Jersey, to catch a West Shore Railroad train up the Hudson to the location of my new school. Getting to Weehawken was a bit roundabout and involved taking the 42nd Street ferry from New York to the railroad terminus. As the ferry pulled away from New York, I got my first look at the pride of prewar France, the liner *Normandie*, surely the most beautiful ocean liner of its time. Built in 1935, it had in 1937 held the transatlantic crossing record of just under four days. Now, it had been tied up at the pier since August 1939. I wondered that day when it would sail again. Alas, it never did, as it was destroyed by fire at its pier the following February.

The West Shore Railroad was even then approaching museum status with its steam engines and old coaches. On that beautiful May day, though, it didn't matter; I sat on the Hudson side with my window open, totally relaxed and with no threats of "Swabs out" to break the mood. The train stopped at every station—Hastings-on-Hudson, Nyack, Haverstraw, Stony Point, Tomkins Cove—and then we came to the Hudson highlands, the American equivalent of the Rhine. After the West Point station, we descended into the long tunnel under the plain where the cadets paraded, and then out into the most beautiful part of the highlands. Ahead were the mountains—Crows Nest and Storm King—that in time I would know well. In the middle of the river Bannerman's Island with its castlelike structure reminded me of lines we memorized at St. Joe's from Longfellow's "Children's Hour": ". . . till I think of the Bishop of Bingen in his Mouse Tower on the Rhine."

I was the only passenger debarking at the next stop, Cornwall-on-Hudson. Luckily, a cab was sitting there to whisk me up the long hill and through the town to the slightly larger adjacent town, Cornwall. Stopping in the circular driveway of a large white house with a nearby three-story brick building, the driver announced that this was Stanton. The house contained an office, where I was greeted and then escorted over to the brick building.

On the way over, I was told that Colonel Stanton was in Washington, expecting to be called to active duty "to assist in building the expanding Army." It turned out that Hubert Stanton had graduated from West Point in 1911, had taught there, and, after an early retirement, had founded the school I was now attending.

After depositing personal effects in my assigned room, I was introduced to a Mr. Hennessy, the math teacher. He explained that most of the students had left after the regular entrance exams in March. Besides the five of us preparing for the June validating, another five had stayed over from the earlier group—some for personal reasons, some waiting the results of their physical exams. These five were preparing themselves in certain first-year subjects taught at West Point.

After handing me my math texts and study schedule, Hennessy took me to the office of the English teacher, a Mr. Bradford, who struck me as both sharp and prissy. The validating exam, he said, covered grammar, spelling, and literature in the sense of knowing authors, titles, plots, and principal characters; it also required writing, usually a book review. He handed me the Kittredge and Farley grammar, and three large notebooks: one had spelling lists; the others covered in short-answer form American and English literature. For the book to review, after a long discussion we finally selected Kenneth Roberts's best-selling historical novel of a few years back, *Northwest Passage*. I could use a copy from his shelf.

By now it was time for dinner and a chance to meet my colleagues. Three of the other four taking the validating exam with me were football players sponsored by the Army Athletic Association (AAA): Cas Myslinski from Steubenville, Ohio, who had an AAA-secured "at large" appointment; Carl Anderson from New Orleans, a high school all-American back who had an appointment from Illinois, a state he had never been in; finally, "Quiffy" Empert from Pittsburgh, for whom the AAA had not yet secured an appointment. The other member of our validating exam group was Jim Gould, who had recently received an appointment from Delaware and, like me, was there on his own.

Study hall was a large, well-equipped classroom where our classes also took place—math in the morning and English in the afternoon. With the end of study hall that first evening we had a visitor from West Point, specifically from the Army Athletic Association, Earl "Red" Blaik, the new Army football coach who had come to chat with his three football players.

Red Blaik had just arrived that spring with his entire coaching staff from some very successful seasons at Dartmouth. A West Point graduate in 1920, he left the Army a few years later and was assistant football coach at West Point from 1927 to 1934. After coaching for a while at Dartmouth, he was at the beginning of a new career and fame at Army. (This would last eighteen years and would soon include those seasons when the cadets were a powerhouse in football.)

Cornwall's attractive natural setting invited walks during breaks in our schedule. Ken Rothwell, awaiting word on his physical exam, knew the area and was a great guide. We walked to Cornwall-on-Hudson with its magnificent views of the river far below. One day we walked to the nearby campus of the New York Military Academy to view a full-dress parade. Ken was an interesting guy who had lived in China for several years. About ten days into my stay he received word that he was physically disqualified for admission and soon left for home.

There were no requirements for us on weekends, though study hall was open for our use. As time went on, I became confident about the exam and decided to take some trips to West Point. Ken had pointed out a bus that one could catch at Cornwall-on-Hudson to go over old highway 9W along the side of Storm King and Crows Nest mountains and into West Point. The views were spectacular, and it was fun to observe cadet parades and other activities that I would soon be part of—if all went well.

The Stanton teachers were very effective but the pace was not for everyone. Quiffy Empert was obviously not going to do it on math. He and the other two football players disappeared each weekend somewhere into West Point, courtesy of the AAA. They said little about their stay there but I gathered that they ate well and received a bit of exam coaching as well. One day Empert, looking rather puzzled, asked Mr. Hennessy which leg of the triangle was the hypotenuse. This brought about a Hennessy-Blaik telephone call that evening and Quiffy's exit to Pittsburgh.

Frequently, in the evenings after study hall the four of us remaining would walk through town, pick up newspapers, and stop at the only bar for a drink or two. We tended to talk about matters featured in the newspapers that day. In the spring of 1941 this was most often the war.

That May London suffered its heaviest bombing of the blitz (as it was now called), but that story was pushed out of the news by even more dramatic events. On May 20 the German airborne invasion of Crete seemed to foretell a new form of warfare, vertical envelopment. That same month the accelerating war in the Atlantic led to the sinking of an American merchant ship by the Germans. On May 27 President Roosevelt declared an "unlimited national emergency."

All this news was preliminary, though, to an event that began about the time we left for West Point and our entrance exam—operation Barbarossa, the German invasion of Russia. Without declaring war, Hitler began, across a thousand-mile front, the greatest land war in recorded history. None of us realized that day the full implications for the United States, but it was obvious that they would be profound.

On Saturday, June 21, a car from the Army Athletic Association arrived to transport Cas Myslinski and Carl Anderson to West Point for the examination. At Cas's suggestion the driver offered Jim Gould and me a ride, and we readily accepted. En route my thoughts on the exam were that three of us would pass and that the fourth, Jim, had a 50-50 chance. The car deposited us at our billets, South Barracks, convenient to the academic building where the tests would be given. West Point was the only site for the June validating exam; fewer than one hundred principals and alternates participated. In looking over the lists I found the name of my first alternate, Saul Levine from Passaic. Hope springs eternal.

Sunday the English test was given, and on Monday the math.

The questions were so familiar that Messrs. Hennessy and Bradford could have written them, even down to the book review, for which I naturally chose *Northwest Passage*. Except for those who still had to take physicals the next day was a period of waiting.

During the wait I toured parts of the academy I had never seen, including the Flirtation Walk, forbidden to plebes. As I stood under Flirtation Rock I wondered what girl it would be and when. For a moment I was Dick Powell in the movie of the same name as the walk. Hearing male and female voices approaching, I returned to reality and headed for the library. That evening a group of us walked to Highland Falls, the small town that lay beyond the south gate of West Point. We had heard that the high school prom was on, but our uninvited arrival there was greeted with mixed feelings (girls yes, boys no). I decided to be discreet and, along with some of our group, headed for the local theater.

On Wednesday afternoon came the results of the exam. On the list of all participants, some were lined out in red. These included my first alternate and, unfortunately, Jim Gould. When I went by his room to wish him well, he said that he would try again the following year. The following morning the rest of us received letters of invitation to report on Tuesday, July 1, before noon. With that I headed for Paterson.

One invitation awaiting me at home was a farewell event for Ray Janeczek, my fellow appointee from Passaic. All I knew of Ray was from the Paterson papers, which carried our pictures and short bios. He was well-known in his town as a high school baseball and basketball star, and his father was a director of the Polish Roman Catholic Union of America, important in the heavily Polish community of Passaic.

The Saturday evening event was crowded and, to my genuine embarrassment, I was assigned to the head table, where I was then pleasantly surprised to see Congressman Canfield on my left. Hoping I would not be called upon, I nevertheless tried to think what I would say to all these strangers if I had to speak. Minutes later I was saying it. Extolling Ray briefly, I shifted my remarks to how thankful I and my Paterson friends were for the fair way in which Congressman

Canfield and his predecessor Seger awarded their appointments to the academies. That made a big hit, especially with the congressman, and I was off the hook.

One final event was of my own choosing. On Sunday evening Jim Farrell, Walt Kennedy, and a couple of other friends from St. Joe's and the Scouts got together for a fun evening. I think we all sensed that this might be the last time for the foreseeable future. Between drinks and singing though we tried to talk of the future, at least our hopes for same.

On Tuesday, July 1, 1941, with my father driving and Aunt Annie and Toots in the back seat, we journeyed to West Point. On arriving mid-morning we found the Hudson Valley hot and humid, and were able to park about a hundred yards from the spot at which I was to report in. My father offered to walk the remaining distance with me. My mind saw a symbolism immediately—here was the man who had dropped me off with Annie fifteen years before now taking me from her and depositing me in my new life. The irony was a bit too much, and I refused his offer. Instead I opened the back door of the car, kissed Aunt Annie, and insisted on being the one to wave them off.

Proceeding toward the reporting-in area, I walked up to a sergeant seated at a table and gave him my name and letter of instructions. "You are assigned to Sixth Company New Cadets; go through that door to your left." Here we go again, I thought.

7. West Point at Peace and War

The door symbolized the start of a new life, but for the moment it led, after a cursory physical exam, to still another door and Beast Barracks, twenty-five days of hell. As soon as an enlisted guide left me, an immaculately uniformed first classman, "Francois" Roberts, greeted me. "Drop that bag, mister, and pull back those shoulders. Has anyone ever taught you how to stand at attention?" Unable to suppress a smile, I assumed an exaggerated position of attention. This, of course, brought down Roberts's wrath. "Wipe off that smile, mister—throw it on the ground—step on it and don't let me see it again!"

All over the area of South Barracks, where I was standing, similar scenes were enacted. The din sounded like Times Square without car horns. That day I was one of 539 new cadets who would, after swearing-in, constitute the West Point Class of 1945. Cadet Lieutenant Roberts, my welcomer, was one of the first classmen assigned to the Beast Detail. He directed me to "proceed on the double" and report for duty to the Cadet First Sergeant, Bill Smith. Trying to be military on reporting, I was greeted by Smith with "Get your slimy eyes off me, mister, and look straight ahead." He then assigned me a third-floor room to which I indeed proceeded on the double.

Already there was my roommate, one Ollie Becker from St. Louis. After quickly exchanging greetings, we were off on the first of many trips that day to the cadet store. This meant joining the end of a long line, and as we waited to draw bedding, clothing, field gear, and so on, the heat and humidity went steadily up.

The West Point system of that time was in the mode and tradition that had governed the academy all through the interwar years. By the time of the 1918 armistice, the Great War had turned the academy into an officer training school similar to Sandhurst in England. The changes came in 1919 when Brigadier General Douglas MacArthur, late of the 42d Infantry Division, AEF, became superintendent. Reestablishing the academy as a four-year school, he gave new direction to the school's programs, especially academics, athletics, and the plebe system into which I was being indoctrinated. While West Point was very much at peace on that July day in 1941, the new plebes of the class of 1945 were anything but.

Soon it was time for the noon formation of the entire new cadet class in Central Area. Out in front stood the corps senior cadet, Carl Columbus Hinkle, whose nom de plume for July was King of the Beasts. Hinkle, known by his classmates as "the Big Hub," had been all-American in football at Vanderbilt before his academy days. On this day, as he supervised our first formation as a class, the simultaneous corrections of plebes in all six companies made the area sound like a huge pit of rattlesnakes, all hissing at once.

It was hot as hell. Standing in a brace with the sweat pouring over my eyes I could see three classmates running continuously around the area. By the third time they passed, I wondered how they could keep from falling. By the fourth time I noticed that all three were Blacks. Later I learned that black cadets were run off as soon as possible; in fact, of the three I saw that day only one survived past the first week. The few who were able to stick it out (only one in my class) were "silenced" by the corps. They lived alone and no one was allowed to speak to them. In many respects West Point in 1941 was a Southern institution—a new experience for me.

We headed to the cadet mess in Washington Hall, an imposing structure that had been built in 1929 in the shape of a Vee. On one of the huge walls was a brilliantly colored mural, 75 x 35 feet, depicting twenty great battles and generals of the Western world, ending with Gettysburg in 1863. On that day, though, my world centered on my assigned table at which nine Beasts sat with one first classman, Mac Patch, an Army Brat. His instructions were precise: Sit at attention on the outer four inches of the chair, head up, shoulders back, fork down after every bite. As we ate, he began checking out our plebe knowledge—miscellaneous and nonsensical matters that we should commit to memory, such as the definition of leather and what do plebes rank: "Sir, the Superintendent's dog, the Commandant's cat, the waiters in the Mess Hall, the Hell cats, and all the Admirals in the whole blamed Navy." As our knowledge was not yet extensive, he told us to bone up on these and other matters. We should use *Bugle Notes*, also known as the plebe bible, a copy of which had been given to us that morning.

The afternoon was like the morning, with a little close-order drill thrown in. By four o'clock the skies began to darken and we were ordered to our rooms to get ready for the swearing-in ceremony. We put on our "plebe skins," which meant gray shirt and trousers, black tie, and white belt. Because the rain had by now started, our oath would not be administered on Trophy Point looking up the Hudson as planned; rather, we gathered in what was called the theater, a large hall in the gymnasium. After the adjutant general administered the oath, General Eichelberger, the superintendent, gave us a short talk. From where I stood, I could scarcely see him, but his words of both challenge and encouragement came through with warmth and even some inspiration—the only such we had on that day.

That evening, when we were allowed time to straighten out our rooms, I got to know Ollie Becker a bit. Older than I, he had attended Washington University in St. Louis for a couple of years. He had apparently memorized a good deal of plebe knowledge before arrival. Without forming a definite opinion I felt initially that he was something of a bore. As taps ended the long day, and in the moments before sleep came, my only thought was how in the hell did I ever arrange for a second fourth class year as a cadet!

Beast Barracks went on for twenty-five days, beginning each morning with a gun firing at 5:30, followed by the noisy playing of the Hell Cats, a fife, drum, and bugle corps element of the West Point band. First classmen were there and waiting, of course, when we fell into ranks for the reveille formation less than ten minutes later. Every minute of the day and evening was scheduled for something. One item on the schedule between reveille and breakfast formations was listed as "necessary ablutions," for which ten minutes were allowed. This seemed overscheduling to me until I thought of the alternative.

The days were a blur of endless sessions of close and extended order drill, lectures, inspections of rooms and equipment, exercises and athletics, unpleasant meals sitting at attention, filling out endless forms, and usually ending with the evening shower formation (frequently with double timing in place while awaiting one's turn). The commander of Sixth Company—a tall, imposing cadet from Providence, "Bunkie" Scofield—provided us a bit of reading for our spare time. Entitled "Customs for New Cadets," it listed twenty-two "wills" and eleven "will nots." He, along with our tactical officer, Major W.H. Sterling Wright, always lurked in the background during our informal exercise sessions in the showers, probably to make certain the exercises were not overdone.

On July 4 came a break of sorts. We spent most of the day working on our equipment, getting rooms ready for inspection, writing a required letter home, and, in groups of about twenty, getting a marching tour of the academy. Guiding my group was Bill Smith, our cadet first sergeant, who came from Birmingham, Alabama. As the tour reached some landmark or view, Smith would command "eyes right," then give a brief description such as "That building is the hockey rink, also available for pleasure skating in season, eyes front." Actually a nice guy, Smith would garner fame of a sort in the final moments of his life when a bomber he was piloting plowed into the fiftieth floor of the Empire State Building one foggy morning in July 1945.

Each morning we double timed out to a huge greensward, the Plain, for calisthenics, with our mass formation facing toward that million-dollar view up the Hudson. In front of us were three six-foot-high stands on which stood three impressive physical specimens: Major Harmony, Master of the Sword (a title going back to 1816 and referring to the individual responsible for the physical aspects of our training), and two of his assistants, Captains King and Messinger. They rotated daily in leading us in calisthenics. On the third day came Messinger's first turn. He would give the commands, some of which we repeated for voice training. Between exercises we stood at parade rest. That day at the end of the first set of exercises Messinger in a booming voice commanded, "Bring the class to PAWADE WEST." So help me, five hundred-plus voices commanded PAWADE WEST. We had not lost our collective sense of humor. Even Major Harmony could not suppress a smile.

During our new cadet period we received a half dozen lectures on the cadet honor code, at first given by the 6th Company commander, Bunkie Scofield, who also was chairman of the cadet honor committee. The basic principles were that a cadet does not lie, cheat, or steal, or tolerate those who do. The goal: honesty in academic work, and truthfulness in official statements spoken or written. Violators of the code came before the cadet honor committee; those found guilty had to resign. The later lectures came from John Short, a tough Irishman from Boston, who was the L Company Honor representative (6th Company new cadets were at the end of Beast Barracks to be assigned to L and M Companies.) Wrapping up his final lecture on practical examples of the code, he asked rhetorically, What happens if a cadet found guilty of an honor violation refuses to resign? The answer was that the cadet was silenced and required to live by himself. "In fact," he said, "there is such a case in the corps today, a third classman in another company whose name I will give you. In the event you encounter him, you are not to speak to him. His name is Timothy Leary."

About halfway through Beast Barracks the Beast Detail changed. Our new company commander was a Georgian, "Judy" Garland, who was also captain of the West Point baseball team. One evening during the shower formation he called me aside, saying that he had read all the background forms we had filled out on arrival. He had noted my attendance at the Coast Guard Academy and wondered if I had been recognized (i.e., given the status of an upperclassman; in other words, no more hazing) at the end of my Swab year. I explained that I had left on May 10 before the end of the year, so the answer was no. He thanked me, and discussion of the subject ended for then.

Toward the end of Beast Barracks we had a sizing formation to determine our permanent company assignments. The taller of the 6th Company group went to M Company; those slightly shorter to L. The purpose was to exploit perspective at parades, making the corps from a distance appear to be all the same height. The two flanker companies, A and M, would have the tallest, with the "runts" in F and G. I ended up in L Company. Thus, a quarter inch or so in my case determined my interpersonal relationships and, in effect, my home for the remainder of my cadet years. In fact, I got into L Co by hunching down a bit, having observed that my most compatible classmates in 6th Company seemed to be going to L Co.

On Friday afternoon, July 25, with the Hell Cats playing, our entire class in its new company formations marched out to the Plain. The upper classes were already there, and we lined up facing them. After the band played retreat, we came to "present arms." The upper classes returned the salute; and we marched over to join them. Now part of the corps, we passed in review with our permanent companies. As the companies left the parade, they marched to Camp Clinton at the northeast corner of the Plain. When each company reached its camp street, a roar came from the third class yearlings, who immediately fell out of ranks to pounce on us. We had been raised from the rank of new cadet to plebe.

Cadet summer camp originated in the early nineteenth century and in the summer of 1941 it still had some old touches: the wooden sentry boxes around the periphery looked like stage props from a

Gilbert and Sullivan production. But there were more recent facilities such as an underground shower and toilet complex, called the Sinks. Our accommodations were walled tents with wooden floors, each tent holding three or four cadets. Outside each tent were two washstands and inside folding cots and footlockers, with a uniform rack in the rear. Each company had its own street, and we were warned to stay away from runt companies, where we would be hazed unmercifully for being flankers. Fortunately, we were adjacent to the sinks, and I frequently heard an L Co yearling stop one of my classmates from a shorter company en route there. "You, little man, halt. Where are you from?"

Although there were always some first classmen present between their summer training trips, most of our supervision came from yearlings. Reveling in their newfound power at meal formations and during the long march across the Plain to the mess, they were a snarling pack behind us. In my case, two in particular were dedicated to my proper development: Gabby Ivan from Pennsylvania and his roommate from Down East, Hal Cloudman. For some reason I found Cloudman particularly irritating, and I was not always able to keep from being "BJ," as he called me. (This was cadet lingo for "bold before June," that is, before recognition.) Naturally, he always won our verbal tilting, usually by requiring some pushups.

Generally, we kept our same roommates in summer camp; added to ours was one Buck Melton from South Carolina, who had just completed a year at the Citadel. I assumed, or more precisely hoped, that at some future time I would be able to choose my own roommates. Mornings meant military training, such as close or extended order drill, practice marches, familiarization firing of weapons, and gas mask drill. The afternoons were something else.

One afternoon, for instance, the first classman in charge of the company that week, Tom Galloway, decided that the L Co plebes were not "on the ball," so he ordered a "clothing formation." To warm up, we did double timing in place. Then he ordered us to repair to our tents, change into a different uniform, and be back in ranks, all in a very short time. This went on for an hour or more. The uniform directed might be a regulation one or some outlandish combination such as "dress gray coat over underwear under arms" or "T-shirts and shorts with cross belts." Any deficiency required going back to the tent to make corrections. Late arrivals did pushups. Since speed was urgent, we tossed uniforms on the cot or the floor. When the formation finally ended, it took forever to arrange the tent in the required inspection order. For several days I found myself wearing items belonging to Becker or Melton.

On two afternoons a week we were required to attend dancing classes in Cullum Hall close by the camp and overlooking the river. Our instruction took place on an upper floor in the ballroom used for hops and entertainment. Just below the frieze on the upper walls of this room were emblazoned the names of battles in which West Pointers had fought. I felt an emotional tug as my eyes focused on Antietam . . . Gettysburg . . . The Wilderness, where graduates of what was now my school had fought on both sides.

Our uniform for dancing included hop shoes and white gloves. Mr. and Mrs. Roberts were our instructors; our classmates were our dancing partners. Mrs. Roberts kept telling us to "twinkle." It was not clear to me how one twinkled, but I was damn sure I couldn't do it dancing with a football player with enormous feet who kept stepping on mine.

One afternoon our company was marched up to the Cadet Chapel, an imposing structure built in military gothic and architecturally dominating the academy grounds. The purpose of the required formation was to try out for the choir. As I stood in line waiting my turn, I studied the stained glass windows. One large grouping was dedicated to the graduates who had been killed in the Great War and its inscription read, "Proudly their Alma Mater claims her own, may she have sons like these from age to age." How could a new plebe help from being moved?

At the end of the line, sitting at a piano placed there for the occasion, was Fritz Mayer, who had been the organist and Choir Master since the chapel had been dedicated thirty years before. What he wanted each of us to do was to sing a four-note scale with the words "Glor-ry-to-God" as he played. Those who did well would report to the first choir practice at the end of the summer. Before I finished the first note, I was excused with a "thank you—next."

On the last Sunday of summer camp I had my first visitors, Aunt Annie and Walter Kennedy, who had driven her up. The visit consisted pretty much of a tour conducted by me, after which we sat on a bench near Trophy Point. While Annie rested, Walt and I walked to a spot affording a better view of the river. How did I compare the plebe systems of West Point and Coast Guard, he wondered. My reply: Coast Guard's was tougher physically and West Point's mentally. The main differences, I opined, were based on scale: Because West Point had six times as many cadets as New London, its fourth-class system was much more impersonal and kaleidoscopic in terms of personalities. There was, I added, one more intangible for me. I was beginning to feel a tug of tradition and history in my new surroundings. Walt's reply was pragmatic Paterson: "Careful, Doug, you came here for a college education, not to join a priesthood." Something to keep in mind, if one could.

The next week we went on maneuvers, marching west out of the Military Academy through Cornwall, Middletown, and Goshen. Our uniforms would have been familiar to cadets twenty to thirty years before us: felt campaign hats, heavy gray shirts, riding breeches, and leggings. Our backs held full rolled packs, and we carried our model 1903 Springfield rifles. The tactical officers and some of the first classmen rode horses.

Overnight stops were in fairgrounds or farmers' fields. During this rainy week, nights in a shared pup tent went from moist to wet. Very early each morning came reveille, announced with loud blasting by Benny the bugler. A member of the enlisted detachment at West Point, Benny had become something of a tradition. Interspersed with the bugle blasts, his foghorn voice bellowed, "Drop your _ _ _ _ _ and grab your socks."

The pace of the maneuvers was fairly leisurely and relaxing— especially after Beast Barracks and Camp Clinton—affording a good opportunity to get to know our classmates. After the last exercise, an all-night attack, we had the next day off. We had all been issued two dollars (normally only cadet chits were legal tender) at the start of the maneuvers to "enjoy yourselves." Some of the more adventuresome made it to New York City, but most of us were content with local wanderings.

I made a point of arranging that day as a get-together with three compatible L Company classmates: Harry Grace from Brooklyn, Phil Toon from Tacoma, and Pat Neilond from San Francisco. Our day consisted of hitchhiking to Newburgh, where we wandered around and ate to the limit of our pooled eight dollars. Though a town well past its prime, Newburgh possessed a beautiful setting on the Hudson. Its ferry provided a major crossing (now spanned by an interstate bridge) to Beacon. Since Newburgh was the terminus of the West Shore Railroad, the ferry also gave cars and some foot passengers access to the main line of the New York Central across the river.

Mostly, we spent our day off talking and relaxing in a way we had not been able to do since June. We discussed everything: from our upperclass tormentors to how little we had been able to keep up with the world outside our monastery. We were aware, though, that the German invasion of the Soviet Union was rolling along. According to Pat Neilond, Germany was about to capture Smolensk, but none of us, including Pat, was quite sure where that was. We had also heard the previous week that the Churchill-Roosevelt meeting on a cruiser off Newfoundland had resulted in a joint declaration of principles called the Atlantic Charter. Though we knew little about the subject, we discussed the point that I brought up: that the declaration was probably aimed at the large percentage of Americans who were still isolationists.

Inevitably, our discussion ended up on girls. Each of the others claimed to have a special girl at home, although the only one who would be at the football games that fall was Harry Grace's. The other two were in the letter-writing category. When my turn came, I had nothing to say except to ask for suggestions. Phil suggested that since his girl was a continent away, the two of us go to see the cadet hostess for introductions. Pat opined that the line would be too long; maybe the three of us should go down to the pier, where the "ginch boat" (Hudson River steamer) docked with tourists on Sunday, to try our luck.

My hidden agenda that day was not girls but to find a new roommate. As it turned out, Phil and Pat had been together at Fort Scott, an Army prep school in California, the previous year and planned on living together. Phil, though very military in appearance, was a great kidder, whereas Pat impressed me as a smart guy and a wheeler-dealer. Harry was calm, precise, and very pragmatic. He had already been designated as one of the two company clerks for the coming academic year; these two would be required to live together. Even though I did not find a roommate that day, I got to know three colleagues with whom I would interact both professionally and socially during cadet years and intermittently for many years thereafter.

On Saturday, August 23, we marched back to West Point. Meeting the tired column at the gate was the West Point Band, leading us all the way to Central Area. Their repertoire included a medley of Army football songs, a reminder that the training of that long summer was finally over. Joining our class the following Monday were thirty-six new classmates, turnbacks from the class ahead of us. This caused a shuffling of roommates, but I kept Becker and Melton for the present.

To some extent, upper-class attention to the plebes slacked off, but it picked up briefly again on August 28 when the cows (second class) returned from their summer furlough and spent some time getting to know us and establishing their authority. One cow from our company, Kearie Berry from Texas, came down our ranks asking, "Where from, mister?" After I answered "New Jersey, sir," instead of passing on he added rhetorically, "No shit." I could not resist responding, "No shit"—long pause—"sir." Behind me an Army Brat classmate, Frank Mahin, doubled up in laughter. Not knowing which of us to discipline, Berry headed for Frank. Later I apologized to Frank, who said no need, it was worth the fun, and anyway I proved that I really was from New Jersey. He became a good friend.

At the noon meal on the Friday before Labor Day weekend the

cadet adjutant, after calling us to attention, published an unusual order: "Paragraph one, in the case of Timothy Leary the Honor Committee removes its silence. Paragraph two, the resignation of Timothy Leary from the Military Academy is accepted this date." Not one of us could have possibly guessed the bizarre career this ex-cadet would follow—ending over five decades later with his ashes orbiting the earth.

Academics began on Labor Day. During the fall semester, indeed during the entire first year, mathematics dominated the academic program. The good news was that I had covered the entire two-year math program in my tree-sitting days at the Coast Guard Academy. The other courses that fall were English and French. Though both were fairly straightforward, French was new to me and posed pronunciation difficulties in going from New Jersey English to West Point French, which, while not Parisian French was a long way from the Paterson patois.

Class sections were small, with only about a dozen cadets, and—to put it mildly—precise in format. Each cadet received a daily grade based on a recitation. The instructors, mostly West Point graduates, kept their opening discussion to a minimum, then had us go to the boards to tackle our assigned problem before reciting. Rarely used, a lecture was considered a form of instruction in which "ideas went from the notebook of the instructor to the notebook of the student without going through the mind of either." The somewhat formal recitations worked fine in math but not as well in, say, English. Consider the following: "Sir, I am required to explain the beauty in Keats's poetry. There are four elements of beauty, which are illustrative, first . . . etc." Illustrating with three, or perhaps five, elements might be more to one's liking, but experience conditioned us not to deviate from the "approved solution."

A regular part of the daily schedule was a morning class in physical training supervised by Major Harmony and his assistants, including PAWADE WEST. Each period began on the large main floor of the gymnasium with a tough session of calisthenics and related exercises. Next came a session, alternating daily, in one of the specialties: gymnastics, swimming, fencing, boxing, and wrestling.

Gymnastics required developing some facility with flying rings, parallel bars, long horse, high bars, rope climb, and tumbling mats. I was able to survive all except the mats. I simply could not throw my body through the air and arrive upright at the end. Once I even defied gravity on a memorable backward flip, staying absolutely horizontal until colliding with the gymnasium wall. I settled for an F on that requirement.

In boxing, Billy Cavanaugh, the boxing coach, used exhausting drills to teach us how to move in the ring: "to the right," "to the left," on and on. Then every few weeks came bloody Tuesdays, when we traded blows with some classmate for a grade. One day, to my regret, I got overly enthusiastic, knocking down (and effectively out) Hymie Kaplan from Brooklyn. I could never convince him that was an accident. For a while after that I was known as the Paterson Kid.

Tom "Pop" Jenkins, the wrestling instructor, was a real character who had been at West Point since 1905. In his earlier days he had been world wrestling champion; before that he was once pitted against a Barnum and Bailey bear. In his last professional match, he explained, one of his eyes had been gouged out by his opponent, the Terrible Turk. Pop went on, "At that point, I realized the Turk weren't no gentleman, so I went back in the ring and broke both his legs!" His favorite advice to us: "Remember, there ain't no holt that can't be broke." He was right, even in matters that have nothing to do with wrestling.

With academics beginning, upperclass attention to the fourth class slacked off. To be sure, we still walked with an exaggerated posture and made "calls" to upperclassmen's rooms to recite knowledge; we still endured endless inspections of our rooms and of our uniforms when in formation. At the first full dress parade I was reported for not knowing the name of a particular march—my Sousa was not yet up to par.

The mess hall was not a place to relax, either. Each plebe had a table duty: keeping the water glasses or coffee cups filled or hailing down a waiter with a serving plate to be filled. Along with this came requests for plebe knowledge. "Mr. Kinnard, let's have the Jersey poop," which in part went, "along came Hoit with a skoit named Goit who woiked in a shoit factory in Joisey City sewing poil buttons on poiple skoits." Though there was a bit of nonsense for most states, none matched the vulgarity of the Arkansas poop, an imaginary tirade against the speaker of their legislative chamber that began: "Mr. Speaker, Mr. Speaker, you blue bellied son of a bitch . . . ." Probably this sort of outlet was a good device to keep us from taking the plebe system too seriously.

The one relaxed meal each week was with the Catholic Squad after Sunday Mass while the rest of the corps was at the main cadet service. The Catholic chapel, consecrated in 1900, replicated one in England erected by Carthusian monks. Our religious destinies were guided by two interesting Irishmen: Monsignor George Murdock, who had been pastor since 1932, and Father Joe Moore, his assistant, who had arrived in 1939. As they were not on the West Point staff, but rather part of a New York diocese, they were in a unique position to play—some thought overplay—an *amicus curiae* role in cadet affairs. I liked them both, especially Moore, who took himself a bit less seriously than the monsignor did.

The only black cadet in our class who had survived Beast Barracks, Minton Francis of Washington, DC, was assigned to our company in early September. He had arrived after a gross hazing episode directed against him in his previous company. Ours was hardly more hospitable, as our instructions were to give him the silent treatment. This attitude was a totally new phenomenon to me, since there had been no black cadets in the Coast Guard Academy during my year there. The few blacks at Eastside High had, as far as I knew, been treated like all other students. (Larry Doby, a couple of years behind me in high school, was quoted on this matter when named to the Baseball Hall of Fame: "I was sort of the school hero at Eastside High, always one of the crowd, going everywhere with my white classmates, parties, dances, shows.")

With that background I understandably failed to grasp the intensity of racial feeling at West Point. Before long, though, something drove it home to me. A few weeks into the semester the plebes at my table, including Francis, were allowed to eat in a normal way one evening because of some athletic victory. Without thinking, I exchanged a few words with Francis. For the next several days I accumulated an alarming number of demerits from first classmen at room inspections. Perhaps naively, I did not connect the two events. On the fourth day Karl Wolf, a third classman who lived across the hall from me and who had recognized me because of my swab year, stopped by when my roommates were gone. Did I know why I had been getting all the demerits? When I said no, he explained: I was seen talking to Francis in the mess hall, and that was forbidden. Thereafter, survival took precedence; I complied with the silence. So much for the free spirit of the Paterson days.

In keeping with Douglas MacArthur's vision "every man an athlete" I became a member of the L Co intramural lacrosse team that fall. Never before having seen the game played, I understood by the end of the first week why the cadets called it "intramurder" competition. As a neophyte I became a combination water boy/assistant manager when competition with the other companies became keen. I did look forward to those three afternoons a week when all four classes from L Co mixed together as a team.

One lacrosse classmate who played at my level was Munson Pardee from Long Island. Munson had been to Colgate for two years and was a flying enthusiast, already having his pilot's license. We were very compatible and soon became good friends. Deciding that we would like to room together, we were able to work it out with our current roommates; apparently, a number of such moves were in the works. Judy Garland, our company commander, set the weekend of December 6-7 as the time to carry them out.

Autumn, with its riot of color and crisp beautiful days in the Hudson Valley, heralded a major event at West Point: Army football. The previous season had been Army's worst, with only one victory—and that against tiny Williams, 20-19. That disastrous season had brought new coach Red Blaik and his staff to the Military Academy to see what could be done. As it turned out, plenty—Army won its first four games. In the fifth game we tied Notre Dame but with so many injuries that Army lost three of the remaining four games, including the last one against Navy. Still, it was considered a good season.

Irene and Walt came for the second game, then took me to dinner at the Thayer Hotel on the southern end of the academy grounds. As usual, Irene had many questions, but this time also had a message of sorts. They had just moved to West Orange, New Jersey, into a house that looked impressive in the picture she showed me. She suggested that I spend some time with them on my first leave, even though that was still over a year away. Also, I should think about using their West Orange address with "social contacts," as Market Street in Paterson "was not impressive." Getting the message, I tucked it away for the future when social contacts would develop.

My battalion (Companies I, K, L, M) went to the Yale game in New Haven, and the entire corps attended the Notre Dame game in New York as well as the final game against Navy in Philadelphia. While football games called for big rallies the night before in the mess hall, the Notre Dame and Navy matches meant a week of hijinks in advance. We might, for example hang bed sheets out of barracks windows; many had humorous cartoons, all, of course, predicting an easy Army victory.

During the fall I managed to catch up on world events since June, mainly through the *New York Times*. I devoured the news about Europe, my focus of interest since the mid-1930s. In the autumn of 1941 that meant reading about German operations into the Soviet Union. By early October the Nazis had advanced to Moscow, putting it under attack. Then things began to change when the early and brutal Russian winter descended. With the German offensive lagging, the Soviets counterattacked, forcing the invaders to fall back. Operation Barbarossa had failed, the first such setback for Hitler since beginning his military adventures in 1936.

I had never systematically studied the Pacific area, though I had a vague idea of U.S.-Japanese relations. From the 1930s on, it was fairly clear that Japan wanted to be the overseer of Asia and the western Pacific but that this conflicted with the U.S. view. Their goals, I assumed, were to relieve the crowded conditions of their own islands, to access cheap, ready sources of new material to feed their population, and to produce goods for the world market. In September 1940 Roosevelt went from words to deeds with Japan by halting America's export to them of scrap iron and steel, commodities vital to their industrial output.

In November, through the *Times* and newsreels, I followed the high-level talks going on between a Japanese envoy named Nomura and our Secretary of State Hull. Japan, of course, wanted us to lift our embargo and to end our aid to China. They also wished for a commanding place in the Far East, a position we did not want to grant. All this, however, was far from my own concern on Saturday, December 6, when Melton and Becker moved and Munson Pardee became my new roommate. That evening we and several L Company classmates went to the theater to see Gary Cooper in *Sergeant York*. Cooper was well cast as the country boy, Alvin York, who became one of our greatest World War I heroes. Returning from the movie, we hummed an old hymn from York's Tennessee days, "That Old Time Religion!"

Sunday, December 7, was a cold, crisp, beautiful day on the East coast. By early afternoon, after Munson had all his belongings arranged in inspection order for the next day, we decided to take in a movie that began about 2:45. We stopped by Phil Toon's room to ask him to join us, but he declined because he was concerned about academics and needed to study. His small radio was tuned to the Philharmonic concert. We arrived at the theater a bit early and were standing in the lobby when along came Phil, almost at a trot. We assumed that he had changed his mind, deciding to join us. Before reaching us, he blurted out, "The Japanese have bombed Pearl Harbor." Too stunned to grasp the real impact, we merely stood there while Phil went off to play Paul Revere. No movie for us now! We went out to walk—all the way to the Thayer Hotel and back—scarcely talking. It was a day of generational importance.

As L Company formed for dinner that evening, Judy Garland put a quick end to a bit of hijinks. President Roosevelt's "day that will live in infamy" speech was not until the next day, but we knew already that we were at war. And with us constantly now was the sobering thought that all of us, sooner or later, would be involved. Some of our group would not "grow old as we that are left grow old." Among those in L Company that night were many who would later be killed in action. Let me list just one from each class. *First*: Captain Mac Patch, France, October 1944; *Second*: 1st Lieutenant Benny Mills, Belgium, September 1944; *Third*: 1st Lieutenant Bob Foisey, Germany, September 1944; *Fourth*: 2d Lieutenant Johnny Hazen, Italy, February 1945.

A few days later came word of the first academy graduate killed in action, Captain Colin Kelly (also from L Company), class of 1937, shot down as his bomber attacked a Japanese naval convoy headed for the Philippines.

As the days of December moved along, there was no good news about the war. All that we could be glad about was to anticipate Plebe Christmas, almost at hand. Although we were not allowed to leave the academy for the holidays, we could celebrate being without the upper classes who would be on leave for almost two weeks. Once again we would be members of the human race: eating in a normal way in the mess; strolling around the academy without bracing; and using Boodlers, the cadet soda fountain.

At breakfast on Friday, December 19, the last day of classes, came a surprise. Judy Garland, who as L Company Commander was authorized to leave the mess hall early, asked me to accompany him outside. There he explained that because of my swab year at the Coast Guard Academy I could get early recognition when the first class thought I was ready. He intended now to take me to the first captain's room, where the "Big Hub" would recognize me for the corps. I had some vague misgivings as we headed to our meeting with Carl Columbus Hinkle. After a brief introduction Hinkle reached out his hand with a "Nice to meet you, Kinnard." I now joined the academic turnbacks as one of thirty-seven recognized plebes.

Plenty of activities, including visitors, enlivened our monastic holiday. One day my brother Harry drove up from the greater Paterson area, where he had a job with one of Curtis Wright's wartime expansion units. Besides an extensive tour and lunch in the cadet mess, we had, for once, a good opportunity to talk. A matter-of-fact guy, Harry opined that it would not be long before the draft caught his age group, twenty-five, and indeed brother Jim's, then thirty-four. (He was right; both of them were inducted in mid-1942.) He was already talking of his postwar plans: to return to Sussex County in northern New Jersey, where he had grown up; there he would start his own construction business.

Christmas day brought Aunt Annie and Toots, driven up by my sister Daisy and her husband Steve. After exchanging gifts in an alcove of the Thayer lobby, we had our Christmas dinner in the hotel dining room. It was a grand day both for Aunt Annie and for me, almost like going home for a few hours. My first actual visit back to Paterson would not be for another year.

New Year's brought Jeannie Marie Carton, my date at the Coast Guard Academy weekend the previous spring. With her was a girl from Jeannie's home on the Jersey shore. Munson, who had reluctantly agreed to double-date, was much less reluctant when he actually met this good-looking friend. The high point of their visit was the New Year's Eve dance. My impression was that Jeannie, an attractive but quiet young lady, was very interested in continuing our relationship. I was less certain. Though we corresponded a bit during the spring semester, I never saw her again.

After New Year's came what the cadets called the "gloom period"—dark, often snowy days. Events that year contributed to the gloom. Japanese forces were on the march and by late December were invading the Philippines, Wake, and Guam; on the continent they had seized Shanghai and had landed in Malaya and Thailand. By January 2 they had occupied Manila. Then a few days later came news from the fighting on Bataan: the first Medal of Honor of the war was awarded to 1st Lieutenant Sandy Nininger, KIA, class of 1941. He had been a member of our L Company less than three weeks before we reported the previous July.

The war was coming home. The commandant of cadets, Colonel Irving, spoke to the corps: "I know many of you are anxious to get into action . . . . The superintendent has asked me to inform you that no resignations will be accepted. Your duty is to complete your education as cadets and qualify for whatever may lie ahead." It would be many months before we knew how our own program would change; meanwhile, changes occurred in our senior leadership. General Eichelberger left in January to command a division and was replaced by Major General Francis Wilby, somewhat older, who was to remain superintendent for the war's duration. The following month the Commandant, Colonel Irving, was reassigned and shortly became a division commander himself. His replacement as commandant was Colonel Philip Gallagher, with whom in time I was to have an interesting and, for me, defining encounter.

Whatever the world situation, we had our day-to-day problems to manage. My new one that winter was horseback riding, required each year of cadet life. I had never been around a horse except to observe those pulling milk wagons in Paterson during the late 1920s. What was show-off day for some Army Brats and others with horsemanship experience, was to me a horror. We were lined up in the riding hall, a big dark building, with the horses lined up opposite us. The instructor, a cavalry officer, appeared mounted, redundant in pinks and greens, and wearing highly polished Peel boots. Without giving us preliminary instruction, he said simply, "Gentlemen, these are the horses. Mount up." He might as well have asked me to dive into a flaming pool. I took the one horse left and, after watching the others mount, tried to imitate their style. My horse was a small mare named Mary Ann who seemed to understand my plight—or did my desperation make me hallucinate?

Once mounted, we began to walk around a large ring, then moved to the trot, and finally at the command "gallop hoooooo" we became an undisciplined mounted mob. The instructor brought us under control and had a sergeant from the cavalry detachment take over. "Put this rabble in a slow trot without stirrups until I return." This ranks as a form of torture for certain parts of the anatomy, and for several days thereafter I walked with difficulty.

As the instruction progressed, Mary Ann and I became buddies, remaining so through my riding years as a cadet. Phil Toon and Pat Neilond, who were good riders, ragged me about my lack of style. Then one day toward the end of our riding instruction, the officer in charge commended me for doing well with Mary Ann on some difficult jumps. My two tormentors were astonished—as was I. Of course, it was Mary Ann who deserved the commendation, and I told her so out loud.

The annual 100th Night Show, which was held early in March, traditionally ended the gloom period. The title of that year's show, "Yeah Furlo," was greeted by moans from the yearlings, since Pearl Harbor had put an end to the two-and-one-half-month furlough that normally came between the second and third cadet years. An upperclassman recruited me to be on the curtain and rigging crew that year, so I had a good chance to watch the musical evolving with each rehearsal. The theme was, naturally, a cadet fantasy and included satires in song and dialogue on certain tactical officers. The names were, of course, coded, but the cadets (and probably the officers) understood "Ming the Merciless," "Porky," "The Jaw," and the like. The highlight of the show was the dancing chorus of football players dressed in women's costumes borrowed from a New York show.

By April the buds emerged, setting the stage for a beautiful spring in the Hudson Valley. On our outdoor surveying class I had a hard time keeping my mind on the problem at hand. Phil Toon, Munson, and I constituted one crew, and until the instructor came along, I enjoyed giving them a visual tour of the valley based on my time at Stanton the year before. Phil, though a model cadet in many ways, was having a tough time with academics. Recalling my own Coast Guard experience, I sympathized with him. What a difference a year makes; now I was easily in the upper half of my class and considered a "hive" in mathematics.

Munson was smart in technical subjects and, in his two years at Colgate, had already taken many of the courses in our curriculum. His antipathy toward physical exercise, though, showed up in gym classes. One day I overheard Mayor Harmony, standing near him, say, "Mr. Pardee, you are dying on the vine." I could not help breaking into a laugh, which made the major scowl at me. Since Munson's real love was the Air Corps, I once asked him why he didn't go directly there from Colgate. Apparently, his mother had prevailed on him to seek an appointment to West Point instead. An interesting person, Munson could be very personable and was a good roommate if I resisted his cynicism toward the "system," as he referred to the West Point culture.

From far away in the Pacific that April came grim war news. The Japanese in their drive toward Corregidor, our last outpost in the Philippines, had captured thousands of American and Filipino troops on the Bataan peninsula. Their captivity began with the notorious Bataan Death March, a sixty-five-mile trek north to a temporary internment camp. This nightmare of beatings, torture, and starvation killed six hundred Americans and perhaps ten thousand Filipinos. Sixteen thousand more Americans and Filipinos died in their first few weeks at the camp. Some details did not come out until the summer of 1943, but even then the world knew about the inhuman treatment and the wholesale deaths. To many cadets and faculty, this was a personal matter involving relatives and friends—a time for sadness and renewed determination to meet the challenges lying ahead.

Our job, though, as the commandant of cadets had told us, was to complete our education as cadets before joining combat units. And our education—at least for my classmates—included the inevitable "spring buck-up" imposed by the upperclassmen. By late April the atmosphere resembled Beast Barracks and Camp Clinton, but with one difference. This time the end was in sight.

As a recognized plebe I was not subject to upperclass harassment, but in a strange way I regretted my new status. These were my classmates; unlike the other thirty-six recognized plebes, I had not been part of the yearling class. Since my recognition I had played my privileged state in low key. In the mess while sitting at ease I kept silent—just like my classmates—unless an upperclassman started a conversation with me, as the yearlings were apt to do. I met first call for formation with my classmates but stood off on the side as they braced to face the inevitable upperclass inspections. In a captivity different from theirs, I looked forward to their recognition, when we all could be the same again.

At last, June week arrived, although, because of the war, it was in May that year. "How many hours to graduation?" the table commandant asked some plebe at every meal. Academics gave way to ceremonies, parades, and, for the upper classes, social functions. Alumni began to arrive; so did upperclass dates, some soon to be wives.

One memorable ceremony on Alumni Day began with returning graduates marching by class to the Thayer monument. The oldest living West Point graduate led the procession; in front of him marched the West Point band, playing tunes of an earlier time including "Pack Up Your Troubles" and "Over There." We listened to the names of graduates who had died during the past year; then the oldest graduate laid a wreath as the alma mater was played.

On the afternoon of May 28 came the most dramatic of all West Point ceremonies—graduation parade. Since it was also the last chance to haze plebes, the yearlings were hoarse from shouting. Music was always the same for this event; the band finished trooping the line with "Auld Lang Syne." After retreat and the command, "Graduating Class Front Center," the first class left their companies for the last time to the tune of "Army Blue." At the command "Forward March" the entire class moved forward in one long gray line, shoulder to shoulder, as the band played the "Alma Mater," reserved only for this ceremony. After they turned and faced the corps, we passed in review led by the Commandant of Cadets, doing eyes right for them as they stretched the entire length of the parade ground. All the while the band played "The Official West Point March." None of us, not even Munson, could keep from being moved.

Next came the event my class had been waiting for since last July 1. Into Central Area the columns marched from the parade ground. After we were halted, the senior second classman commanded, "About Face." Out came the right hands of the upperclassmen with a "Glad to know you." Plebe year was over.

The next day, May 29, 1942, we all attended graduation in the large field house down toward the river. The speaker was George Marshall, Army chief of staff. I remember quite clearly one of his statements: "Last spring I insisted upon a rearrangement of courses in order that our new air force should include as soon as possible a large number of commissioned flyers imbued with the traditions and standards of West Point." That explained the impetus behind the academy's new air cadet program that had been planned during the past several months. A substantial number of cadets from the two upper classes would be leaving the next day for primary flight training in locations around the country.

After General Marshall's address the first class went up to the platform one at a time, in order of class rank to receive their diplomas. When the name of the last-ranking cadet, John Crowley, was read, the first class threw their hats into the air to thunderous applause, always reserved for the class goat. Finally, the first class gave the "Long Corps Yell" for the corps, and Hub Hinkle gave his last command as first captain: "Class Dismissed." We were yearlings!

That afternoon our class and the ground cadets from the new first class moved across the plain to Camp Clinton. Actually, we had the camp pretty much to ourselves, as the firsties were usually off somewhere on training trips. In various ways that summer we experienced West Point's transition from peace to war. "Yearling deadbeat," with afternoons off to lounge or to swim at Delafield Pond, was a thing of the past. We had pretty much a full training schedule: indoctrination in each of the Army branches, particularly infantry; marksmanship training, and qualification with the new Garand rifle, etc. Spit-and-polish still prevailed, though, in our daily tent inspections, guard mounts, dress parades, and the three-a-day marches to the mess hall from Camp Clinton.

Something new in training was added that summer: "flight indoctrination." From a dock on the Hudson each cadet had five observation flights in an old and smelly Grumman amphibian known as "the duck." The plane held a dozen cadets on each of its one-hour trips, frequently bouncing us around when hit by the winds of the river valley. On landing, the plane would hit the water with a sharp impact, necessitating my use on each flight of the paper sack issued in anticipation. After the second flight I renamed the plane "the Puka dive bomber" (after the Stuka dive bomber, a well-known German plane), which stuck with my L Company colleagues for the nonce.

In early June we learned that the class would be representing the corps that month in the "New York at War" parade. Our uniforms would be khakis, newly issued for summer training, along with World War I helmets, field packs, and leggings. In mass formation our class practiced daily marches to the Thayer Hotel and back to camp. Constantly supervising was the Commandant, by now nicknamed Uncle Phil—not a favorite uncle, by the way. Ever optimistic, we looked forward to a couple of hours of free time in Gotham when the parade was over.

As soon as our busses arrived in New York, we formed up as the lead unit. Garands on our shoulders, we marched up Fifth Avenue for what seemed like an endless time. Finally, after passing the reviewing stand, we turned off the route of march and halted next to our busses. Here, after receiving a cup of coffee, we were loaded into the busses for the ride directly back to West Point. Well, at least we got the academy some good publicity. Or did we? Newspaper accounts the next day showed a photo of our formation on Fifth Avenue captioned, "A crack Regular Army Infantry regiment"! Thanks anyway for the cup of coffee, Uncle Phil.

Through radios and occasional trips to the library, fortunately near Camp Clinton, we could keep up a bit with the outside world. Mostly, this meant the war. Early in June came good news for a change, the dramatic victory of our Pacific Navy at the Battle of Midway—a devastating defeat for Japan. Though few realized then the full implications of the battle, we did know that the Japanese had lost four aircraft carriers. Years of bitter fighting remained, but in those early June days of 1942 the United States had placed the Japanese navy on the strategic defensive from which it never fully recovered.

In the European and North African areas, the news was not so good. By late June a German offensive had established bridgeheads on the Don—one with the objective of moving on Stalingrad, the other to seize the oil fields in the Caucasus. At the same time German Field Marshal Erwin Rommel, the Desert Fox, captured Tobruk in Libya on June 21. Then breaking into the open, Rommel's Afrika Korps raced into Egypt, reaching a place called El Alamein by the end of the month. Here the British determined to make a last stand to prevent the Germans from cutting their lifeline, the Suez Canal.

Despite our busy schedule that summer, we had some time for relaxation. Every night we could attend a movie at the theater; on weekends we could swim at Delafield Pond and simultaneously observe the dates—usually in bathing suits—of those classmates lucky enough to have such, for which there were also hops in Cullum Hall on Saturday evenings. What a difference from plebe summer! On one of my trips to Delafield Phil Toon pointed out a classmate from the other half of the corps—John Eisenhower. John's father, Phil said, had recently been named Commanding General of American forces in Europe—at the moment this meant England.

Essentially the only class in residence, we had plenty of space; like others, Munson and I had a tent to ourselves. The relaxed atmosphere and inevitable horseplay (water fights and the like) provided opportunity to get to know my L Company classmates. There were summer visitors, too, among them my sister Daisy and her husband Steve. During a dinner conversation at the Thayer, Daisy mentioned that Steve's boss Stan Kron who lived in Upper Montclair had a daughter Ginnie almost my age. Would I be interested in a date during my Christmas leave? Without giving the matter any thought I agreed, indirectly setting in motion a long-range chain of events in my personal life.

In mid-July one phase of our summer activities ended as we prepared to move for one week to Pine Camp near Lake Ontario in upper New York State. On the morning that we loaded on trucks taking us to our train, we got one last look at our camp. Tents were already being struck, this time for good, ending a century-and-a-quarter tradition. Assembly had sounded for the final time for the march to old Camp Clinton; we had been its last occupants.

The week at Pine Camp allowed us to observe the training of the 4th Armored Division as it prepared for its eventual role in the European Theater, including handling some of its equipment. One day, when my turn came, I drove one of their tanks without bothering to inform anyone that I had never driven a car. It went fine. I can recall, when observing a training exercise of the 37th Tank Battalion one afternoon, overhearing a sergeant say to one of my classmates, "The battalion commander is Major Creighton Abrams, one of the best officers in the Army. Someday he will be famous." How right he turned out to be in the Vietnam era.

From Pine Camp we headed back to the academy, but to a part we had never seen before. The West Point reservation had been expanded to the west by some ten thousand acres. The new Camp Popolopen with barracks constructed along the shores of Lake Popolopen featured extensive firing ranges. During our two-week stay we fired 105 mm howitzers, mortars, and various types of machine guns.

Meanwhile, during this eclectic summer of ours the new plebe class had arrived, this time in two echelons. Congress had mandated a wartime expansion of the corps from 1,960 to 2,496 cadets. The first increment, about the size of our class, arrived, as we had, on July 1; the second increment, of about the same size, arrived on various dates in July, August, and even into September.

We met the first echelon of plebes, after the two weeks in Popolopen when they left with us and the ground-force firsties by motor convoy on maneuvers, held that year at Pine Camp. These maneuvers hardly resembled the leisurely ones of our plebe summer. With little sleep we spent four days marching and "fighting." The only holdover was Benny the Bugler, who roused us in base camp before and after the maneuver. His raucous manner was the same, but with a toned-down script (which we attributed to unwanted wartime censorship): "I know you're tired and sleepy too! I don't wantcha but the major do."

The day after our return from maneuvers, August 17, 1942, was Reorganization Day at West Point. The expanded corps went from a regiment of twelve companies to a brigade of two regiments totaling sixteen companies. For many, this meant new roommates—for all, it meant new companies. Gone was old L Company; I was now in G-2. Though many of my L Company friends ended up in F-2, I felt fortunate that my roommate Munson and my closest friends—Toon, Neilond, and Grace—all ended up with me in G-2.

Company reorganization was just the beginning. Next came the reduction of the academy course from four to three years, which had been rumored since the past spring. The new firsties would graduate in six months and henceforth be known as the class of January 1943—their air cadets would remain away and not rejoin the corps until just before graduation, by which time they would also have their wings. The cows would now be known as the class of June 1943; their air cadets would return to West Point to take flight training at Stewart Field (called during the war the Wings of West Point) near Newburgh, while remaining at the academy to take a modified academic schedule. They, too, would graduate with their wings. We were now the class of 1944, and the plebes took our old designation, 1945. By the late summer of 1942 West Point had established the mode it would operate under during the Second World War.

Understandably, the increased size of the corps—over 25 percent—had some impact on our lifestyle. For yearlings it meant three-man rooms, at least until the January class graduated. Harry Grace, whose former roommate had ended up in another company, joined Munson and me. Perhaps, though, the most noticeable change was in the now crowded and noisy mess hall. At peak volume it sounded like a warehouse filled with tobacco auctioneers all chanting at the same time.

By that fall the staff and faculty were not only larger but also more diverse in background. Many of the Regular Army officers stationed at the Point had been transferred to line units scheduled to be deployed overseas; by the beginning of the academic year fewer than half of the 350 officers assigned to the academy were regulars. The balance, many of whom held reserve commissions, were mostly academy graduates from civilian life. In addition, a number of academics without any military background received commissions and became faculty members.

Before the fall term started on August 31, the academic board had reworked the remaining three years of our original course into a two-year program. Some of the engineering courses were reduced in scope, but the main cuts came in the social sciences and English. As it turned out for me, yearling year was my best for class standing, primarily from having stored up calculus, physics, and chemistry in my tree-sitting year at New London.

Both Munson and I wanted to relax that fall; in particular, we wanted nothing to do with the plebe system, which Munson had always despised. Harry, though a yearling corporal, was laid back, whereas I simply needed a break after two years of swab and plebe experience. Moreover, since we were meeting the academic goals we had set for ourselves, our study hours were relatively brief and our conversational periods long.

One day in English my assignment was to prepare and present a short talk on the con side of an issue. Since I could select the issue, I settled on tackling the academy's requirement for horsemanship. In preparing my assignment I was egged on by Munson, an admirer of E.B. White's sharp, satiric style. I also kept in mind the instructor's stress on the attention, or opening, step of a talk. All I now remember of my effort is that opener: "Horseback riding is for cowboys, sons of cavalry officers, and damn fools!" My argument seemed to amuse the class and instructor. When I finished, the instructor, with tongue in cheek, asked, "Mr. Kinnard, in which of the categories in your opening statement would you put polo players?" That stopped me momentarily; then I answered, "All three, sir." With that bit of illogic, school was out.

With the two early graduations that academic year, members of our class accelerated into leadership positions in cadet activities. Two of these involved me. The first was as company representative on the class ring committee. Important in academy tradition since 1835, class rings were usually presented in a formal ceremony at the beginning of first class year; they were worn from then on. Who has not heard the term "ring knocker" applied to West Pointers in the Army?

The other activity had to do with the cadet publication *Bugle Notes*, also known as the plebe bible. I knew its editor, Al Toth from Clifton, New Jersey, through an acquaintance of Daisy and Steve's at home. Al appointed me as one of his yearling helpers that year, but when his class accelerated to January graduation, this once-a-year spring publication would no longer be on his watch. In October, when he named Mike Davis of the June '43 class as editor, I became Mike's assistant. Being on the ring committee was basically an honorary position, but *Bugle Notes* would involve a good deal of work.

The war that fall did not slow down enthusiasm for football; if anything, we had even more rallies with their related hijinks. The 6-3 record of the "big rabble," as cadets called the team, was little different from the previous season's, but some of Blaik's recruits began to foreshadow what Army football would be in a couple of years. My two Stanton colleagues, Carl Anderson and Cas Myslinski, had an outstanding season. Andy, a breakout back, was unfortunately injured along the way; but Cas was a rock at center, sixty minutes against both Notre Dame and Navy, presaging the All-American he became in 1943.

The Notre Dame game on November 7 attracted a crowd of 78,000 in Yankee Stadium. I had secured four good tickets for Walt and Irene, rabid Notre Dame fans. They brought along friends of theirs whom I had not seen since my Hopatcong days in Sperry Springs ten years before. Afterward, we all went to a cocktail lounge in the Taft Hotel and later to dinner at an Irish restaurant. During the singing that celebrated Notre Dame's victory, I, of course, was silent. Drinking was verboten for cadets—especially with tactical officers waiting on the boat for our return—but the outing was great fun, anyway. Such, then, was life for me in the fall of 1942, as the war approached its first anniversary.

It was a time when Harry, Munson, and I had frequent discussions about the war situation on the Russian front and in North Africa, and sometimes about the prolonged American campaign for Guadalcanal in the Solomons, initiated in August. The German offensive begun on the Don in early summer had by November ground to a halt. Though the campaign had cost the Russians some oil fields as well as industrial and agricultural areas, the Nazis had failed to reach their objectives and were overextended, especially near Stalingrad. It was here that the Soviets prepared for the major counterattack that came on November 19.

In North Africa, Rommel failed to break the British line at El Alamein in early September, and on October 23 Montgomery's counterattack began pushing Rommel into a retreat. But the most important news to us came on November 8, the day after the Notre Dame game. American and some British forces, under command of Lieutenant General Dwight Eisenhower, landed in French North Africa—at Casablanca, on the Atlantic and in the Mediterranean at Oran and Algiers. Despite scattered French resistance the landings were successful, and Eisenhower was able to begin his race for Tunis. Though many months of fighting lay ahead in North Africa, the giant pincer that would destroy the Afrika Korps was taking shape.

As the days of December passed we concentrated on the forthcoming Christmas season. During the reprogramming of the course into three years the academy authorities had decided that our class would get only one leave of any duration: fifteen days during the Christmas season of 1942. On Saturday, December 19, we left our monastery of the past eighteen months to head home. This meant my first extended stay in Paterson since leaving for New London almost two and one-half years before.

Like most parts of the country after a year of war, Paterson had changed. The Depression had disappeared with the war boom, as Curtiss Wright and related war industries in the area brought an influx of workers. Many workers were older than usual, like Walt Kennedy's father, who had given up his tailor shop for employment at Wright.

The draft had reached, or was about to, most young men from eighteen to thirty-five years (twenty-six was the upper limit if married). Both of my brothers had been inducted: Harry was en route to North Africa in a mortar unit, while Jim's outfit in Texas was training for the Pacific. Of my Paterson friends only a few were around that holiday. These included Walt Kennedy, waiting for a January induction; Jim Farrell, home from a Naval unit for Christmas; and Jim McLaughlin, who was a 4-F, not physically qualified for military service. Most of the others: the Gallaghers, St. Joe's, the Scout troop, and Eastside High, were in one of the services; many were already overseas or soon headed that way. Mothers hung little flags with a blue star for each son in service. As time went on, too many were replaced with gold stars after receipt of a telegram beginning: "The Secretary of War (or Navy) regrets to inform you . . .". By the end of 1942 our generation had already established our identity for future historians as "the GI Generation."

At home, people were talking about matters hardly mentioned at West Point such as War Bonds, Victory Garden plans for the coming spring, shortages of some items like sugar, and, especially, gasoline rationing. The government had stopped all private car and truck production, and each vehicle being used was required to display a sticker identifying its ration category. Based on usage priorities from low to high these were A—pleasure, B—drive to work, C—used in work, and E—emergency vehicle.

Travel restrictions in general dictated that most leisure activities took place at or near home. This in turn caused record-breaking attendance at movie houses. Among the hits that fall and into the holidays were *Yankee Doodle Dandy*, *Mrs. Miniver*, and *Casablanca* (with Ingrid Bergman and Humphrey Bogart at their best and with Dooley Wilson's classic rendition of "As Time Goes By"). Movies in those years influenced people in the same way that television does today. These movies and scores of others, by depicting us fighting the good war against evil, helped to unite public opinion behind the war effort. In entering the public's imagination, they may have also shaped viewers' expectations for the postwar world.

Despite the absence of many friends I had more than enough to do. For this brief vacation I could replay the low-key but enjoyable activities of home: midnight Mass at St. Joe's with Aunt Annie; lunch at the Alexander Hamilton with Toots; and long hikes to Passaic Falls and later to Garret Mountain with Johnny Bustard, where I could view again all of Paterson with the beckoning New York skyline. One innovation was a stay with Walt and Irene at their new home in West Orange. Through Walt's American Legion activities they had acquired many new friends, several of whom had us come for cocktails. It was a long way from Market Street, more symbolically than geographically. Irene again emphasized that for "social reasons" I should use their address, and I agreed, at least for nonofficial matters. Thereafter, I increasingly became a resident of 69 Edgewood Avenue, West Orange.

One evening a few days into my leave I set out with Daisy and Steve for dinner at the Krons' lovely home in Upper Montclair. Their daughter Ginnie, a senior at Montclair High and a prospective art student, was personable, bright, and attractive. After an excellent dinner Ginnie and I went to another room for a pleasant get-acquainted conversation before I left, and she invited me to a small party she was hosting the evening after Christmas. It turned out to be a buffet supper with plenty of records for dancing afterward. With some of the records we just listened ("Paper Doll" had recently been revived from its origins in the late twenties); with others, like "White Christmas," we sang along; and some others, like "You'd Be So Nice to Come Home To," put us in the dancing mood.

As the evening ended, Ginnie mentioned that a friend, Peggy Cushman, who lived nearby, was having a party on the 29th. Would I like to take her? Indeed I would. We were greeted that evening in the foyer of her parents' home by Peggy who dispatched Ginnie upstairs to a coatroom and me to a nearby study to dispose of my cadet overcoat.

Afterward, I found myself in a large room from which most of the furniture had been removed. After glancing around, I focused on a girl sitting on a divan directly opposite me. Wow! She was beautiful—long dark-brown hair, large brown eyes, lovely features—and nicely assembled. Certainly this was the most beautiful girl I had ever seen. I was captivated—no, smitten! All this took place in less than a minute. My normal reticence with girls evaporated, and I was about to head across the room to introduce myself when Ginnie, who had come up from behind, tapped on my shoulder. In trying to compose myself, I blurted out something about glancing around the house. Her response: "I noticed." We headed off into a large room where couples were already beginning to dance to music from a concealed record player.

Most of the dancers appeared to be a year or two younger than I. Although none of the men was in uniform that carefree evening, I suspected that most were only months or perhaps a year away from induction. The music was mainly currently popular numbers such as: "Serenade in Blue," "That Old Black Magic," and lively numbers such as "Don't Sit under the Apple Tree." There seemed to be no cutting in or switching of partners and, try as I might, I was never able to steer us close to the pretty brunette during a break in the music. At one point I asked my date about her. As she was younger, Ginnie did not know her but thought she might be a cousin of Peggy, our hostess.

Later, as couples began to leave, I became desperate. At the price of being a boor, I said I would like to meet the young lady I'd asked about. Reluctantly Ginnie fetched her from the coatroom, and we chatted briefly. Young indeed, but she was even prettier close up. Her name was Diana Hamilton and she lived nearby on Upper Mountain Avenue; now she had to leave. Just the same, I had all the information I needed. "A journey of a thousand miles begins with a single step."

Sunday, January 3, we were back at "Hell on the Hudson" and into the gloom period: cold, windy, and snow-driven. Fifteen days in the real world had had its impact, though. All of us had been with friends who had been or were about to be drafted; this thought, combined with news of American fighting and dying in faraway places, engendered a slowly growing restlessness. Countering that for a time was a challenge we would face soon. In less than five months the two classes ahead of us would graduate, and we would assume responsibility for commanding and administering the Corps.

The January class was even then preparing for its graduation on the 19th. In late December the "fly boy" contingent of the class returned. After six months spent earning their wings, some demonstrated a new attitude. One who walked into Central Area to sign in had apparently been in the cockpit too long. He had removed the grommet from his cadet hat, which was tilted back on his head; he wore his hair longer than regulation and was smoking a cigar. Within minutes he was surrounded by tactical officers who gave him a brief reprise of his opening day in Beast Barracks: "Put out that cigar, mister . . . stand at attention; you're not a civilian!" Within hours he reported to the battalion board (a group of officers whose legal code we interpreted as "a cadet is guilty until proven guilty"). The next day he was walking punishment tours.

The academy did everything possible to replicate the normal June Week activities for the graduating class. At every formation I heard the Hell Cats or the academy band include a popular song of the 1940s, "June in January." There were hops, a baccalaureate, and a ceremony for the presentation of pilot wings. Because of snow on the Plain, graduation parade was a "band box" review held in Central Area. Joining the traditional music at that event (and continuing throughout the war) was a West Point football song, "On to Victory."

Graduation left a dozen empty rooms in G-2 company, a void promptly filled by yearlings. Harry moved across the hall with Jim Connell, while Munson and I remained in place. Excited all winter about a girl from Long Island he had dated during Christmas leave, Munson described his condition as having "the hots for her." He was amused by the intensity of my feelings about someone I had scarcely met. Trying to counter his skepticism, I dredged up a Christopher Marlowe quote from my days in Kathleen Westman's class: "Who ever loved, that loved not at first sight?" Munson's riposte, which he reserved for those indulging in fantasies, was the title of an old song, "Meet Me Tonight in Dreamland." Regardless, I wrote my first letter to 369 Upper Mountain Avenue.

That fall, with chemistry and mechanics added to our fall program, we carried the heaviest load of our three-year course. I was doing fine in academics but unlike Munson and many others found the emphasis on engineering dull. What stimulated me that semester was the English course, particularly a supplemental text *Modern Short Biographies and Autobiographies.* Assigned to give a short talk, we could choose a subject so long as it was suggested by one of the sketches in the book. As soon as I looked through the table of contents, I had mine: John Reed's autobiographical essay "Almost Thirty."

I chose as my discussion topic Jack Reed's role in the great Paterson silk strike of 1913. In particular, I emphasized how he organized the "Pageant of the Paterson Strike" held in Madison Square Garden. Reed had drilled a thousand men and women "to act out before an audience of twenty thousand people, the wretchedness of their lives and the glory of their revolt." When I finished, the instructor asked the source of my material. My answer was that I had grown up in Paterson. When grades were posted at the end of the week, I was curious to see how I had done—a max!

The academy's stress on physical fitness increased in wartime. Sometime that winter the Master of the Sword discovered that we had a bit of free time after our last class. To fill the gap, his torture team devised not only a course in judo but also one in "watermanship": jumping into the swimming pool from overhead rafters while holding a shirt over one's head; the shirt supposedly ballooned out and became a flotation device. Not to be outdone, Uncle Phil came up with "fit to fight" training. We had to double-time in field uniform, complete with boots, up and down the hills, regardless of the weather. Munson began counting the days until he would leave for air cadet training.

Between the *New York Times* and occasional evening lectures we could keep reasonably well informed on the war situation. We did not, though, have the perspective or insight to sense that the campaigns of that winter and spring marked a strategic turning point in the war.

The Soviet winter offensive of 1942-43 was on a grand scale, its most dramatic event being the turnaround at Stalingrad, where in early February over a hundred thousand German troops were forced to surrender. Meanwhile, in North Africa enemy forces were gradually compressed into Tunisia by Montgomery's Eighth Army from the east and Eisenhower's expeditionary forces from the west. This was really the first large-scale test of the new American army, which, though bloodied at Kasserine Pass in February, was holding its own. By May a quarter of a million enemy forces had surrendered, ending Hitler's ambition to close the Suez Canal. The Pacific saw equally significant victories, most notably in Guadalcanal. After seven bloody months of fighting there, the Navy and Marines forced the Japanese to evacuate the island.

All these Allied successes that winter and spring can be best understood by one of Churchill's famous summations. It is not, he said, the beginning of the end of the war, "but it is, perhaps, the end of the beginning."

During all our activity, I still had to find time to work on revising the plebe bible, *Bugle Notes*. The editor, Mike Davis, and I decided that we had a dual mission: to keep pace with the wartime changes at West Point and, most important, to retain and pass on to the new class the core traditions of the Military Academy. In a final discussion, after we went to press, Mike and I acknowledged that only in the next edition could all the ongoing changes be incorporated. Turning to me, he said, "That will be your job; yesterday the Commandant approved your selection as editor effective June 1st."

Because of my work on *Bugle Notes*, I got to know a number of cadets from other parts of the corps. Some of my colleagues did not have this opportunity during our compressed and intense wartime program (something I felt was not—could not—be considered when the program was planned). In fact, we had little time to get to know our own classmates in other companies and, at least as important, no time to read or—to state it straight—to think.

My other writing project that semester, while not time consuming, certainly had as high a priority as, say, studying physics or chemistry—letters to Diana. The initial exchanges brought the facts: sophomore in Montclair High, sixteen, artistically inclined, played the cello, and, oh yes, liked to dance. Would she be interested in coming to West

Point for a hop? Evasive reply, but it gave an opening. It seemed that her mother had dated at West Point, including a hop about the time the class of 1915 was graduating, and remembered meeting "Ike" Eisenhower. Well, would Diana be interested in coming to graduation hop that spring? Long delay in responding—apparently an older sister had just been forced to turn down a weekend invitation to Dartmouth. Then came the answer, yes—apparently West Point was considered safer than Dartmouth for a young daughter. Whatever the validity of that premise, I was delighted and we began working out the details.

In mid-March came the event Munson had been waiting for. Our class was given the opportunity to volunteer for flight training, if physically qualified. Over half took the option for a variety of reasons: some just wanted to get away from our "rockbound highland home" for a while; some were curious to find out what flying was like; but most, like Munson, had from the outset wanted to be pilots and would have chosen the Air Corps at graduation had there not been an air cadet program. All were aware of the potential cost: five members of the class of June 1943 had been killed in air cadet training. In late April 256 of our classmates left for primary flight training at one of ten civilian flight schools, mainly in Texas and Oklahoma. Those who passed were scheduled to return to Stewart Field near Newburgh for basic flight training during July and August, though we would not see them again until September 1. Two different subcultures within the corps were in the making.

Since Harry Grace had left for flight training, his roommate Jim Connell moved in with me. Jim was the front runner for company commander when June '43 graduated, and we talked frequently about our future. There were about 230 ground cadets for what would constitute the new first class. Below us would be about nine hundred new yearlings and, of more concern, about the same number of new plebes reporting into Beast Barracks on July 1. Whatever one's personal feelings toward the plebe system, it would soon be time for all of us to take it seriously. The carefree days were almost over. First, though, the fun period I had been waiting for—June week—was upon us.

By Sunday, May 30, the alumni portion of June week was over.

After baccalaureate and lunch I was in my room reading the *New York Times* when the call came: "Cadet Kinnard has a visitor in Grant Hall." In the large reception room I saw many dates and cadets moving about, but where was mine? Finally, I spotted what looked like someone's younger sister leafing through a magazine. It was Diana, as beautiful as I remembered, but even younger looking in casual attire. Moving into Boodlers, we sat down with cokes to get acquainted.

She was fun to talk to and had a good sense of humor. At one point I glanced up and saw Johnny Hazen, a classmate from my company, sitting at the table behind Diana. The big grin on his face alerted me that I was in for a cradle-snatching remark at his first opportunity. I did say to my date, "If anyone asks your age, tell them you're seventeen." "Why?" she asked. "Well, uh . . ." I lost my footing on that one. That evening after a buffet dinner at the Thayer we went to the movie. A special showing of *This Is the Army*, the movie featured Irving Berlin's music and a number of stars, including Ron Reagan. The one I remember most, though, was Joan Leslie. At that point she and Diana seemed to have a distinct resemblance. I had obviously gone through the looking glass!

Monday was one of those unbelievably beautiful days in the Hudson highlands. At West Point upperclassmen were out in full force with dates, some of whom would soon be brides. Diana and I toured the grounds, occasionally stopping at points of interest such as the library, Trophy Point for picture taking, and the cadet chapel. Overnight I had decided against taking my sixteen-year-old down Flirtation Walk to its well-known objective, Kissing Rock. I surmised that by next year she would find more credible the threat of its tumbling down should a femme refuse to kiss her cadet. Instead, we hiked from the chapel up to Fort Putnam. Part of the defenses of the Hudson during the Revolutionary War, the fort had a magnificent view of the academy and the highlands. Here we found a quiet spot and had no difficulty finding matters of mutual interest to discuss—while I suppressed my natural instincts. Later as we headed back to the plain I knew that my immediate judgment "across a crowded room" at the Christmas party had been correct.

That afternoon was graduation parade, and since the firsties had recognized the plebes just before the ceremony, it was up to us to give them their final working over before recognition. Though they outnumbered us four to one, never had so few done so much yelling at so many. As the graduating class left the company for the last time, Jim Connell came out of the ranks and assumed command of G-2. After we completed our eyes right for the long gray line of June '43 and passed into Central Area, the shouting at the plebes reached a crescendo. Then the command, "Company halt, fall out," followed by the handshakes of recognition for the class of '45.

In early evening when I met Diana for dinner and the hop, she again looked like my beauty of last December, this time wearing a demure high-necked gown with plaid skirt. The dance went well, though I got tired of cut-ins by several just-recognized plebes; and in each case I cut back in less than a minute. During the break we chatted with George Daoust, a plebe I had recognized the previous summer, who was with an interesting and most attractive date named Lee Lauterbur. A dancer from Ohio, Lee had recently moved to Manhattan and now was in hopes of a part in the chorus of a new Broadway musical, "One Touch of Venus."

Back dancing, my restraint began to crumble, and "As Time Goes By" pushed me over the brink. Potential demerits or not, I tried for a kiss and was rebuffed with a not only "No," but "Hell, No" look on Diana's face. Was she a prude, or was it my usual ineptitude with such matters—or both? Oh well, there would be other times and places. Her smile returned but with that wait-till-third-date look of determination. Soon the orchestra was playing "Army Blue." ". . . to the ladies who come up in June, we'll bid a fond adieu . . ." and then "Goodnight, Ladies." It was over. Walking back to the bus we talked about her coming back during my first-class year. There was no way of knowing that a crisis in my cadet career in early fall would change that and any other plans I might have for the fall and beyond.

The next morning we exited from graduation into another beautiful June day, made more so by our knowing that we were now the first class. That was soon reinforced when the ground cadet "make list" came out with our summer ranks. In G-2 company Jim Connell was commander, with Phil Toon second in command; Pat Neilond was a platoon leader; I was first sergeant. For the moment, though, these titles meant little, as our class was heading out the next day for a long training trip to three major army posts.

First stop was Fort Knox, Kentucky, home of the armored force. In the five days there we covered the waterfront: visits to maintenance and repair shops, participation in tank crew drill, and firing the tank-mounted weapons. Climaxing the training was a spectacular demonstration of an armor regiment attacking with artillery support. Despite the impressiveness of the new armored force, successor to the cavalry, we could still look forward to another year of horsemanship, as though preparing for a second try at the Little Big Horn.

On June 8 we boarded a train for Fort Benning, Georgia, home of the infantry school. The train to Knox had been clean and comfortable, with excellent food. In contrast the trip to Benning introduced us to wartime travel, courtesy of the Southern Railway with its antique rolling stock. When we opened windows because of the heat and smell, in came the coal dust. In the distance I heard a tactical officer sounding off to some of my classmates: "Don't you know there's a war on, men?" He was right; as I sat by an open window smoking a cigarette and watching the South roll by—a small empty station platform, a road with few cars but with Burma Shave signs—suddenly another troop train passed, going in the opposite direction. At that point it was driven home to me that there must be many troop trains like that one all over the country carrying thousands of men to new and strange places, and eventually to where we were all headed, the war itself.

From time to time many of us moved about the train, trying to improve our comfort level. Though that proved impossible we did get to meet classmates from distant parts of the corps. While I was musing, a classmate sat down opposite me and held out his hand: "I'm John Eisenhower." We talked for about an hour. He struck me as being interesting, personable, and perhaps a bit self-effacing. When I mentioned the *Bugle Notes* revision I had ahead, we launched into a discussion of plebe customs. He related some anecdotes his father had told him about his own cadet experiences. I gathered that Ike had not taken the system too seriously.

Meeting us at Benning was our transportation for the next ten days—long "cattle cars" with low sides and three hard wooden benches running from front to back. Next morning after drawing field equipment we were integrated into the Officer Candidate School training cycle with two groups who were already several weeks into the course.

Precisely patterned, instruction began with a lecture and demonstration. After that came practical application such as an attack on a village, firing mortars or some other weapons, or sample airborne training. One night we were dispatched individually on a compass course through some wild terrain. All in all, the ten days at Benning gave us our most intensive training since Beast Barracks. It also showed us how thousands of young men coming from the ranks would train to become platoon leaders and, in time, company commanders in our combat divisions—in effect our colleagues in about a year.

After two days at Benning we heard that the Americans and British had landed on Sicily. This Mediterranean strategy had been confirmed by Roosevelt and Churchill the previous January. At their Casablanca conference, they had decided that an invasion of Western Europe would not be possible until 1944. During the successful thirty-eight-day campaign in Sicily came news of Mussolini's downfall on July 25. This political development triggered military action on the Italian peninsula itself. It also spawned a new wartime slogan: "One down, two to go."

On June 19 we headed to the Army's antiaircraft center at Camp Davis, North Carolina. Our five days there seemed like a vacation after Benning. Although we had the opportunity to fire various antiaircraft weapons, mostly we attended demonstrations of ground-to-air capabilities and techniques. On some days, work was over by noon but always by late afternoon, and the Atlantic beaches beckoned. Each evening the officers' club held a dance at which the hostess had (to steal one of Claude Rains's lines from *Casablanca*) "lined up the usual suspects." On June 25 we headed back to West Point where seventy of us, along with some yearling corporals, would comprise the beast detail to face the approximately nine hundred members of the class of 1946 on July 1.

Thursday morning, July 1, found me installed behind a table on the steps of South Barracks. Now I was functioning as first sergeant of Eighth Company, New Cadets, at the same spot where I had reported in to Bill Smith exactly two years before. I did my best to emulate him. "Is that any way to report to the first sergeant, mister? Start over, and this time speak clearly and try not to look like the hunchback of Notre Dame!"

On this hot, humid day, typical of July in the Hudson Valley, putting the plebes through their initial paces was hard work. This was nothing like our previous experience though; no longer on the receiving end, we were instead dishing it out.

Each evening after taps for the new cadets, the beast detail went to work planning the next day's instruction: close order drill, manual of arms, athletics and other basic training subjects. My own work dealt more with administration, such as going over the endless forms the fourth class had to fill out and setting up duty rosters. Since I roomed with the company commander, Jim Connell, we frequently spent part of our evenings discussing how things were going and who or what needed shaping up.

These sessions inevitably focused on personalities. Generally, we had a good group of fourth classmen, and we assumed that the system would eventually solve a few problem cases one way or another. At the other end of the spectrum and watched closely was plebe Andrew McCoy from Pennsylvania. One of the two or three most impressive new cadets in our charge, he was also black. In keeping with the custom at that time, McCoy was silenced and lived alone; we could do nothing about that. What our company beast detail could and did do was to see that in other respects he was treated exactly like his other 8th Company classmates. We wanted no repeat of the Francis episode of our own plebe year.

On the afternoon of July 18 we turned over our charges to the second detail and prepared to head out that evening. For two weeks we would be acting second lieutenants at one of five possible replacement training centers. Along with about two dozen classmates I ended up at the antiaircraft center, Fort Eustis, Virginia. Each of us was assigned to a different training battery, where we performed the normal instructional type duties of a second lieutenant: close order drill, weapons firing, physical training, inspections, and occasional lectures on military subjects.

Since these draftees were destined for antiaircraft units, they were understandably somewhat older than those at, say, an infantry training center. As a result, many of them simply could not hold up on the training marches. Educationally, they covered the waterfront from some college to "I ain't had much schooling, sir." In this atmosphere, totally different from West Point, I experienced an absorbing phenomenon that I kept to myself. I was back in Paterson; these draftees were the same as my boyhood friends or their older brothers. I knew instinctively how to work with them, no longer as the cadet first sergeant but more as an older version of Doug Kinnard, senior patrol leader Troop 35.

My roommate for the Eustis stay was Pat Neilond. He and I, along with other classmates, were able to spend most evenings at Williamsburg, fortunately near our center. Though we found the historic buildings interesting to visit; dates with coeds from William and Mary, when available, were more so. At the end of two weeks our group left in several directions on brief leaves; then we were back at West Point en route to Pine Camp for maneuvers. This time we worked with the 5th Armored Division, which, like the 4th of the previous year, was destined for its real test on the plains of northern Europe in 1944.

Reunited with our fly-boy classmates at the end of August, we exchanged tales of quite different experiences. Some of theirs were hard to top; for example, a six-plane night flight of "Wrong Way Corrigans," which ended up in Syracuse out of fuel, rather than back at Stewart Field. Of the two hundred fifty-six aspiring pilots who had left in April, thirty-three had washed out and one had been killed in training.

Munson seemed to have thrived on the experience, and he was not amused at my first sergeant antics in having plebes who needed correction report to the room. Soon he explained that the air cadets were scheduled to fly out of Stewart Field every other weekday in exchange for two hundred and fifty fewer hours of academics at the academy. He felt, therefore, that it would be easier for everyone if he moved in with a couple of air cadets. Both of us, of course, knew the real reason: I had, at least for the moment, embraced the plebe system that he regarded as anathema.

The first weekend in September was traditionally Ring Weekend; the first class received, and wore thereafter, their class rings. After a short and somewhat emotional talk by the Superintendent, each of us on the committee went forward to receive the rings for our own company. At the hop that night the dates of engaged classmates sported miniatures of the ring. Only nine months to go until June 6! The time would go fast—or would it?

The compressed academic program for our final year stressed engineering subjects. Two particularly painful—and, from my perspective irrelevant—courses were electricity and mechanics. I found a little relief in a law course (all officers were expected to serve on courts-martial) and even more in a course on military history. We followed the campaigns of the great captains before Napoleon, such as Julius Caesar and Alexander the Great; then we focused on Napoleon, the Civil War, World War I, and, most applicable, our own war as far as it had gone.

Discussions on World War II did not wait until the end of the course; rather, we were periodically issued "little gray books" on recent campaigns. We could easily divert the instructor from, say, Hannibal's escapades on the Italian peninsula to our current operations there. This campaign had started on September 3 with the British Eighth Army's assault across the straits of Messina. Less than a week later the American Fifth Army made an assault, landing farther north at Salerno. By mid-month that beachhead was secure, and before the end of the month the two forces linked up to begin a long, frustrating campaign up the Italian peninsula.

During the early weeks of September while I was functioning as a mess table commandant, a plebe problem case named Eugene Gibney was assigned to my table. George Daoust, a yearling corporal, worked him over a bit in hopes of improvement. For similar reasons I had sad-sack Gibney come by my room on three occasions between reveille and breakfast. Finally, on September 10 I gave up and told him not to return; the next day, I arranged for his reassignment to another table. On Monday the 13th Pat Neilond walked with me from barracks to the noon meal formation; after wishing me a happy twenty-second birthday, he asked if Gibney had been to my room that morning. Without knowing the reason for the question, I simply answered no.

Next evening, shortly after taps, Frank Moore, our company honor representative, rapped on my door and entered. He informed me that I was needed as a witness at an honor committee meeting. After I dressed, we headed out across the plain, lit by a full moon on this beautiful September night. En route, Moore explained that Pat Neilond had reported Mr. Gibney for lying to him, specifically using as an excuse for not appearing at Neilond's room as ordered, that he had been in mine. At the fourth-class club the honor committee formed a circle in a large, high-ceilinged room with dimmed lights. The atmosphere conjured up images of the Spanish Inquisition. In my brief stay I merely affirmed that on the day in question Gibney was not in my room.

The following Saturday about fifty of us left the academy for a weekend tour of the air defenses of New York City. Such as they were, the defenses—90 mm guns, 40 mm Bofors, and 50-caliber machine guns—did not seem very impressive. I never got to ask the question in my mind: What precisely and whom were we defending against? The day's final stop was Coney Island with its World War I barrage balloon. With liberty until midnight and scheduled to spend the night near there, Phil Toon, Pat Neilond, and I decided to use our free time to enjoy the amusement park.

Our tour eventually took us by that huge, rickety-looking roller coaster, the Cyclone, constructed in 1927. When I kept on walking, the others grabbed me, insisting that I join them on the ride. In motion the contraption felt even less safe than it looked. As we careened around the big turn just before the major plunge, even my tormentors tightened up. Then we began what seemed like a free fall through space. Christ, I wondered, will this metal bar hold us in! It did, and we finally came to a halt. When Neilond suggested that we do it again, I vaulted over him and headed for the exit. They followed and we ended up at Nathan's, eating their famous hot dogs. I had no way of knowing that at West Point a cyclone of a different sort was brewing.

Back at the academy the next afternoon I headed to my room for some sack time before tackling the mysteries of alternating current circuits. My plans were quickly preempted by several notes on my desk, alerting me to a gathering storm: Gibney, found guilty of an honor violation, was awaiting departure. His mother had appeared on the scene, accusing me and George Daoust of hazing her son; she was writing letters to this effect to the Commandant as well as to unnamed Washington officials. Welcome back!

Two days later our company tactical officer, Major Joel Walker, informed me that the Commandant was convening a board of officers to look into Mrs. Gibney's accusations. The following day, September 22, I was summoned to meet with the board, consisting of a lieutenant colonel, as head, and two majors. With very few preliminaries they started quizzing me about my role as table commandant and first sergeant. A sample:

Q. Do you believe a fourth classman can or should get along on any less food than anyone else?
A. No, not in general.
Q. Is there any basis for the belief that a fourth classman should get anything less to eat than anyone else?
A. I did not say that they received less.
Q. That was not my question [repeats above question].
A. No.

After a time the questioning shifted to my requiring Gibney to do pushups. Yes, that was true on three occasions. At the end of the questioning I took the opportunity to sum up my position. As far as the mess hall was concerned, the fourth classmen at my table received as much food as the average fourth classman did. As for the exercises, they had never been carried to excess and certainly never more than I as a plebe had been subjected to. Though both charges could be brought against a large percentage of upperclassmen, what made my case different was that the person bringing the charges was the mother of an admitted liar. While I understood her feelings, to link her son's character failure with any treatment he had received from me was nonsensical. Stony silence from the board. (What now comes to mind is the title of a book published many years later: *Military Justice Is to Justice as Military Music Is to Music*.)

Friends kept me informed of the board's continuing activity during the next couple of weeks. I also learned that similar inquiries were going on in four other cadet companies. Obviously, the academy was under pressure from the War Department or higher to modify the plebe system for classes entering in the wartime environment. No doubt this large plebe class had some members who were not at West Point for the traditional reasons. Why, then were they there? Perhaps a bit uncharitably, I reflected that the Hudson was a long way from New Guinea or Salerno.

On October 7 I received two delinquency reports signed by General Gallagher, both for hazing—one for the mess hall; the other for requiring plebes to do exercises. In my reply I accepted the second charge but denied the first. If the Commandant was trying a pincer movement on me, I was trying to cut off one leg of it. About a week later I was summoned to his office. Though evasive, Gallagher had clearly decided that I was guilty of both offenses. Further, without quite saying so, he implied that I might be turned back a class. As his mind seemed made up, I simply stated that his suggested punishment was, I felt, far out of proportion to the offense. Leaving, I knew that my only hope lay in an appeal to General Wilby, the Superintendant. Over the weekend I thought through my approach.

On Monday afternoon October 18 I was directed to report in full dress to the Superintendent's office. The general's manner was affable, but he got to the point quickly. The Commandant had recommended my suspension until the following August; after that I would join the class of 1945. When he asked me to comment, I made the usual arguments but added a coda. If he decided to suspend me until next August I would resign from the academy and apply for officer candidate school. With one brother in combat in the South Pacific and one in Italy, I could not live with myself if I stayed out of the war for almost two more years. After listening closely, the Superintendent ended the meeting by saying that he would do what he could for me. In any case, he said, I would know the outcome soon.

He was right. That evening shortly after dinner began, Bob Morrison, the cadet brigade adjutant, called the corps to attention to publish the punishments awarded seven cadets for hazing. Mine led the list.

> For "Hazing in violation of paragraph 139, Regulations for the United States Military Academy, 1931": CADET LEO D KINNARD C-1352 1st Class, is awarded twenty-six demerits, confined to restricted limits until the end of current academics, and will serve one hundred and seventy-six punishment tours. He is also suspended from the Military Academy, with pay and allowances, from the end of current academics until two days after the graduation of his Class, on which latter date he will be graduated from the Military Academy if otherwise qualified.

On October 20, Cadet Private Kinnard began walking off his punishment tours at the rate of five hours per week. By rough calculation the 176 hours of walks in the sun would end about June 3, three days before graduation. Each Wednesday and Saturday afternoon the "area squad" formed up in Central Area to begin marching back and forth in silence at a rate of 120 steps per minute, Garand rifle on shoulder. The tour could be viewed as a form of physical exercise but was a bore; I quickly developed a thought agenda to carry my mind far away from Central Area. Fortunately, the tactical department had no way of monitoring subversive fantasies on the part of the "area birds."

The less physical but more onerous aspect of a "slug" (cadet slang for punishment) was "confinement to restricted limits." This meant that you spent free time in your room, at the library, at the gym, or, in my case, anywhere at the academy where *Bugle Notes* business took me. Being slugged meant no visitors, no dates, no dances, no movies, no football games, no leaves, in sum no fun. No end of a lesson in all of this, but I was not yet coming to grips with just what it was.

In only one way was my sentence liberating, at least in my own mind. Delaying graduation by two days meant that my class standing did not matter as long as I passed—so the hell with electricity and mechanics. One course that year, a brief survey of the international relations field, stimulated an interest that became lifelong. Particularly fascinating was learning about realpolitik. One visiting lecturer, tracing this policy back to Thucydides, summed it up with what he called the law of nations: "No permanent enemies, no permanent friends, only permanent self-interest." How refreshing it was to hear someone cut through the rhetoric and tell it the way it was!

The closest area birds got to football games was listening to the cheers echoing from Michie Stadium while walking punishment tours. Still, we could easily detect when Army did well; we could almost tabulate scores: very loud roars = Army score; silence with faint roar in background = opponent score. That bit of idiocy about football occupied my mind on some beautiful fall afternoons while doing penance for whatever it was I was supposed to have done.

Despite information to the contrary, I believed it possible that some portion of my punishment could be remitted. With that in mind I developed a new attitude, centering on how to avoid demerits. I was fortunate that both my roommates, Bob Brundin and Hal Emerson, were air cadets and hence frequently at Stewart Field. The room could thus be manipulated, Potemkin-like, to exude neatness, at least in areas an inspector would reach. I also returned to my yearling year approach to the plebe system—I ignored it. What a relief.

Confined on weekends, I could at least spend time in the library, becoming acquainted with some authors on the new-books shelf. John Marquand's *So Little Time*, dealing with wartime dislocations, introduced me to his lightly satirical style. And I discovered a journalist who was to become famous in the war—Ernie Pyle, who had just published *Here Is Your War*. I could also dig into several journals and magazines on the war, which by late fall had reached the point at which we could sense an eventual victory. The Soviets had regained a substantial portion of their territory as they continued to push westward. On the other hand, though the Italians were out of the war, the Nazis were still holding the Allied advance well south of Rome. In the Pacific we were fighting bitterly for every island stepping stone to Japan. Late October had seen the costly victory at bloody Tarawa—2,700 casualties in a four-day operation. The invasion of western Europe was still ahead, but in December the man who would be its Supreme Commander was named—Ike Eisenhower.

Our class was scheduled for only a few days off at Christmas that year, but being in confinement, I expected no leave. The plebes at my table (where I was playing Silent Cal that fall) had composed a little ditty for my benefit. To the tune of "White Christmas," they sang, "I'm dreaming of a gray Christmas, with Uncle Phil and all the plebes . . . ." Then something happened: General Gallagher was replaced as Commandant by General George Honnen, class of 1920. Shortly after arriving, he decided that all first classmen in confinement would be given the three-day Christmas leave, since no one could tell where they would be by next Christmas.

With Christmas falling on Saturday, the leave was not much more than a long weekend. My Paterson friends were all gone, and with no car I stayed pretty close to home. While shopping I ran into parents of friends and caught up with some names and locations, all a long way from Paterson: the Pacific, England, Italy, the Middle East, India, and many bases in the States. I was beginning to feel like a slacker. Later, as we left St. Joe's after midnight Mass, Annie pointed out something near the plaque honoring those who had served in World War I. Ours would be the next plaque there. At the moment it was only a bulletin board telling about the future memorial, but it did contain a short list of St. Joe's KIAs to that point. The last name showed the location as Tarawa, October 21, 1943.

Back shortly to the snow-cleared area and into the gloom period—but it was 1944 and only five months to go. That thought dispelled much of the gloom. Increasingly, I focused my confinement energies on *Bugle Notes*, meeting with my large staff of yearlings and plebes working on the revisions. Still, confinement took its toll. That winter the cadet lecture committee had arranged a great parade of artists and speakers, including Fred Waring, Risë Stevens, Lowell Thomas, and Alexander de Seversky. My participation was restricted to debriefings from friends such as Harry Grace or Pat Neilond.

As winter progressed, the light at the end of the tunnel brightened. In early March came branch drawing, which determined one's future occupation for a long time to come. Class standing affected the selections, with the engineers going out first and antiaircraft artillery—which got the goats—last. I got my branch choice, field artillery, even though I had slipped thirty places in my class standing, thanks to my idiosyncratic defection in electricity and mechanics.

A more obvious augury of the end was the display of uniforms and equipment for the first class to purchase. The days of Sam Browne belts, Peel boots, and dress blues were over. One tailormade set of pinks and greens, a trench coat, and quartermaster uniforms would do it until the war was over. In any case, a second lieutenant's pay of $150 a month would not go far if one recklessly exceeded the savings in his cadet account on uniforms.

With April the Hudson Valley was in bloom again. In front of our barracks after supper and before study period Johnny Hazen frequently gathered a small group of harmonizers, sometimes swelling to as many as twenty. Songs included "Moonlight Bay," "My Gal Sal," and always "Persian Kitten."

About the third week in April I received a call from Mrs. Lystad, the cadet hostess, inviting me to dinner with the Superintendent and his wife along with the heads of other cadet activities. I explained that because I was in confinement the Superintendent's quarters were off-limits and therefore I could not attend. A call back; confinement was to be lifted that night for the first class, since our yearbooks (*The Howitzer*) were to be distributed that day. Though failing to see the connection, I gladly accepted the invitation. As the only cadet private present at dinner I took a good deal of ragging from my classmates. My reply was the old Brooklyn Dodgers' watchword, "Wait till next year." Taking advantage of my brief freedom, I went from the dinner to the Howitzer Hop at Cullum Hall. No date, so I adopted a new approach, cutting in on my friends. They allowed me about as much time as I had allowed interlopers with Diana—not much. At taps I turned back into a pumpkin.

All through that winter and spring we followed closely Allied actions against the two Axis powers. Even without access to classified information, we could figure out the strategy of Admiral Nimitz and General MacArthur in the Pacific. Nimitz was battling to take Kwajalein and Eniwetok in the Marshall Islands in the central Pacific before heading for the Marianas: MacArthur meanwhile was conducting a series of amphibious operations up the New Guinea coast. The two forces would not converge for a while, but it seemed obvious that they would meet in the Philippines.

At the same time the Russian winter offensive had recaptured the Ukraine, gained control of the Black Sea, and raised the siege of Leningrad. What was most important from our perspective was their inflicting of enormous casualties on the German forces—losses that would be impossible to replace.

Italy was a different story. Here the Allies ran into logistic and strategic difficulties while facing a tough German force. In January we conducted an amphibious assault behind enemy lines at Anzio, designed to link up with a push from the south. The southern force, however, ran up against stubborn resistance at the Rapido River and at Cassino. By late March the two forces had still not linked up. Finally, in May the overall commander, British Field Marshal Harold Alexander, amassed enough power from his Allied force to achieve a breakthrough; along with our Anzio Corps he headed for Rome.

In that spring of 1944 we focused on the big strategic question: When and where would the invasion of Western Europe take place? Our interest heightened at the end of April when we received our first assignments as second lieutenants. Those of us in the field artillery were distributed among nine infantry divisions scheduled to be deployed to Europe in the fall or early winter. My assignment was to the 71st Infantry Division at Fort Benning, Georgia.

On Monday, May 1, I was summoned to our company tactical officer's office, this time for some great news. Major Walker had just reviewed the peer and tactical officer ratings of the first class; mine were all in the top category, superior. Because of that, my few demerits, and my editorship of *Bugle Notes*, he would recommend removing that portion of my slug pertaining to late graduation. (Don't celebrate yet, though; the Commandant and Superintendent both have to approve.) This reprieve came out of the blue, and my immediate thought was one of appreciation to my classmates; obviously they had somehow organized their ratings with this possible outcome in mind.

The following Saturday, during my scheduled break in the area tours, the officer of the day summoned me. He wanted me to know that the Superintendent had just approved the Commandant's recommendation that I graduate with my class. Even though required to walk the remaining forty-nine punishment tours, I was on a high the rest of the weekend. The remaining month of punishment tours was nothing for an area bird who had seen the leaves fall from the trees, the snows come and melt, and the leaves return. Liberation was almost at hand!

The remainder of May 1944 was, and is, kaleidoscopic in my mind. Numerous letters: from the Commandant and Superintendent congratulating us on the revision of *Bugle Notes*; from Congressman Canfield to his first West Point appointee; from my family, the most treasured being one from brother Jim on V-mail written by candlelight in New Guinea; from my real family, Annie, Toots, Irene, all of whom would be at graduation along with my father and sister Daisy; and, surprisingly, from my two Eastside High mentors, Hallie Turner and Kathleen Westman, who wanted to drive up to West Point on Sunday, June 4. Since my last punishment tours would be walked the day before and they could attend both a Superintendent's reception and a full-dress parade Sunday afternoon, I readily agreed in a wire back, which I signed Kinnard. This brought on some twitting from Kathleen Westman, my former mentor, who accused me of imitating Patton. As usual, her message to me stuck and I never tried that again.

Saturday morning brought the most unusual review in our three years. While the corps (less our air cadets) paraded in full field equipment on the plain, our 170 air cadets flew overhead in some one hundred training-type aircraft. This large formation of multi-engine and single-engine planes was probably dangerous, but it was spectacular.

Monday, June 5, shortly before the alumni ceremonies, Major Walker assembled the G-2 firsties on the steps of barracks to swear us in as second lieutenants, U.S. Army. That afternoon we arrived at graduation parade early to recognize the plebes; then we lined up with G-2 for the last time. After retreat came the command, "Graduating Class Front and Center"; and, though marching at attention, we shouted our goodbyes as we left our companies. Then came the command moving us forward into the long gray line of '44, followed by the Corps' passing in review—the end was in sight.

Our graduation hop that night featured a special treat: Glenn Miller and his Army Air Corps band provided the music. At the last minute a classmate who found out I had no date asked me to take his sister to the hop. Though no Diana, she was personable and we both enjoyed Glenn Miller's traditional hits: "In the Mood," "String of Pearls," "Moonlight Serenade," and so on. For the last piece he played in honor of our graduation his special arrangement of "Army Blue." The old familiar words from *Bugle Notes* went through my mind: "'Twas the song we sang in old plebe camp, when first our gray was new . . . . Now, fellows, we must say good-bye . . . ."

Tuesday, June 6, was a beautiful day in the Hudson Valley. Many West Pointers may not remember what their graduation speaker had to say, but all 474 men of '44 would remember the electrifying way in which General Brehon Somerville, chief of Army Service Forces, began his.

> This is an historic hour. Today, these walls, these hills, take on a new meaning and a deeper significance. Only a

few hours ago, the mightiest undertaking ever attempted by our Army was launched against enemy entrenched along the shores of France. Today our forces begin that grim, tough, and bloody march from the shores of the Atlantic to Berlin. Many of you will join in that march.

On their feet, his listeners shook the rafters of the field house with waves of applause. It went on and on. Ever after we would be known as the D-Day class of 1944.

8. The Farthest East Seventy-First

Just after the train passed Peekskill, the Hudson appeared, then the familiar buildings of West Point silhouetted against the gathering dusk of the highlands. Ten days after graduation, the second lieutenant was heading north to Lake Placid for rest and some reflection before entering the wartime army.

Graduation leave was speeding by. I ushered for two G-2 Company classmates' weddings: Harry Grace's at West Point the day after graduation and Scotty Solomon's in Providence the following weekend. Aunt Annie and her family hosted several dinners for the graduate, as did Walt and Irene. Increasingly, the latter were becoming role models and mentors regarding social matters; this meant that my address would be 69 Edgewood Avenue, West Orange, from then on.

One day on a whim I had gone to New York and called Lee Lauterbur, then in the chorus of Cole Porter's *The Seven Lively Arts*. Yes, we could meet after the show . . . how about the Waldorf Roof? Xavier Cugat's orchestra there made the evening even more enjoyable. Lee was attractive, pleasant, a great dancer, and a live wire—but what about Diana? Though very much on my mind, my seventeen-year-old high school senior was away somewhere with her family; in any case, without a car I could not get to her town. She was, though, definitely on my reflection agenda for Lake Placid.

As the train wound up the Hudson, I heard an increasing din in the next Pullman car. Investigating, I found a prewedding party headed for Tupper Lake (part of the Tri-Lakes area that includes Placid and Saranac). The men, all naval officers, spotted my uniform with its shiny new bars. "Come in, soldier, and have a drink." The groom, a Yalie, was still recovering from wounds received at Tarawa the previous fall, and between the songs, a few war stories came out. As the evening wore on, they insisted I come to the wedding in two days. Naturally, I accepted, knowing that next morning none of them would remember me or the invitation. After the third rendition of "The Whiffenpoofs Song" I slipped back to my berth.

The inn where I stayed at Lake Placid was appealing, especially the first-floor social room with its large glassed-in veranda. The big furnished space allowed for everything: dining, lounging, card playing, conversing, there was even a library alcove for reading. My own room, one flight up, had a private screened-in porch with writing table. The inn's arrangement and the affable proprietors made it easy to get to know the other guests, many of whom had been coming there for years.

The main street of the small but vibrant downtown consisted of shops, small hotels, and restaurants, all reflecting into Mirror Lake, a tributary of Lake Placid. Interesting remnants of the 1932 Winter Olympics showed up everywhere, like the skating rink where Sonja Henie first dazzled Americans as women's figure skating champion, replicating her 1928 victory at St. Moritz. My main recreation, outside of reading, was in the hiking trails and, when I could find another able and interested guest, canoeing on Lake Placid. Only a few young men were about, and most of the college girls were busy working in the hotels and restaurants.

The proprietors of the inn also operated a smaller version near the lake. As the only meal served there was breakfast, its guests frequently appeared at my location for the evening meal and stayed on in the lounge. One such was Jane Matthews, who appeared to be a couple of years older than I. One evening, when we struck up a conversation over coffee, I learned that she was from upstate New York and had been teaching the past academic year at the local high school. She planned to leave the day after graduation for Corpus Christi, Texas, to join her naval aviator husband. Before leaving that evening she asked if I would like to go with her to the graduation a couple of days hence. Of course I would.

The graduation evening brought home to me the contrast between the monasticism of my last four years and the social scene of wartime. After the ceremony—with its decorous, traditional marches and speeches—I was introduced to the changing world of looser moral codes and tentative relationships occasioned by couples' long separations and the scarcity of young men.

On the way home I suggested to my personable, attractive "date" that we have a drink at a local bistro. She readily agreed, but after the second one felt it was time to go back to her room to pack. En route, as we passed through a small park by the lake, we engaged in about a twenty-minute "wrestling match." Afterward, she wondered if I would like to take the bus with her to Syracuse, where she would be spending the following evening. I thought about it for a few moments, realizing that the trip would mark the end of my virginity. That would, I felt, be good, but not worth two days on a bus. I declined, my usual reticence on this matter preventing me from saying what was really on my mind: Why wait for Syracuse, how about tonight?

In the solitude of my porch and the hiking trails during my Lake Placid stay I conducted a kind of self-seminar. The central question was Where from here? The immediate answer was easy: Be the best artillery lieutenant I could in the 71st Division. The real question, though, was one that I shared with most young servicemen: What direction should my life take after the war? In my case I could opt for a career in the regular Army—West Point had motivated me in that direction—still, there were two other possible careers that appealed to me. The GI Bill, signed that month by President Roosevelt, would facilitate either one: college teaching or law. Best, I concluded, keep all three possibilities in mind until after the war. Anyway, I had a legal commitment to serve in the Army until 1947, which would certainly postdate the war's end.

Ever since the previous October I had delayed pondering still another question: What was the lesson of the eight-month slug? My answer: Don't stick your neck out except on a matter of principle or for the welfare of those under your command.

Then there was the matter needing no agenda: Diana! In some ways I hardly knew her, and yet I was unquestionably in love. "Who can explain it, who can tell you why?" All I could do for now was to continue our correspondence. After all, most of the soldiers with whom I would be serving were in the same situation. We could all hope that the competition at home was "either too young or too old."

Before joining combat divisions, artillerymen of the class of '44 had one more school session together, the basic officer course at Fort Sill, Oklahoma. From whatever direction we came, most of us ended up in the Oklahoma City railroad station on the morning of July 8. Here we boarded some ancient railroad cars recalled to duty for the duration by the equally ancient Rock Island Railroad.

Leaving behind the city with working oil wells on the state capitol lawn, we headed into rolling prairie country. My knowledge of the state was pretty much limited to high school history: acquired by the United States as part of the Louisiana Purchase; home in the 1830s for the "five civilized tribes" at the end of the "Trail of Tears"; opened for homesteading by runs and lotteries late in the nineteenth century; and entered the Union in 1907 as the forty-sixth state. Many had acquired a more subjective view of the state from John Steinbeck's *The Grapes of Wrath* describing the hardships of the Okies during the 1930s dust bowl. This was supplanted with a more cheerful feeling about the state after the Rodgers and Hammerstein's 1943 musical, *Oklahoma* and its enormously popular songs like "Oh What a Beautiful Morning" and "The Surrey with the Fringe on Top."

Sometime after the train passed through the town of Chickasha, we saw in the west a row of bare mountains that my seatmate identified as the Wichitas; then came an oasis with trees—Fort Sill. Busses were standing by as we debarked onto a dirt road. Our first reaction was that it was hot as hell.

Established in 1870 when Oklahoma was still Indian Territory, Fort Sill was chosen in 1911 as the location for training artillery officers. Rightly named the School of Fire, it turned out artillery officers for Pershing's AEF. In 1930 the War Department, designating the post as the permanent home of the Field Artillery school, expanded its size to a huge 75,000 acres, largely open rolling prairie. When we arrived in the summer of 1944, the school was at its wartime peak, housing an enormous military population of officers and enlisted. All these transients were, like us undergoing some kind of training related to field artillery, the branch with the reputation as "the greatest killer on the battlefield."

The busses dropped us into a vast Hooverville, our housing until our departure at the end of September. Our home-away-from-home consisted of screened, tarpaper huts of about 250 square feet, with a cot and field table for each of the four occupants. My roommate was Pat Neilond, who had prudently arranged that our hutmates were Harry Grace and Scotty Solomon, who would actually be living in Lawton—the town adjacent to Fort Sill—with their June brides. At the end of our street a temporary building housed sinks, showers, and latrine. Beyond that was a large cafeteria-style mess, which surprisingly served pretty good food.

After dropping off our belongings, Pat and I were off by foot in search of greener pastures, meaning the permanent post, a mile or two away. We discovered a library, movie theater, and officers' club with bar, all air-conditioned. Another find was a club swimming pool, decorated by an interesting assortment of young wives, all clearly off-limits except for viewing opportunities. In any event, those of us without cars would have adequate off-duty diversions to escape from our tarpaper village.

A couple of days after arrival we began the course for new officers whose purpose was to teach us how to function as artillery junior officers in a combat division. We worked on communications, tactics, motor transport, but the crux of our training had to do with directing and controlling artillery fire. Particularly interesting were the ten or so occasions when we were taken out in small sections to an observation post overlooking the firing range; there we played the role of artillery forward observers.

The instructor would begin each problem by selecting a target some three thousand or more yards away. Then one of us, called on at random, was expected to come out of the bleachers shouting commands to a telephone operator for transmission to the firing unit. As the student adjusted the fire to destroy the target, the instructor usually shouted something to simulate the pressures of combat. The entire exercise made for stimulating afternoons, and afterward the return bus was the scene for humorous critiques and pantomimes, especially for the victims who had scored Unsatisfactory.

Without personal transportation I made only a few forays into Lawton except for an occasional meal with a married classmate and wife. The main social event each week was a Saturday night get-together at the officers' club's dinner and dance. Some classmates found dates among the post's Army brats, but most of us could merely watch the young wives (previously admired in bathing suits) glide around the dance floor to "I'll Be Seeing You" or show their stuff to "Please No Squeeza da Banana." Invariably, most of us ended up in the bar, sometimes singing with Johnny Hazen when he appeared with his young bride.

Since we were all heading for Europe in early winter, we naturally kept up with the fighting in France. The various beachheads of D-Day had all been linked up by the 12th of June, and despite fierce German resistance, particularly in the hedgerow country, the Normandy campaign was over by late July. Allied forces were now poised for a breakout, which came in the early days of August. Patton's Third Army, previously kept under wraps, broke out and in the first three days of August raced seventy-five miles into enemy territory. Whenever we could, we were glued to the radio, an imperfect but exciting source of battle reports.

All through August Eisenhower's forces moved onward. On the 25th came the liberation of Paris with its joyous pandemonium and "The Last Time I Saw Paris" sung over and over again. Our forces kept advancing toward the German border until lack of supplies and fuel forced a halt at the west wall of the Reich. An abortive attempt to jump the Rhine at Arnhem proved to be "a bridge too far." By mid-September the lines were stabilizing.

The campaign in France was one of the great Western battles of all time. Though not yet beaten, the Germans had lost enormous numbers of troops and even more materiel. In Italy they were holding on with great difficulty and in Eastern Europe the Soviets were essentially at the frontiers of the Third Reich. All this was happening when we completed our course at Fort Sill at the end of September.

The last week of September brought orders sending the class to our divisions with ten days leave en route. Eight of us, including Harry Grace and myself, were assigned to the 71st Division at Fort Benning, Georgia. Pat Neilond headed to the 69th Division at Camp Shelby in Mississippi; Scotty Solomon and Johnny Hazen were off to the 10th Mountain, then at Camp Swift, Texas.

Departing Sill on Saturday the 30th meant a weekend on train coaches crowded with servicemen in every conceivable uniform, occasionally with families along. Sleeping was difficult, but I felt lucky to have a seat, especially on the second leg from St. Louis to Grand Central. Food was catch-as-catch-can, the best treat being a night stop at a station in Indiana where some nice ladies on the station platform were dispensing homemade snacks to servicemen. From New York to Paterson I was back on one of the same Erie locals that my buddies and I had used for our forays into New York in the 1930s.

This was my first October in Paterson in five years, and its moderate temperature was especially welcome after an Oklahoma summer. Since this would be my last leave for a long time, I spent most of it with the family in Paterson and West Orange. Toots, who liked movies, talked me into a three-hour saga, *Since You Went Away*, a sentimental and nostalgic view of the American home front during the war, well acted by Claudette Colbert and Jennifer Jones. Some parts of the story, such as the loss of a fiancé at Salerno, were all too real.

That very month Diana and her family were grieving. Her twenty-one-year-old brother, Dick, who had left Rutgers to become a naval aviator, was killed while on a training flight out of Daytona Beach. Not wanting to intrude and not having friends with cars around seemed to be good reasons not to try to see Diana.

In the late afternoon of 11 October I began my rail journey from New York to Benning. This time I was fortunate to get a Pullman as far as Atlanta. At last, after years of preparation I could get into the game, albeit as a second lieutenant in an army of eight million I was not exactly in the role of a quarterback.

My seatmate on the two-hour local train ride from Atlanta to Benning was an infantry lieutenant returning from leave in Virginia. He had been with the 71st division since June and in a very articulate way enlightened me about how the 71st had been formed.

In 1942, in planning the World War II buildup, Army strategists had proposed a light division for specialized missions with fewer troops than in the standard infantry division (nine thousand versus fifteen thousand), limited transportation, and reduced firepower. In 1943 they organized three such divisions and early in 1944 tested this concept by sending the 71st and 89th divisions to rugged California country for maneuvers against each other.

By then both units had serious reservations about their capabilities: they had a lack of equipment and personnel, inadequate firepower, and serious transportation problems. The 89th had a company of jeeps as its primary transport, while the 71st, with about 1,700 horses and mules, had perhaps only a dozen jeeps in the entire division.

Although this most difficult of World War II stateside maneuvers was supposed to have had six phases, it never advanced beyond the third, though the maneuver lasted fifty-six days. Supply was impossible. The 71st artillery spent its time hauling C-rations to the infantry rather than its own ammunition, although its normal mission is to supply the infantry with firepower rather than with beans. At one point the 89th had to assign six of its infantry battalions to supply the remaining three. In short, the light division could not sustain itself.

By mid-April everyone had had enough, from the lowest privates in the divisions all the way up to Chief of Staff George Marshall. Accordingly, both units went to new locations for conversion to standard infantry divisions. The 71st was in Benning by June and during the summer increased its strength almost 50 percent by adding replacements and some combat support units. The mules, sent out to pasture in Nebraska, were replaced by motor vehicles. By the time of my arrival the division was just reaching its authorized strength and was into unit training preliminary to its final before-combat maneuvers. It was one of the thirty U.S. Army divisions in the states scheduled to join Ike's command by early winter 1945 to fight alongside the thirty-one sent earlier, some of which had been in combat since D-Day.

The arrival of new officers was so routine that within an hour of stepping off the train I was en route to my assigned room in the Division Artillery bachelor officers' quarters. I opened the front door of the building onto a poker game in full swing. One lieutenant whose IOUs had run out helped me locate my room and over a beer briefed me on arrangements. The rooms were sparse but adequate—cot, table, chair, and locker. In any case it was home for the nonce. About six-thirty the following morning I headed next door to the mess hall prior to reporting for duty.

Being the first arrival, I had already started eating when another officer seated himself at the far end of the table. He said nothing to me but quickly gave his order to the enlisted attendant: "Eight over easy now, and four later." Was he talking about eggs, or was this a code or some joke between them? Surely no one would begin a workday with a dozen eggs. I was wrong. Soon eight, with appropriate extras, came out. I could not help staring as they were devoured, and I felt slightly bilious. As I made for the exit, the attendant was heading out with four more, over easy!

When I arrived at Division Artillery, the adjutant advised that the commander, Brigadier General Henning, was away; I was to see Colonel George Scithers, his executive. Meanwhile, he informed me of my assignment to the 608th Field Artillery Battalion. This was one of the three light (armed with 105 mm howitzers) battalions in direct support of each of the three infantry regiments; each had a total personnel strength of about five hundred. There was also a medium battalion (155 mm howitzers) for general support as needed.

Entering Scithers's office I spotted a short, craggy-faced mule-packer prototype, cigar in mouth, bent over some work on his desk. When he looked up, I saluted and reported for duty. Returning the salute, he eyed me closely for some seconds without responding. Then: "I'll tell you, Kinnard, if you do well, we'll promote you; if you don't, we'll kick you out. Any questions?" "No, sir." Whereupon the "meeting" ended.

Totally different was my reporting at the 608th to a personable battalion commander, Major Clarence Clapsaddle, a 1940 graduate of West Point. He early on discussed the condition of the battalion, which he thought was good and about ready to go into combat. He assigned me to Captain Stanley Jagoda's B Battery, one of the three firing batteries. (The battalion also had headquarters and service batteries.) Jake, he said, had at one time been a mule packer in Panama. From there he went to officer candidate school before being assigned to the then newly activated 71st at Camp Carson, Colorado. After introducing me to the fire direction personnel at the headquarters, Clapsaddle pointed me in the direction of Baker Battery.

Jagoda turned out to be about thirty, a big guy with a crew cut and an outgoing manner. He wasted no time going into my assignments. I was to be the assistant executive to Lieutenant Charles Wheeler, currently away at a packing and crating school. "You two are in charge of the guns" (each firing battery had four gun sections). On Monday, he went on, we would have our final battalion firing test, and a Lieutenant Brigham from battalion headquarters would be the executive in Wheeler's absence; being new, I should simply observe the exercise.

Oh, yes, there were some other duties. I was to be the battery motors officer also. We would be having a motors inspection in a couple of weeks—but, not to worry, Sergeant Richardson in charge of the motor pool knew what he was doing. There was one other matter. Because packing and crating for overseas might start before Wheeler's return, I would be in charge of that for now. At that point only an hour and a half had elapsed since Scithers's charge, but it looked as though my agenda contained enough to keep me fully engaged for some time.

Giving me a tour of the battery area, Jake introduced me to the other junior officers in the battery. Rudy Kehren, like me a second john, had graduated that year from Iowa State. Short, very young-looking and friendly, he was our forward observer. In combat he would normally be with one of the rifle companies we were supporting, adjusting artillery fire on their targets, usually enemy or enemy weapons. In fact, though, all four lieutenants in the battery would be expected to take their turns as forward observer; either Wheeler or I, though, would always be in charge of the guns.

We had a job locating the other officer, a first lieutenant, Norman Persson. As the reconnaissance officer he would help select new positions for the guns to occupy as the forces moved forward, backward, or sideways; at the same time he had to provide survey, which tied the weapons into the fire control system. "Here is Persson now," announced Jagoda, and I focused on the approaching person. He looked like—he was!—the man of the dozen eggs at breakfast that morning. Norman Edward Andrew Persson came on as a character—sharp but appearing a bit eccentric, like someone walking on stage in an Oscar Wilde society comedy.

I took the first weekend to settle in, draw field equipment, and get acquainted with Sand Hill, the division cantonment area. Fort Benning was a huge post with perhaps sixty thousand personnel at that point. I knew the main post from the time spent there as a cadet, but Sand Hill with its red clay, sand, scrub pines, and bugs was a long way removed from that. Self-sustaining, like all the World War II cantonment areas, it had its own living and training facilities as well as the amenities: clubs, movie theaters, and post exchanges. A lodge near our living area served as an officers' club. The word was that George Patton had had it built when he commanded the Second Armored Division at Sand Hill earlier in the war.

Monday morning I followed the battery out to the test area on the firing range after Lieutenant Brigham cautioned me to observe but stay out of the problem. As the guns went into firing position, I noticed an anomaly from what we had been taught at Fort Sill. The howitzer, firing the registration on which all later firing would be based, did not seem parallel to the other artillery pieces. Was this perhaps an advanced technique that the unit had developed? Following my orders I remained silent and observed. On command of Kehren at some distant location on the range, all guns eventually fired on the assumed target. "Cease fire!" commanded an excited umpire after receiving some word on his radio. Suddenly a half-dozen jeeps arrived with umpires, Clapsaddle, and Jagoda. The battery had fired out of the target area. Much discussion. The anomaly I had noticed was not an advanced technique; it was a screw-up. As the jeeps left with one additional passenger, Lieutenant Brigham, Clapsaddle and Jagoda came by, telling me to take over. With the help of Sergeant Joe Glissner, senior gun section chief, we managed to get through the remainder of the problem. We barely passed the test, since the initial fiasco had put us in the hole. Anyway, for better or worse, I was now executive in charge of the guns until Wheeler returned. ("Won't you come home, Charles Wheeler, won't you come home?")

For the next couple of weeks we concentrated on maintaining vehicles and weapons, but we kept training in small sections on survey, communications, and howitzers. Also tossed in were classes for the troops on such matters as defense against gas attack or on troop information (for example, "why we are fighting the war").

In the days after the test I had a good opportunity to get acquainted with the men in the battery; if I didn't talk to each of the hundred, I came close. They were a diverse and interesting group: some were young, not long out of high school; a larger group, a few years older, included several with a year or two of college; and among the more senior sergeants were a number who owned, or had owned, their own businesses. Though they came from all over the country, Illinois for some reason provided the largest contingent. As time went on, I became impressed with their competence and teamwork; never did I have any question about going into combat with them. Even after I got to know many as individuals, I was never able to identify them by their nicknames for one another, such as "Hammerhead," "the Mole," "Undertaker," and "Hog."

About ten days after my arrival Charles Wheeler returned from packing and crating school. He resumed his role as executive officer, but Jake decided that I would be the packing and crating (for movement overseas) officer—my reward for being the last junior officer on the scene! A western Oklahoman, Charlie had attended the University of Oklahoma law school before coming into the Army. Humorous and seemingly laid back, he was really both sharp and competent.

The nearest city to Benning was Columbus, where officers such as Jake and Charlie lived with their spouses, although their duties required them to stay in the BOQ on some nights. On weekends GIs on passes flocked to Columbus, outnumbering the residents about two to one. Spatlen's Pool and Barn on the outskirts of town was a popular spot for dancing and for picking up a girl. On Sundays Georgia law closed the gin mills, but not to worry, soldier, there was a solution. Adjoining Columbus, on the other side of the Chattahoochee River, was Phenix City, Alabama.

The music heard as one crossed the bridge to Alabama was not Sidney Lanier's "Song of the Chattahoochee," rather the noise emanating from the slat-sided beer joints and a place called Idle Hour Park, which operated seven days a week. Ever-present B-girls hustled the upstairs trade as they dished out drinks to soldiers. Therefore, the division troop information program included frequent VD lectures, sometimes accompanied by films. The more explicit of these, holdovers from World War I, were designed to shock men into abstinence. Some, though, always had to learn the hard way.

Both Columbus and Phenix City brought together soldiers from various organizations including the divisions and young paratroopers in training at the airborne school. These young paratroopers, who followed the custom of blousing their trousers over their boots, had decided that they alone would do so. As a mule-pack division the 71st had needed to do the same; now the blousing had become part of the division culture even though the mules had retired to Nebraska. Inevitably, weekend clashes occurred, especially in Phenix City after the booze started flowing. The mule packers prevailed physically over the kids with wings, a few of whom landed in the Chattahoochee. To make it official, the commanding general of the 71st issued an order that members of the division would always blouse their trousers; supposedly, he had added, "Anyone who doesn't like it can lump it." From such is a division's esprit de corps developed.

The days of October and November slipped by rapidly, in a kaleidoscopic way while I did the typical duties of an artillery lieutenant: preparing for a major inspection of motor vehicles; training with the firing battery in garrison and in the field, especially on going in and out of position; and teaching such subjects as defense against chemical attack. Then I received a new type of assignment—defense counsel on the Battalion Court-Martial. Armed with the background of the cadet course in military law and the residual chutzpah of a Paterson kid, I secured acquittals on my first two cases. My clients, who were privates first class, were delighted, but Battalion changed my assignment from defense counsel to prosecutor!

Keeping up with the news that fall was a radio-dependent exercise, supplemented at times with whatever weekly news magazine one chanced upon. The major domestic story was Roosevelt's campaign against Thomas Dewey ("the man on the wedding cake") for an unprecedented fourth term. Most of us never doubted the outcome. FDR had become a way of life; he had been my president since I was eleven years old. His running mate, Harry Truman, was not so well known. As I recalled, when he was first elected as senator from Missouri 1934, the Paterson papers referred to him as "the senator from Pendergast." Beginning in 1941 he began to receive favorable national attention as chairman of a special Senate committee investigating the national defense program. In any case, he would be only the vice president, right?

War news from the Pacific that fall was good. Late October brought MacArthur's promised return to the Philippines, along with a major defeat of the Japanese navy in the Battle of Leyte Gulf. Contrasting with that was the picture from our area of interest, Europe, where we would soon be fighting. There the heady optimism of the August days had faded. After the failure of the Arnhem operation, Eisenhower's great offensive had slowed, and the battle line was essentially along the Franco-German frontier. The concept of a major thrust into Germany along a northern axis had been replaced with a broad-front strategy, aimed at occupying the Rhineland, prior to seizing bridgeheads across the Rhine. From there Eisenhower planned to mount the final drive into Germany itself.

By October the Rhineland campaign had become a bitter war of attrition. Aachen, birthplace of Charlemagne and of great symbolic importance in Nazi ideology, was the scene of a bloody battle beginning on October 2. By the time the city finally surrendered on the 21st, we had paid a heavy price—about ten thousand American casualties. One spot along the front, though, the Ardennes Forest, was judged to be a relatively quiet area; there some battle-weary units could recover, and new units could gain some seasoning. Surely, it was felt, in such terrain no heavy fighting could occur during the approaching winter.

December at Sand Hill brought our final maneuvers before our departure for overseas. For us this consisted of a series of four- or five-day tactical problems under division control. One goal of the maneuvers was to simulate actual battle conditions: foxholes, camouflage, communication networks, medical clearing stations, and so on. Last but not least, sleeping, if one could call it that, on the cold, cold ground of a Georgia December.

Personally supervising the maneuver, including a visit to my firing battery, was the new division commander of the 71st, General Willard Wyman, West Point class of 1919. He came to us from the battles in France, where he had been assistant commander of the 1st

Division since the D-Day invasion. Impressed with his appearance and in what he had to say, we felt fortunate to have someone with European war experience to lead us there.

In the middle of one tactical problem came some startling news. On December 16 a powerful German force had struck our lightly held front in the Ardennes. As the days went on, news reports became more ominous; this was clearly the Germans' attempt to reenact their great breakthrough against France in 1940—this time to cross the Meuse River and head for Antwerp so as to trap and destroy the northern Allied armies.

Our forces reacted strongly, however. The 101st Airborne's defense of Bastogne and the redisposition of Allied forces by Eisenhower slowed the German attack, and eventually halted it. When the weather cleared after the first week, our air forces began hitting the enemy's forward units and their lines of communication, averaging three thousand sorties a day. This, combined with attacks by Patton's armored divisions on the southern flank of the Bulge, as the battle was now called, halted the German advance by the day after Christmas.

Shortly before Christmas we completed our portion of the maneuvers and began the slow, tedious task of packing and crating our equipment for the trip to France. The only interruption came when division headquarters imposed an additional requirement: several hours of training on how to defend artillery positions against direct attack by infantry or armor units. This was occasioned by the SS massacre of eighty American artillerymen captured at Malmedy on the second day of the Battle of the Bulge. Needless to say, the troops paid close attention to this training.

Since my arrival at the 71st my letter writing had been on hold, but now I tried to catch up with Christmas cards. In cards to Toots and Aunt Annie I added a brief P.S. I hoped they would understand: "Hope to see you briefly in January if I can work it out." Annie's card told of her move from Market Street to a nicer place on Carroll near St. Joe's. (I had been prodding her to do so since the previous summer.) I also heard from my two brothers. From a South Pacific island

Pfc. Jim Kinnard's card was typically upbeat, as though he were on a tour. Sergeant Harry Kinnard's card from Italy included a Mauldin cartoon that caught the mood of his battle weary outfit.

Diana's card had some interesting news. That fall her folks had acquired an old farm in Cavendish, Vermont, with a lot of acreage, which they planned on using summers. With the help of Sergeant Cusson, our only Vermonter in B Battery, I located the area on his map. He was high on the location: "A lot of flatlanders are buying there now." When I asked what a flatlander was, he looked at me quizzically and explained, "Well, someone from New Jersey, for example, who moves to Vermont."

The only battalion officers' social event during my stay at Benning was a New Year's Eve dance at the Patton Club. It was a good chance to meet the wives and to talk to some of the officers whom I did not see in my daily routine. Of particular interest was the new battalion commander, Lieutenant Colonel George Oram, who had replaced Clapsaddle in late November. Oram was a 1930 Princeton grad, who had become a lawyer with a practice in New Jersey. He had come on active duty when that state's National Guard was federalized in early 1941. He seemed personable and a good corporate-type leader, but what he knew about field artillery was not clear to me on the two occasions he had visited my unit during maneuvers.

As the January days moved along, a better picture of the German Ardennes offensive emerged. Their armies had gone as far west as they were going to go by Christmas. Short of fuel, denied critical roads by Allied resistance, and hammered by air forces and armored units, their spearhead into our lines began to recede. By January 21 they would be forced back to their original line. Just as our breakout the previous August had failed to achieve victory, so too the German offensive had failed. The crucial difference, though, was that Hitler could not replace his lost manpower and materiel, while we had been able to. To make matters worse for him, the Soviets began a major offensive into Poland and East Prussia on January 12.

Both sides suffered heavy casualties: for the Germans, 100,000; for the Allies, about 81,000, of whom 77,000 were Americans—the heaviest battle toll in U.S. history. Later I found out that of my seven infantry classmates in the 106th Division (run over by the Germans in the first day of their offensive), five were taken prisoner for the remainder of the war, one was evacuated because of wounds, and one had survived the battle and was awarded the Silver Star. The class of 1944 had received its baptism of fire.

By the second week in January our advance detachment and most of our equipment had departed. The men used their time now to tidy up affairs such as updating allotments, wills, and next-of-kin addresses. The officers also had time now to relax a bit. In the evenings I began going to the movie theater close to my BOQ and was especially impressed by two pictures: *Laura* and (on my last night in Benning) *Experiment Perilous.* Technically, the first, a suspense yarn enhanced by a love story with an excellent cast headed by Gene Tierney and Dana Andrews, was the best. The theme music was a haunting melody, "Laura . . . but she's only a dream." I wondered if with a change of name the song would apply to my own situation. The other movie, with Paul Lukas and Hedy Lamarr, was an atmospheric vintage mystery. What impacted on me were two scenes in the Vermont countryside—one early in the movie with a young Hedy; the other at the end back in Vermont, this time married to George Brent. The Vermont scenes rather than the story caused me to focus on Diana; they inspired something I had been thinking about for some time—writing her a long letter. From the movie I went to my room and began writing.

My pen flowed. I was sorry I had not been able to write her more or see her, and now seeing her would be impossible for a while. I thought of her often and of things I would like to say to her. I wondered if she would have the time to be a regular correspondent to my new address (APO 360 c/o Postmaster, NY, NY). I had no other girlfriend and hearing from her would mean a lot to me. For my part I promised to be a regular correspondent also. I closed with "Always," thinking of the words of Irving Berlin's song with that title. The letter was postmarked January 17, our last day in Benning.

The 608th was scheduled to depart by train in early evening. The men spent the day turning in post property such as bedding, rolling their packs, and policing the area down to the last cigarette butt. After the post inspectors gave their okay, the troops marched to the train. Behind they left memories of hot Georgia afternoons, firing problems, battalion tests, fights with paratroopers in the local towns, numberless inspections by 2d Army and finally the mad whirl of packing and crating. Somehow in those months the 71st had molded into in infantry division out of an experimental light division. We were ready to fight.

On the train the battalion officers had a car to themselves. Soon some illegal bottles and paper cups were produced and singing started, led by George Oram, who had a pretty good voice. As usual, we ended with what would always be our song, even though the mules were long gone, "The Mountain Battery": "Oh, I'd rather be a soldier with a mule and a mountain gun, than a Knight of Old, with spurs of gold, or a Roman, Greek or Hun. . . ." Afterward, while we were sleeping, the train sped on to our destination—cold, snow-covered, Camp Kilmer, New Jersey, our port of embarkation.

Camp Kilmer took its name from the schoolteacher-poet Joyce Kilmer, born in nearby New Brunswick, and killed in action in France, July 1918. He was best known for his twelve-line poem "Trees" ("Poems are made by fools like me, But only God can make a tree."). Less poetic were the other aspects of the camp, a sprawling conglomeration of temporary buildings for units to stay briefly before boarding troop transports to Europe. Scribbled on the walls of our barracks were hundreds of names with dates of stay such as "arrived 12 Sept '44—left 15 Sept." Those of us hoping for a pass preferred the more optimistic "arrived 6 Oct '44—left 14 Oct."

We spent our time at Kilmer on various preembarking requirements: lectures on censorship regulations; lifeboat drill, including climbing down nets; checks on individual equipment; issuance of gas masks; and final personal matters such as wills and insurance. All ranks also went through a kind of physical examination: walking through a long line of medical personnel who asked a few questions and stuck typhus and typhoid shots into us. Apparently anyone who reached the end of the line—meaning everyone—was considered fit to fight. Some relevant GI humor overheard in our barracks: "A civilian janitor, discharged during the last war for physical disability, had been mistakenly sent through the examination line and found combat serviceable."

Like many officers, I had to attend a lecture about censoring the outgoing mail of men in our units. During this first opportunity to see any of my nine infantry classmates assigned to the 71st, I happened to sit next to one, Pierre Bontecou; an impressive-looking guy who had completed three years at VPI before entering the academy. He tried his best to update me on the others, including John Eisenhower, and I did the same for the other seven artillerymen. After the lecture we parted with "See you in Europe."

On Monday the 22nd Jagoda offered me a pass from noon until reveille next morning. After a telephone call home I headed for the Kilmer bus station with its big sign, "Broadway and 42nd St." From there the Paterson express delivered me to Annie's new location on Carroll Street by mid-afternoon. Toots was there, too, soon to be joined by Johnny Bustard; we all kept the conversation light. I took the opportunity to use the phone, including calls to Irene and sister Daisy, who promised to be good correspondents. Dinner featured foods well beyond the limit of wartime rationing guidelines. By seven-thirty I was off to catch the New York bus, leaving a stiff-upper-lip group behind.

Near the bus stop on the corner of Park Avenue and Summer Street was a snowy empty lot I knew well. During the summer it was the site of evening tent revival meetings—off-limits to those of us from St. Joe's except to watch from the outside. But in the fall, with the lot empty, we fellows of the early-to mid-1930s would gather there many an evening to play "pick up and tackle." The only equipment required was a football and a tough body. Now, in my mind's eye, the snow disappeared and a fall night returned. I heard the familiar voices, shouting and laughing, of friends now scattered all over the world: Johnny Sproverie, Red Gallagher, Lefty Lefkowitz, Bradner Riggs, Billy Moran, and others. The game ended and they left one by one with our usual farewell: "See you after." The approaching New

York bus burst into my reverie, along with the realization that there would be no "after."

As the bus headed toward Manhattan I had no desire to head directly back to Kilmer. Why not a few hours in the city? But with whom? On impulse I made a call from the bus terminal to Lee Lauterbur, not seen since graduation leave. By luck she was at her hotel doing some work on a dancing part she hoped to get in a new show. I could meet her at the Lexington to go somewhere for a drink and dancing.

The place she selected had a big bar and a moderate-sized dance floor, both packed. Every male had on some kind of uniform. The small but good orchestra kept us dancing to "This Heart of Mine," "Jersey Bounce" and, in honor of Glenn Miller (the forty-year-old leader of the Air Force Band who had disappeared on a flight over the Channel the previous month), "In the Mood."

During a break in the music we ended up next to a Coast Guard officer and his date. There was instant, mutual recognition: he was Glenn Murphy, a Coast Guard classmate. When I asked what he was doing, he looked at my uniform with the 71st Division patch, smiled, and said "Convoy duty." The orchestra resumed, but soon Lee had to call it quits, and we headed back to her hotel.

En route she mentioned that the new show of her dreams was a Rodgers and Hammerstein musical, *Carousel*, to open in April. Lee was especially excited about this work possibility, as the choreographer was Agnes de Mille. Back in the lobby we headed to a hidden corner for about a twenty-minute necking session. Its intensity surprised me; perhaps it signified the serviceman's last opportunity for a while. We exchanged addresses and promises to write. By two or so I was in bed at Kilmer for a short sleep before checking in with Jake at reveille!

On the morning of January 25 I was part of a small advance party leaving Kilmer on a short train trip to the Hoboken ferry. Not exactly a routine commute as we were each loaded down with about seventy-five pounds of gear: winter clothing, an extra pair of combat boots, two blankets, a small tent, a pistol, as well as personal items such as a mess kit. The waiting ferry to Manhattan brought us to a west-side pier, where the U.S. Army transport *Christobal* was tied up to be boarded that evening by the artillerymen of the 71st Division.

Formerly in the service of the Panama Lines, the *Christobal* was a sturdily built modern vessel with one large stack amidships. Once aboard I was assigned a bunk on Veranda B, fortunately above the water line. Fabricated out of two bedrooms and a sitting area, it was now packed with thirty double-decked bunks for junior officers. Not bad, except that there was only one bathroom. After unloading my gear I headed down several decks to find compartment six, which was to be the nautical home of B Battery. It is unbelievable the number of men who can be packed into a single compartment when the bunks are stacked five tiers high.

The *Christobal* was one of five ships transporting the 71st to the European theater of operations. These five were only a small part of one of the largest convoys going to Europe that winter. We later found out that ours had about sixty ships as well as nine Navy destroyers and destroyer escorts. The latter along with air—when available—would protect against the German U-boat threat. By that stage of the war these efforts had been fairly successful in keeping the U-boats at bay along the northern Great Circle route, which we were to follow. More difficult for convoys was the approach to the British Isles, where the Germans were then focusing their efforts. On Christmas Eve, a month before, the transport *Leopoldville*, carrying part of the 66th Infantry Division, had been torpedoed while trying to enter Cherbourg harbor. About eight hundred of the troops lost their lives. Three members of the class of '44 were fortunate enough to survive as well as to help rescue some other members of their units.

Sometime during the night we left New York harbor to head for the Atlantic. On the first day, as we rendezvoused with the convoy, the roll of the ship was not bad, but the second day, as we headed out into the North Atlantic, brought a dramatic change. The mess line became noticeably shorter as seasickness became epidemic. Only the hardier sailors—and I was not one of them—were fully mobile.

By the fifth day most who still had mal de mer could make it to the rail in an emergency; the remainder fitted themselves in with the routine. The working day began by cleaning up the compartment and then, for those who could, some group exercises on deck. Occasionally, we had a practice alert and lifeboats would be swung out. At unpredictable times the routine was broken by the high-pitched "Feee-EEEE-Feeee" of the bosun's whistle followed by "Now hear this" and an announcement such as "Sweepers, man your brooms" or "The smoking lamp is lit."

Those who could handle food went to two meals per day; waiting one's turn in line was interminable, but the food was good. Below deck the troops had plenty of sack time and the poker games reached gigantic proportions. Many men spent time on their backs reading or just thinking. Everyone had been issued (besides the paper sacks for sickness) a Red Cross ditty bag containing a book or two to read on the way across.

During daylight on deck we could see some of the convoy's other ships: transports, cargo ships, oil freighters, and destroyers. From time to time the destroyers made sharp turns, racing to the rear or flank. The convoy was shaped like a large rectangle, probably four times wider than its length. The Navy had evidently determined on this arrangement for maximum protection against the U-boats.

On the approach to England two genuine submarine alerts came, both at night. We raced out onto the deck with field jacket, Mae West (life jacket) with the little light on it, wool cap, and boots unlaced. We stood on the deck for about an hour, during which the destroyers dropped depth charges; then came the "all clear."

The seriousness of the situation was made even clearer to me later when I heard about an incident on the 14th Infantry's transport. One night during the crossing a man fell overboard, but no effort was made to rescue him. A doctor and a chaplain proceeded to the fantail of the ship. After a few minutes the doctor pronounced him dead of cold in the frigid North Atlantic; the chaplain said the burial prayers. The convoy never budged from its course, nor would it, had the *Christobal* or any of the other ships been hit with a German torpedo.

What a relief for everyone when on February 5 we sighted land—the harbor of Southampton, England. The *Christobal* dropped anchor off the Isle of Wight, but our view of the lovely English countryside that afternoon was as close as we were going to get to England. On awakening next morning we were approaching our destination, the port of Le Havre and we could see the French coastline.

After a bitter fight five months earlier, the city was now a smashed and shattered ruin. The harbor contained many wrecked vessels, some with masts and even damaged superstructures showing above the water. In this environment the pilots really had to know their business to get ships to the docks. As we approached ours, a small vessel passed us, heading in with General Wyman and a small group of officers. Though I did not know at the time, one in that group was my classmate Johnny Eisenhower. The higher command had decided that the son of the Supreme Commander should not be in a frontline infantry platoon where he would be vulnerable to capture; thus, he was reassigned elsewhere.

The evening before, Jake had alerted me to be prepared to leave the ship shortly after docking. I was to be part of an advance party heading to the division's tent city, where we would be billeted while preparing to move to the front. My task was to guide the various sections of B Battery to their tents when they arrived the following morning. Accordingly, shortly after the *Christobal* docked I loaded myself and my seventy-five pounds of gear into a 3/4-ton vehicle along with a number of lieutenants with similar missions. Lafayette, in case you missed it, the 71st is here!

Le Havre was a beehive of American army activity such as unloading and storing, some in the open, some in half-destroyed buildings. Soon we were out in the Normandy countryside with its characteristic hedgerows and old thatched-roof farmhouses. As we drove along, I noticed many large draft horses pulling high-wheeled carts across the farms. One of my colleagues called them Percheron horses and said that they had originated in Normandy. There were church spires everywhere as well as roadside shrines, testifying to the Catholic faith of most Normans.

Our destination, some forty miles northeast of the port, was a massive tent encampment known as Camp Old Gold. Units were so widely dispersed that the 608th, like others, had its own self-supporting area. We later learned that Old Gold was one of several similar staging areas known collectively as the "cigarette camps." The 89th Division, some thirty miles north of us along the Norman coast, was at Camp Lucky Strike.

Dominating our impression—and my memory—of that month at Old Gold was the all-pervasive mud. The hillsides on which we camped had turned into acres of mud, meaning that we must constantly exert ourselves to keep the drainage ditches open as well as to prevent the tents themselves from collapsing. Naturally the troops were always griping about the mud.

Once established in Old Gold, we worked on our major goal: to get our trucks, guns, and other equipment in combat-ready condition. Drivers sent to Antwerp to retrieve our trucks arriving there from the states returned with tales of German V-1 buzz bombs still being fired at that port from German-occupied Holland.

Our artillery shells came from a different direction. Rudy Kehren and some troops were dispatched one evening to a rail point where the 608th would assume responsibility for guarding the ammunition train on its final leg to our area. Since the train was not ready to go, Rudy released the vehicle that had brought his group there and they waited in the caboose. Time passed and the guard detail slept. When they awakened, the train had left for its destination near the 608th, but without the caboose, which someone had failed to attach. Several hitchhiking hours later Rudy and group arrived at Old Gold just as the train pulled in. About fifteen minutes later the battalion supply officer and his assistants arrived to take over responsibility, apologizing for not being there when the train had pulled in. (All's well that ends well.) Such was life in the European Theater—Communications Zone version—in early 1945.

Vital after the long layoff since Benning, physical conditioning took up much of our time and effort. Besides road marches we worked on the "road gang," as the troops called our struggle to keep the muddy farm roads passable for heavy vehicles. Everyone was famished after the daily exercise, but there never seemed to be enough chow. Soon the more ambitious soldiers were out into the countryside with cigarettes in hand, practicing their fractured French: "Avez-vous du pain?" and "Avez-vous des eggs?" Inevitably, the more linguistically talented or thirsty came up with, "Je veux boire de cognac."

The B Battery officers ate at a stand-up table at one end of the battery mess tent. Occasionally, Jake used some of these three-a-day sessions as an impromptu officers' call; more often, the conversation was light. Charles Wheeler entertained us with his western Oklahoma witticisms, as did Jake with his tales of mule-pack days. Norm Persson, always out of cigarettes, consistently bummed from our free Philip Morris packs. We accused Norm of being on the French black market, knowing all the while that he smoked like a chimney. At these sessions I learned more about the officers with whom I was going into combat than in all our time at Benning.

About a week into the Old Gold experience came our first mail call, and the clerk handed me several letters. Would there be one from—? Yes, I recognized Diana's artistic handwriting! She was happy to get my APO 360 address and would like to hear about my "adventures" in Europe. For her part she would fill me in on her own activities and plans; at the moment she was focusing on her final semester at Montclair High and on trying to work out a college for the fall. By the time I finished reading her letter, I was already planning my reply. I sensed that our correspondence would provide a way of expressing feelings—not just about her—that I could not articulate to anyone then around me.

A couple of days after mailing my response, I was walking and chatting in the battery area with Jake, who said, "I didn't know you had a girlfriend." Thinking that he had me mixed up with one of the battalion officers involved with one or two of the beauties in nearby Yerville or Yvetot, I replied, "What girlfriend?" Sheepish smile, then, "Well, Diana." How could he possibly know about her? Then it dawned on me that he was responsible for censoring my mail. Not wanting my letters to Diana censored—and still possessing Paterson street smarts—I "borrowed" a censor stamp each time I wrote. It was either that or feeling inhibited in writing her. This covert operation made, I think, for much better letters and certainly a better outlet for my feelings.

During our third week at Old Gold I was designated, along with many other division lieutenants, to attend a mine and booby trap school on the Normandy coast. Though special teams had been trained to remove these deadly devices, we needed to learn enough about them to supervise their removal during combat if it became necessary. The trucks dropped us off near the small town of Cany-Barville, about eight miles from the coast; there we would have our preliminary instruction.

As one of the other lieutenants was Harry Grace, we became roommates again, but this time in a pup tent on the cold cold ground. Our camp and instruction took place on the grounds of a small château. The inside of the building was off-limits to us, but glimpsing its elegance through the terrace's French doors we envied the absent owner, supposedly an Englishman.

In the evening several of us walked into the small town in hopes of a little excitement before facing the night in a pup tent. Not even one mademoiselle was at the bar, only eight or ten unfriendly Frenchmen playing a game with greasy cards on zinc-topped tables. We stayed long enough to drink some cider, which though not alcoholic enough to bring on any euphoria, turned out later to be an excellent, if untimely, diuretic.

On the afternoon of the second day with our belongings on our backs, we headed out on an eight-mile hike to St. Valéry-en-Caux. St. Valéry was about fifteen miles west along the coast from Dieppe, famous because of the August 1942 commando raid. There the Canadians, who suffered about three thousand casualties, had barely gotten inland off the beach before they had to evacuate. From that time on the coast in that area was seeded with German mines and booby traps. St. Valéry had become a ghost town with booby traps in every house, and one dared not get off the streets. It was as weird as an Alfred Hitchcock movie.

For two days and one night we were immersed in the practical portion of our course: with probing devices like long skewers we located and disarmed German mines and lethal devices in the coastal area near St. Valéry. We knew, of course, that we had to be extremely careful, especially considering the age of the mines and booby traps, but after our initial successes we became a bit casual. Then, as we looked at a nearby lieutenant shouting, "I've got one," we knew something that he didn't—he was sitting on an object with a trip wire attached. As soon as we alerted him, he became like a statue. One of the instructors helped to disarm the device, which turned out to be a booby-trapped double Teller mine. After that we were even more cautious than we had been initially.

En route from Benning to France, keeping up with the war news had not been easy, but at Old Gold this became easier in a broad-brush sort of way, thanks to the daily *Stars and Stripes*. News since the Bulge had been both dramatic and good. For one thing the Germans had cracked before the onslaught of the Russian offensive that had started on January 12. Within ten days the Russian forces had moved forward almost two hundred miles, essentially from the Vistula to the Oder; in February they occupied most of what was left of Prussia. The Red Army had developed into a superb fighting machine, and they had a score to settle with the Germans. In our area, Hitler had turned south with a new offensive into Alsace Lorraine after his failure in the Bulge. Despite some German gains in January, the Seventh Army held. The Germans had again wasted resources needed for the defense of their homeland.

The German offensives in the west in December and January had bought them time, but for what purpose? By the time we were established in Old Gold, Eisenhower was ready for his drive to the Rhine and beyond. From early February until early March our forces hit the enemy with a power and ferocity that they could no longer withstand and we cleared the Rhineland north of Coblenz.

Then on March 7 came one of the great surprises of the war in the west. At Remagen, not too far north of Coblenz, a unit of the U.S. First Army captured a bridge across the Rhine, and before the Germans could destroy it, we had established a secure bridgehead on the eastern side—the great river barrier had been breached. Now overrunning what remained of German-occupied France and Germany west of the Rhine would be the task of the Third and Seventh U.S. Armies. It was into this operation that the 71st, as part of the Seventh Army, was to be committed to combat.

On March 6 the division began moving forward with the infantry boarding disreputable old "40 and 8" boxcars of World War I fame (they could hold forty men and eight horses). But because of our size and equipment they could barely hold thirty men of our generation; fortunately, there were no horses. The artillery moved in its own vehicles, with the 608th departing Old Gold on the afternoon of March 9. We skirted north of Rouen and Paris and south of Nancy, ending the 347-mile journey the following day at the small farming village of Bidestroff in Alsace.

We were to remain there until the infantry regiment we supported (the 14th) had replaced a comparable unit of the 100th Division on the front. B Battery officers were billeted in a farmer's home where, to make matters interesting, there actually was a comely farmer's daughter. However, the farmer made it clear, to Jake especially, that she was off limits.

Soon after our arrival the mail clerk distributed letters he had received just before we departed Old Gold. He gave me one from Scotty Solomon, who was in Italy with the 10th Mountain Division. It was brief: Johnny Hazen, our G-2 Company classmate, had been killed in action there while serving as a forward observer with the infantry. While trying not to think too much about this guy who loved life, my mind's eye kept picturing him leading us in song as he so often had—maybe in his favorite "The Persian Kitten": "'Cheer up,' said the Tom Cat with a smile . . . ."

Waiting to move forward into our first firing positions, we knew little of the big picture; later we found out that our division was part of the XV Corps. Its job was to deliver the big punch in Seventh Army's offensive to break through the German West Wall. In conjunction with the Third Army to its north, it was to clear the Saar-Palatinate area while moving to the Rhine. Before achieving that, though, it must push the enemy out of their positions in the old French Maginot Line; and then penetrate the Siegfried Line, which was just inside the German border.

My recollections of one division in combat in World War II are, of course, from an artilleryman's perspective. We were the primary supporting arm of the infantry, but they had the mission of closing with the enemy and capturing or destroying him. All soldiers in combat are in life-threatening situations routinely; however, it is the infantryman, the "dogface soldier," who takes the brunt of ground warfare every day—a dirty, nasty experience. With the enemy intent on firing a loaded weapon at your head, you had better fire first!

After dark on March 12 the battery moved the last forty-one miles to the front at Montbronn without lights. On arrival, still in blackout, we immediately started replacing a comparable artillery battery of the 100th Division. One by one, our four gun section chiefs (Sergeants Joe Gliessner, Kentucky; Glenn Tracy, Oregon; Delmar Bohr, South Dakota; George Orseske, Chicago) supervised the emplacement of their weapons and prepared to fire. At dawn the cannoneers cheered loudly as our first artillery shells went out against the enemy.

Besides our unit, many others were replacing 100th Division units; all this truck movement by both divisions must surely have been noticed by the Germans. Sure enough, no sooner had we fired than we began experiencing incoming rounds; they were telling us that they knew where we were and what they had in store for us. Fortunately, they missed.

Later in the morning what we identified as an American P-47 passed over our position, circled back, and began strafing us. We had not known that the enemy was now employing our crashed P-47s. We were lucky that no one in B Battery was hit, but we did hear that two soldiers up the road were killed. A couple of days later some of our P-38s shot down the returning P-47s.

By the following day the 14th Infantry was in contact with the enemy on the right flank of our division. Its immediate goal was to participate in the division attack driving the enemy off the ridge lines in the old Maginot Line area and back across the German border. Now was the time to send out forward observer teams; three—headed by Persson, Kehren, and Wheeler—were dispatched from our battery. Jake had decided that Wheeler and I would rotate as observers while the other commanded the firing battery.

On the afternoon of the 16th Jake and the other battery commanders went forward with the battalion commander to select new gun positions for supporting the attack. I was left to prepare the battery for displacement, and to move it forward after dark over an assigned route. At some point along the route Jake would meet our column and guide us into the new positions. It turned out to be one of the two most memorable displacements our unit experienced in combat.

The night was really black as our battery, in advance of the other firing batteries, headed out to rendezvous with Jake, who presumably had selected our new firing position. Our vehicles' peep lights helped very little, especially as this Vosges Mountain road narrowed; fortunately, though, military police with small flashlights marked particularly dangerous turns on the route. At last we seemed to be coming to one side of a town, whether Bitche or a nearby one I never knew. At a crossroads Major Thaler, the battalion executive, appeared, signalling us to turn right.

The road seemed to be leading into town, but within a few hundred yards we could hear, and then see, gunfire exchange directly ahead. What the hell—something wrong here—we were heading directly into an infantry firefight! Halting the column at an intersection, I conferred with Sergeants Gliessner and Tracy. Leaving Gliessner in charge, Tracy and I headed out on foot to find a way to circle the column back to the "Thaler crossroads." The road's tape marks indicated that it had been cleared of mines, at least to the ditches (fingers were crossed on that). When we found a route, Tracy hoofed back to bring up the column while I waited to be certain that a key intersection remained clear. It did, with the help of a few Hail Marys.

About an hour after we had first passed there, we were back at Thaler crossroads—but no Thaler. A captain I had never seen before pointed us in the same direction as before. "We are not going that way, Captain," I began and then recounted what had happened earlier. Confusion! At this point Thaler arrived in a jeep. Acting as though he had never seen us before that evening, he directed us to a road straight ahead; there, he said, I should find Jagoda.

We wound up on a one-way unpaved road, where within a quarter of a mile I sighted a soldier with a light, standing on a rock. It was Pfc. (or was he a private again?) Mills, Jake's driver. "Go down that way, Lieutenant," he said while pointing toward a lane to my left. "Is it clear of mines?" "Don't know, Lieutenant, but Captain Jagoda has been up and down it several times in a jeep."

In about a hundred yards, as the lane ended, I finally found Jake. After walking me and the gunnery sergeants through the firing position he had selected, he gave me a general direction of fire. There was, he said, no communication as yet to battalion fire direction center and he was not certain where the battalion headquarters was. Shortly after, he left to find out, or at least to find a communication team laying wire from battalion to our position.

As the howitzers were being prepared for firing and the ammunition was being unloaded from the trucks, Gliessner and I discussed how to register the battery (registration was a method of establishing the accuracy of firing data). We decided that without communication with either fire direction or an observer we had only one option: to register on high bursts that we would fire ourselves. Though we knew the technique, neither of us had actually done it before. When Sergeant Tracy said that he had, we converged on his gun position and proceeded to register the battery.

After that we focused on improving our position's security by establishing listening posts and digging foxholes. We did this in blackout as quietly as possible; everyone was tense. Suddenly a GI digging a foxhole yelled, "Christ, it's black as ape shit!" We all laughed, breaking the tension, and then we went back to minimum noise and conversation, at least until dawn, when we could begin to get a better appreciation of our situation.

At first light we could see that we were in a small valley with two ridges on either side. Up ahead each ridge contained two large bunkers, remnants of the old Maginot Line. At a much greater distance straight ahead was the fortress of Bitche, which must have gone back many centuries. This Franco-German border area had changed nationalities several times since the Franco-Prussian War of 1870; we were there to see that it did once again.

As I studied the terrain in front of us, a soldier tapped me on the shoulder and said, "Turn around, Lieutenant." To our rear, where the ridges converged, we saw coming down a road in the middle an advance patrol of an infantry unit, their fixed bayonets pointed straight toward us. It was the 14th Infantry, the unit we supported. Somehow we had ended up in the front lines between our infantry and the enemy. Later we found out that the enemy in this case was an SS Panzer Grenadier Division—wow! To say that we were relieved to see friendly infantry pass through our position is to put it mildly. Still, we could not suppress a little GI humor; as the initial group passed by, our waving handkerchiefs welcomed them to the fray.

Later that day I found out what had happened. In the course of the blackout displacement, the battalion commander, along with his headquarters unit and at least one other battery, had gotten lost. Becoming suspicious, the division artillery executive, Colonel Scithers, had set out to find the battalion. He located Lieutenant Colonel Oram and the others pulled off the road, parked next to an area marked "Achtung Minen." A witness later described the conversation: *Oram*, "Well, we are lost and it's mighty embarrassing." *Scithers*, "It's more than embarrassing, you're relieved!" Soon after dawn Oram was en route to a new assignment, which turned out to be with military government. Within a few hours we had a new commander, Major Clay Collier, a former mule packer who had come up from the ranks.

Scithers knew him well enough to assume that he could find his way around in the dark.

Before long, communication was in to the "lost battalion," and after registration by a forward observer we had our hands full with fire missions. By now Jake had taken over a nearby abandoned farmhouse for the mess and his post. Mills appeared with coffee for the troops to accompany the dry K-rations they carried along for such occasions. In passing by my area, he stopped and pretended to be fixing my collar as if my insignia were slipping off. He handed me a piece of paper that Jake had given him promoting me and the Class of 1944 to first lieutenant as of March 1. Fiddling with my collar had been a ploy for the purpose of pinning on my new insignia. The ceremony for my first promotion was thus presided over by Pfc. Jack Mills of Florence, South Carolina.

By midday Jake was out to spell me, and I headed for his command post to get some sleep. As there was no furniture, I tossed my sleeping bag on the floor and sat on a couple of empty ammo boxes to relax for a few minutes with a cup of coffee. What a relief that we had gotten through the night with no injuries or worse. Was it really only nineteen hours since we had left Montbronn? As I was getting ready to crawl into my sleeping bag Mills appeared again, this time with some letters. One of them I had to read before dozing off—it was from Diana, full of news, upbeat and entertaining. Even so, I was by now almost asleep and slipped it into my pocket for many future readings.

When I returned to the firing battery, I learned that the 100th Division had been given the task of taking Bitche, with the 5th Infantry Regiment of our division in support. The bulk of the 71st division would attack south of Bitche. In the course of the attack we displaced forward several times in the next few days and by the 21st we were firing missions over the German border. The immediate objective ahead was to break through the famous Siegfried Line and to help eliminate the final German pocket west of the Rhine.

Shortly after he occupied the Rhineland in 1936, Hitler ordered the construction of a defensive barrier, which he called the "West

Wall," between Germany and France, extending into the Low Countries. This barrier, known to most Americans as the Siegfried Line, stretched about five hundred miles from Holland to the Swiss border. Its miles of tank barricades, often called dragon's teeth, and pillboxes helped create the illusion of being impregnable to attack from the west. Whatever the reality, the hugeness of it was of immense propaganda value to Hitler both at home and abroad.

During the fall of 1944 some of our First Army divisions had paid a heavy price when they attacked through the Siegfried Line at its strongest point west of Aachen. By the time we arrived to confront its still intact southern portion, we found its defense greatly weakened. The troops and weapons that the Germans needed to man the line were—thanks to Hitler's Ardennes offensive—inadequate in numbers and quality. Just the same, to the north of our division the 3d and 45th infantry divisions had experienced three days of heavy fighting before they succeeded in breaching the line.

The "lucky 71st," and particularly the 14th Infantry Regiment that we supported, hit the line at perhaps its weakest point. We crossed the border at 8:10 A.M. and began moving through the Siegfried Line at 10:30 A.M. As we moved through the line we were sometimes slowed down, sometimes stopped by obstacles. Occasionally, we went into firing position but did not fire. Where had all the Germans gone?

As we passed through the bands of blockhouses, pillboxes, tank traps, and dragon's teeth, I could not help but admire how skillfully the German engineers had used the terrain. We would have paid an enormous price had all this been defended, but the earlier efforts of our troops in other areas made our own Siegfried experience a pursuit rather than an assault.

As we moved east, we could tell that the German forces were fleeing to get across the Rhine while they still could. In retreating, they had created all kinds of obstacles: trees dropped across the roadway, craters were in the road, and blown bridges. To our north the first German city across the border, Pirmasens, had been taken by our division's 66th Regiment with minimum fighting. After getting out of the Siegfried Line area we skirted around the southern edge of that city and picked up the road leading east toward the Rhine.

A few miles down that road we came upon a slaughter. Our Air Force and Corps Artillery had caught some German columns in the open. Strewn about for several miles were hundreds of trucks, wagons, artillery pieces, and even some tanks, in most cases destroyed. We saw many bodies of German soldiers and horses—some of the horses still being put out of their misery—and none of us would ever forget the smell.

For the 14th Infantry and the 608th Field Artillery the specific target on the Rhine was the city of Speyer and its surrounding area. Here we were to prepare for an assault crossing of the river. The other two regiments of the division and their supporting artillery were to target the city of Germersheim south of Speyer, and their mission was to capture the last intact bridge over the Rhine.

Obviously, the goal of the enemy was to get as many of their troops over the bridge at Germersheim as they could, then to destroy it before we arrived. For this the German Seventh Army could be expected to fight like hell, and they did. The main German defense took place at the town of Lingenfeld, where the 71st attacked early on March 24. Bearing the brunt of this bloody fighting that went on until the early morning hours of the 25th, the 5th Infantry sustained twenty-three killed and sixty-nine wounded. Then, at the last minute as our troops got close to the bridge at Germersheim, the Germans blew it; but they, too, had paid a price in killed, wounded, and captured.

While the action was underway at Lingenfeld, we took up firing positions near Speyer and fired our first missions over the vaunted Rhine defensive barrier. In the early morning hours of March 25 the 14th Regiment, not without some casualties, feinted a Rhine assault; our part, along with the other artillery battalions of the division, was to fire continuously for several hours. The feint was to cover the 45th Division's actual crossing north of us. As the morning wore on, we participated, along with perhaps as many as twenty-five other battalions, by shifting our fires to support that effort.

Even further north, Patton's Third Army in a surprise move on March 23, had slipped the 5th Infantry Division over the river without employing either air or artillery support. Though our division had some mopping up operations west of the river for a couple more days, the battles on the Rhine were over. The campaign for central Europe was about to begin.

At this point the 71st had pushed some 180 miles in its first twenty days of combat. B Battery had experienced so many firing positions that we could go from movement on the road into position and be ready to fire almost without any discussion. Working and living with the men of B Battery, usually twenty-four hours a day, made me even more appreciative of the competence and initiative of the World War II artillerymen. It did strike me as an inconsistency that the younger soldiers, though old enough to fight for their country, could not vote or, for that matter, even buy a drink!

Taking advantage of a few days without a move, I had my first shower in almost three weeks in a jerry-rigged arrangement we set up in what was left of a nearby house. Then to the battery "barber" for his best effort (probably more accomplished in his previous occupation as a muleskinner). About that time the B Battery First Sergeant, Bill Summers, whom we rarely saw at the firing battery, appeared searching for Jagoda. Apparently, the battalion commander wanted to see all the battery commanders right then. As Jagoda was not around, I headed out for the meeting. This was the first time I had seen Major Collier, a tall, impressive-looking guy, and what he had to say was most interesting.

Collier told us that this evening the 103rd Division would begin replacing us in our present positions along the Rhine; as soon as our division was relieved, we were assigned to Patton's Third Army! Sometime on the following day, March 29, the 608th would go out of firing positions and move to an assembly area in the town of Rockenhausen north of us. On the following day we would cross the Rhine as part of a Third Army column and then be committed to combat again at a location to be determined.

That was indeed a significant meeting. I headed back to the battery to brief the now-located Jagoda and to get them ready for the new mission. During the next twenty-four hours the forward observer teams rejoined us, and the mail arrived. Though I had no letter from Diana, I did receive plenty of Paterson news from Annie, mainly in the form of newspaper clippings. My sister Daisy recounted the latest on Jim's escapades in the South Pacific and Harry's adventures in the Italian campaign. We also received several back issues of *Stars and Stripes*. We were supposed to receive daily copies of the European edition in sufficient copies to have one for every seven or eight soldiers. I did not recall seeing a copy for a couple of weeks, so during the lull I tried to catch up on the news.

Filling the most recent issues were pictures and articles on Operation Plunder, the far-north assault over the Rhine by British Field Marshal Bernard Montgomery's 21st Army Group on March 23/24. This long-planned operation, employing an American and a British airborne division, had, of course, been overshadowed by our First Army's surprise crossing at Remagen on March 7. Even more to our own delight was Patton's coup in slipping our 5th Infantry Division over the Rhine on the night of March 22.

The night at Rockenhausen provided our first chance for a good sleep and, beforehand, an opportunity for the five battery officers to shoot the bull about on our experiences. I found the forward observer stories, especially Rudy Kehren's, really interesting. Earlier I had mentioned to Jake that this might be a good time for Wheeler and me to change positions for a while, but he declined. We all knew our jobs, so why change, especially as we were going into a new environment? He did promise, though, that later on he would consider making the change.

Early on Good Friday, March 30, we crossed the fabled Rhine near Oppenheim on a pontoon bridge cloaked in smoke screens. At this point every Allied army in the west was passing across this last major defensive barrier of Nazi Germany. In our case, as fate placed us in the final climactic campaign of the European war in the west, chance placed us in the center of activity as part of the most mobile and aggressive of Western armies—Patton's Third.

Because of the fluid nature of the situation on the front, the 71st was initially placed in a concentration area southeast of Frankfurt pending a Third Army decision on where to commit us. Our rest was good but short-lived. Early Easter morning we headed out on a long road march that took us through Hanau and across the Main River. Apparently, a German counterattack had developed in the XII Corps area to our north. Dispatching our forward observer teams out to the 14th Infantry, we moved into possible firing positions. Rumor was that an SS division was headed in our direction.

Nothing developed for us that afternoon, but just before dark Jagoda headed out with a battalion reconnaissance group. Returning in the middle of the night, he gave us the word that we would displace forward at first light to a position at the edge of the Thuringian Mountains. The 14th Infantry expected to make contact with a sizeable pocket of German troops that had been sighted by its reconnaissance unit. As we moved forward, I was surprised but happy to see that we had a tank escort, at least part of the way. This was the 761st Tank Battalion, an all-black unit, which had been in combat for several months but had only recently been attached to the division. When we arrived at our destination, Jagoda pointed out the position area he had selected and then left to find Battalion and get an update on the situation.

As we prepared our weapons for firing, I called the section chiefs together to stress the importance of providing ourselves good security, given the fluid nature of the front lines. Finishing up, I said "Remember Malmedy!" Just then Sergeant Orseske pointed beyond our left front and said, "What the hell is that?" Our field glasses shot up, and what we saw was indeed startling—a horse-drawn artillery unit coming over the crest of a hill to the left front of our position, perhaps 150 yards away. It was obviously a German artillery unit.

I immediately decided that we had to take it under fire to prevent their firing on us or escaping. I told Gliessner to get on a small knoll nearby to act as observer; I would control the fire and we would fire as a unit, not by individual pieces. To the radio operator: "Tell Battalion what we are doing, but I can't talk to them now." After about four volleys we had them—their artillery pieces, horses, and some of their troops were scattered along the road. The remainder fled into nearby woods, where our infantry later neutralized them.

About this time we established wire communications with battalion operations, and I discussed the event with Major Gunn, the S-3. At first he seemed a bit put out that I had acted on my own without clearance. When I explained that it was a question of kill or be killed, he finally agreed that I had no option. It turned out that we had destroyed a firing battery of the 6th SS Mountain Division Nord. Artillery was the greatest killer on the battlefield in World War II, but rarely since the Civil War did our artillerymen get in direct shootouts with opposing artillery.

Our division had spent the first few days of April battling the 6th SS, but what was that unit doing behind the front lines; how had it gotten there? Later an interesting story emerged, in some ways illustrating what by that point had happened to the once-vaunted German Army. The 6th SS had been in Finland until the previous summer, when it was moved to the western front. At that time it was considered the strongest and best-equipped fighting unit of all the SS infantry divisions. Before our contact its last major action had been severe fighting against some of our First Army units along the Mosel River in March. Afterward the remaining eight thousand troops of the division (about one-third of its original strength) were assembled and reorganized in an area northwest of Frankfurt. They then headed out, traveling largely by night, in an attempt to break through American lines and get into what was left of central Germany. Our contact with them (a "meeting engagement" in military parlance) was thus essentially an accident—and, as it turned out, an unfortunate one for them.

For the next several days the 71st was involved in a wild running battle with the 6th SS in an area covering many miles. Every unit of the 71st was committed, along with elements of the 5th Infantry Division and the 2nd Cavalry Group. At one point the SS captured one of our hospital groups, but we managed to recover it. In the end the 6th SS Mountain Division Nord ceased to exist, though many of its members escaped as individuals. Over five hundred SS troops were killed, and several thousand were taken as prisoners. Among our own who also paid a price was my classmate Pierre Bontecou, killed fighting with our 5th Infantry Regiment.

With the captured SSers we had our first look at many fallen supermen. Their faces mirrored a wide range of attitude and emotion: many displayed arrogance, bitterness, hate, confusion, and disbelief; they were counterbalanced by others who showed fear and, in many cases, relief that for them at least it was over.

After the battle with the 6th SS we began to experience a different kind of combat as the enemy's situation deteriorated. The German forces to our north, caught between allies coming from the west and Soviets from the east, could not delay their inevitable surrender much longer. In the Third Army area and to our south the enemy had one other option. They held sufficient territory there to fight a delaying action as their forces retreated toward the mountainous areas of southern Germany and Austria. Once into the mountains, they could conduct a last-ditch battle that might go on for some time. To prevent this, our forces' goal was to fight an aggressive campaign of movement. Given the location of the 71st on the southern flank of the Third Army as it headed east, we would inevitably become crucial to the fighting to the south and east. Meanwhile, the division pushed along with the other units in the Third Army toward the Czechoslovakian border.

Moving into the Fulda area and then further east, the 14th Infantry engaged in many small battles and skirmishes, usually at the platoon level. Although constantly displacing forward to keep up with the infantry, B Battery was not called on for much artillery fire in these actions. In the infantry platoons involved, though, each skirmish meant that a soldier could be wounded or killed just the same as in a larger battle.

By the end of the first week in April the 71st had been in the Third Army long enough to feel Patton's impact, though we were many levels below him. His emphasis on aggressiveness and speed of forward movement put a strain on support agencies trying to keep up with us. Patton set the priorities for these: gasoline was tops with ammunition coming next, then rations; other items, including mail, could follow in their own good time.

By April 7th we were almost able to enjoy the picturesque borderlands of the Thuringian Forest as the 608th took up positions near Kaltennordheim. Soon after we were established in firing position some mail arrived, updating me on Diana's life at Montclair High in the early spring of 1945. About that time Jake appeared, saying that since things were quiet, he would like my help on "something" that evening.

It turned out that "something" was a huge backlog of outgoing mail in need of censoring. Near Jake were a couple of unopened bottles of wine liberated from a warehouse in the town. As I viewed the mail, I could see hours of "Dear Moms" and "Dear Myrnas"; in reality they would need about as much censoring as an O. Henry short story. Time to take the offensive: "Captain Jagoda, since we're short of time let me make a suggestion." He looked at me inquisitively as I continued. "I'll seal the envelopes, stopping to read about every tenth letter, then you apply the censor's stamp." After a brief pause he replied, "Don't bother with the one in ten!" It was a pretty good wine.

The next morning we headed out in the direction of Meiningen. In small villages along the way we witnessed a new phenomenon: bedsheets and white flags of surrender hung out of house windows, indicating that the "thousand year" Third Reich seemed to be reaching the end of its millennium. We should not, however, be misled; this was still enemy territory. Although the enemy was relying mostly on mines, roadblocks, and demolished bridges to slow us down during its retreat, there were still enough snipers to make us cautious.

Meiningen itself fell without a fight. The city had been the center of a resort area favored by residents of Berlin. In my brief time there it impressed me as an interesting place with many handsome public buildings including an elegant-looking opera house. I also noticed something that we were to see more and more in the German cities. Children were slinking along, dodging down side streets and avoiding contact with either Americans or Germans. Apparently their homes had been destroyed and their parents killed or taken away by the Nazis to labor or concentration camps. They lived by stealing and sleeping in hovels.

From Meiningen we turned south and east. Since the battle with the 6th SS, we had moved an average of almost fifteen miles a day; in the process we had become familiar with the oddities of German place names. These frequently began with a prefix such as *ober*, *unter*, or *nieder* (upper, under, or lower) before the base name of the location. Then came endings such as *bach*, *stein*, or *hof*. Put it all together and you had results such as Unterschleissheim, unpronounceable in New Jersey English. For obvious reasons we insisted that when calling for an artillery adjustment, we use initial locations by map coordinates rather than by place names.

On April 10 the 71st, along with the 11th Armored Division, received orders to prepare for an assault on the city of Coburg by the next morning. The artillery prepared to provide supporting fire in the form of heavy barrages in front of the attack. Before the assault began, however, the German authorities in Coburg decided to surrender. As the infantry began screening the town they came across a hospital with many wounded Allied soldiers who had been prisoners. Since we had not known of their existence, we were most happy that we had not had to fire any artillery barrages into the city.

On April 12 the 71st, still teamed up with the 11th Armored Division began moving east and then south toward the city of Bayreuth. Within twenty-four hours came the news of Franklin Roosevelt's death at the Little White House in Warm Springs, Georgia. We felt it personally, as he was, after all, the only president most of us had known (I was in the sixth grade at St. Joe's when FDR was elected). But now we had a new Commander in Chief, Harry S Truman of Missouri.

In the same issue of *Stars and Stripes* covering FDR's death two other stories appeared, the full significance of which took a while to sink in. North of us a Patton armored column had captured Weimar, at one time the literary and intellectual center of Germany and home to such as Johann Goethe and Franz Liszt. The news of Weimar that day, though, concerned our tanks' liberation of a concentration camp, Buchenwald, located in the hills overlooking the city. The news item said that over fifty thousand inmates had been "liquidated" in the eight years of the camp's existence.

A related story told of the Third Army's liberation of another camp: Ohrdruf, in the vicinity of Gotha. Pictures showed a grim-looking Ike walking around some of the three thousand or more corpses littered about where they had been slain by Nazi guards just before fleeing.

These news stories, including the photographs, brought home to us forcefully the kind of tyranny we were fighting. Certainly, mixed in with the war news, we had already seen individual photos of atrocities; but now and in the weeks following, we felt the horror of their nature and scale. My feelings of revulsion and indignation were of an intensity that I had never experienced before.

By the evening of April 13 our 14th Infantry Regiment, teamed up with a combat command of the 11th Armored Division, was in position to attack Bayreuth at first light. Earlier attempts to secure the surrender of the city of Wagner had failed. Even now, despite a preliminary air and artillery bombardment the resistance to our initial attack was fierce, especially considering the stage of the war. By evening of the 14th, though, we had reached the middle of the city; the next couple of days consisted largely of mopping up operations and bagging around eight hundred prisoners of war. Evidently, enemy resistance had been aimed at delaying our advance so that their remaining forces could fall back to make a stand at the Danube, around seventy miles to our south.

A story that came out later illustrates who some of those sacrificed to delay us were. As our troops attacked Bayreuth, an early point of resistance was a machine gun placed so that it was almost impossible to approach. The enemy gunner was as accurate as hell, pinning down our attack for some time until a well-placed mortar round silenced the defender. When our troops advanced, one of them checked the machine-gun position. It contained the remains of a girl about sixteen years of age!

Not all the German resistance at this stage fit into a strategic pattern. For example, while the fight in Bayreuth was going on, a battalion of our 66th Infantry Regiment advancing on the division's west flank chanced on a large airport and aeronautical school. As the battalion's forward elements approached the airport, they were hit with intense small-arms and machine-gun fire. The defenders, who turned out to be both Wehrmacht and Luftwaffe personnel, put up a surprisingly good defense. After a number of casualties on both sides the defenders were overwhelmed and around five hundred of them captured.

On April 16 the 608th moved through the outskirts of Bayreuth, B Battery going into position in the nearby town of Laineck. I was hoping that we would be routed through the middle of the town, as I had heard about the annual Bayreuth festival of Wagnerian music. I knew very little about that nineteenth-century composer, or his music, except that it provided the theme music for Hitler's Nuremberg party rallies. I found out later that Hitler had been a frequent guest at the Wagner home in Bayreuth, where he was known as "our blessed Adolf."

At Laineck we had a day or two to work on the maintenance of our equipment, to write brief letters, and to catch up on our sleep. The capture of Bayreuth and our operations in the surrounding area had brought the division up to the Third Army restraining line for the moment. Apparently, 7th Army to our west and south was finding Nuremberg a major obstacle. Pending developments there, we were held up awaiting further orders, except for our reconnaissance elements; they were always out in front of us.

On April 19 the division was assigned to the XX Corps—our sixth corps since entering combat on March 12—but this time it was for keeps. Our new mission was to attack southeast with the objective of seizing a bridgehead over the Danube in the vicinity of Regensburg some seventy-five miles away. The corps had three other divisions: the 65th, on our right, with the same objective; and the 80th and 13th armored divisions, both initially in corps reserve.

In the terrain between us and the Danube, we came across many ravines and heavily wooded areas. The 13th armored probably could not pass through us (a normal role of armor in a breakthrough) until we were over the Danube. Air reconnaissance indicated that enemy resistance would be mostly at the principal road nets and around the key towns interspersed throughout the area.

The division planned to form the regiments into three self-contained combat teams, each with its own artillery, engineers, tanks, and so on. As usual, we were with the 14th. The combat teams would attack three abreast; they would emphasize speed of maneuver to prevent the enemy from organizing a determined stand on the Danube. Our instructions were to bypass small pockets of resistance, leaving them to the 80th division; in effect, we were spearheading a Patton drive.

The infantry jumped off on the morning of the 19th towards its immediate objective, the town of Amberg some fifty miles away. While moving along, the 14th engaged in a series of small actions against enemy strong points set up to delay our advance. Firing in support, we displaced constantly to stay within range, then moved again as the infantry did. Just as the road net became more limited, the rains came. We had to use winches constantly to get our trucks, and sometimes the howitzers they were pulling, out of the mud. It was a close call whether the Germans or the rain delayed us the most, but by the night of April 22 the infantry had occupied most of Amberg.

With this type of fire and movement we obviously consumed enormous amounts of gasoline and ammunition. Given Patton's logistical priorities, food rations had a hard time keeping up with us, except for the canned C and dry K rations issued to individuals. After a time, when we became desperate for real food, our mess personnel added "food acquisition" to their job description. During the lull after the Bayreuth fighting we even had steak when a cow happened to get "hit by a truck" very close to our mess tent. Then, as we moved south, the mess personnel became very skilled in their new task, "requisitioning" eggs, chickens, ducks, and the like. Fortunately, no one was wounded on these forays; it would have been difficult to justify a Purple Heart for action against a German farmer.

Before getting to the Danube the 71st had to contend with two smaller rivers: the Naab and the Regen. The task of securing crossings of the Naab was assigned to the 5th and 66th Combat Teams by division; our objective in the 14th was the Regen. What the 5th found in the city of Schwandorf after its crossing was all too characteristic of German behavior at this stage of the war. In the city's railway yards the troops found a train of securely locked boxcars, which they broke open. They found a trainload of abandoned Russian and Polish prisoners, who had had no food or water for several days. Many were dead; most of the others were more dead than alive—emaciated and understandably hysterical. Why the hell hadn't the civilians in the towns broken open the boxcars?

Our target on the Regen was a bridge at the town of Regenstauf some twenty-five miles away. Rolling toward it, we ignored opposition when we could or eliminated it when necessary. The town turned out to be heavily defended, and the bridge had been blown up before our arrival. While we fired a heavy artillery barrage, one of the infantry battalions conducted an assault crossing. By late afternoon the 14th was engaged in house-to-house fighting, and by the early morning hours of the 25th we had captured Regenstauf. The entire combat team was in position in or around the town. We did have visitors that night, though: one of the remaining elements of Herman Goering's Luftwaffe strafed the town and also tried unsuccessfully to knock out the treadway bridge our engineers had constructed over the Regen.

April 25, 1945, was a memorable day. Well north of us the First Army linked up with Soviet forces near the town of Torgau. That same day Soviet forces fighting in the Berlin area announced that they now had surrounded the city. Far away in San Francisco fifty nations were meeting to draw up the charter of the United Nations. For the 71st that day came an order from XX Corps to conduct an assault crossing of the Danube in the early morning hours of the next day.

During the afternoon we continued our attack south, finally reaching the north side of the river as daylight faded. As the evening wore on, the infantry and engineers had their hands full moving assault boats and other materials through swampy ground in our area. We did find firing positions on solid ground though from which to fire in support of the crossing.

We had moved so rapidly and so far in the last week that good maps were hard to find. An old map of mine showed the English name of Regensburg—Ratisbon—in parentheses. Where had I heard that name? Then I remembered a Browning poem I had read for Kathleen Westman's class that began, "You know we French stormed Ratisbon. . . ." The poem, "Incident of the French Camp," was based on an event that had occurred during Napoleon's storming of Regensburg in April 1809!

The division plan of attack called for simultaneous assaults by the 5th and 14th regiments. From the north side of the Danube we prepared to support the attack. The B Battery forward observer teams were, as usual, with the 2d Battalion of the 14th. Later, Sergeant Gerv Nash, a member of Lieutenant Persson's team, told me what they experienced in that action.

Originally scheduled for 2:00 a.m. the attack was postponed a couple of hours because of problems getting the assault boats in position for the crossing. They got underway in heavy fog and their boat arrived at what they assumed was the far shore. It turned out to be a sandbar in the middle of the river. Eventually, they retrieved their boat and caught up with F Company of the 14th on the far shore itself.

The company, led by Captain Tom Alvey, encountered German troops in foxholes along the shoreline. Advancing while employing marching fire, the company forced its way through these initial defenders; beyond lay open ground sloping toward the river. About this time the fog lifted, and enemy defenders on top of the slope took F Company under fire. Particularly troubling was a 20 mm anti-aircraft gun and near it a large number of German riflemen firing rapidly. At this point Alvey stood up and shouted, "Let's get the sonsofbitches." His unit's charge overran the gun and the riflemen in a bloody fight with killed and wounded on both sides. Later, Lieutenant Lee Barstow and Pfc. Guillermo Rosas were each awarded the Distinguished Service Cross for their part in the action.

Elsewhere in the 14th and 5th Regiments similar actions were taking place that morning. By late in the day the division bridgehead was secure; a bridge constructed over the Danube behind the 14th permitted support units, including the 608th, to move into the bridgehead by dark. Our crossing had placed the defenders of Regensburg in such an untenable position that on the following morning the commanding general of the city's defense surrendered unconditionally to General Wyman.

On that same day the 13th Armored Division passed in front of us, preparing to lead the next phase of our advance ordered by XX Corps: attack southeast with the objective of meeting up with the Russian forces sweeping northeast from Vienna. That night Captain Jagoda told me that I would replace Lieutenant Wheeler as forward observer beginning at first light the following morning, April 28.

The next morning Charlie Wheeler returned to take over the firing battery as I headed out with my own forward observer team: Sergeant Ed Kortnik of Tacoma, about my age, and Corporal "Johnny" Johnson from Great Falls, Montana, about nineteen. Along with the other two teams from B Battery—Rudy Kehren's and Sergeant Gerv Nash's (which had replaced Norm Persson's)—we were with the 2d Battalion of the 14th Infantry. In our case we usually accompanied one of the platoons of E or F Company, depending on where the action was.

Ahead of us lay the broad valley of the Danube. Cutting across our zone of advance were its three major tributaries: the Isar, Inn, and Enns. Moving farther away from the Danube itself we began to encounter many small valleys and ridges, all of them providing good opportunities for resistance by determined or fanatical groups.

When we arrived at the battalion, it was in reserve awaiting orders to move by vehicle to a point ahead; there it would initiate a probe into enemy territory the next morning. On the 29th, when our infantry set out on foot, we followed along behind one of the lead platoons. I had a close-up look at these now-seasoned riflemen. They walked in a slouch, generally with rifle on right shoulder, helmet pulled down. Underneath that helmet, though, were two bright, alert-looking eyes ready to detect any unusual movement ahead or to the flank. When that happened, or seemed to, the rifle was instantly off the shoulder and gripped tightly with both hands.

In mid-afternoon I had my first combat experience in the role of forward observer. As the column moved along a small road, we heard firing ahead and came to a halt. Moving forward to the location of the platoon leader, our jeep came over a small crest. Just ahead on a slightly higher ridge we saw the platoon leader and perhaps a squad of men. At that point we drew fire from somewhere on the other side of the ridge. The platoon leader waved our vehicle down into a low area; I jumped out and moved toward him while Kortnik got the radio into a transmitting position without drawing fire.

The enemy appeared to be located near the road in a small farmhouse with one or two outbuildings. The platoon leader's location did not give me an adequate field of observation from which to adjust artillery fire, but by crawling over to a nearby clump of trees I had a decent view. Luckily, we had a good map that day, and with Kortnik on the radio communicating with fire direction center, the initial rounds I called for were not far from the target. All the while the firing from the farmhouse kept hitting in the general area of the platoon leader's and my location; fortunately, the ridge line protected us. The next rounds were on target! We fired several volleys, and either we got them or they decided to fight another day—I never did find out for certain. Two riflemen going forward to check found no more firing, and we were waved ahead. Our forward observer team was no longer the new kid on the block.

As darkness overtook us, we halted to rest and to prepare for the next day. Both the 14th and 66th regiments were to move to the Isar beginning about 6:00 a.m. and, after conducting assault crossings, to establish bridgeheads on the eastern side.

Interesting outside news filtered into us that night from some infantrymen who claimed it came from the BBC. Mussolini and his mistress, Clara Petacci, had been executed by Italian partisans the day before; their bodies were displayed hanging upside down at a filling station in the center of Milano. Also that very day German forces in Italy had surrendered!

On a cold, clear 30th of April we had excellent visibility as the battalion started forward. Unlike the day before, the column ran into remarkably little opposition, and by mid-afternoon the advance element reached the Isar. In the crossing area assigned to us, the bridges had already been blown; because of the strong and speedy river current crossing by assault boat was not a feasible alternative. But we did find were the remnants of a railroad bridge dipping down into the river and then coming up again. Sufficient bridge girders remained so that by going hand over hand in the middle part individuals could make it across. The decision was made to try this since there was no evidence of enemy on the other side. We would do without an artillery preparation, which might alert any nearby German units. Just in case, though, the infantry set up a base of fire, including heavy machine guns, on our side of the Isar.

Both Rudy Kehren and I were going across at the same spot. When we tossed a coin to see who would be first, I won. Kortnik and I headed out with the lead platoon, each of us with half of the radio on our backs. Johnson would catch up later with the jeep. Except for the noise of the river below, quiet reigned. Reaching the midpoint, we then moved hand over hand. I could not resist looking down. In the water, caught in the remnants of the bridge, were two dead American soldiers wearing armor jackets; the 13th Armored must have tried to get a reconnaissance element over earlier. Just then a sniper bullet from the far shore whizzed by—Jesus, Mary, and Joseph, there was no place to hide! In what seemed like an instant our infantry fire base on the west bank smothered the area where the shot had originated.

No more shots came from there. One way or another, the sniper had, as we said then, checked out of the net.

We reached the east bank and regrouped. Rudy, who had followed, moved out with a platoon to my left, and I headed up a hill straight ahead with another platoon. Shortly, enemy firing started up ahead. As I caught up with the platoon leader on the ridge, he pointed out a large barn from where the firing had come. As Kortnik assembled the radio, I tried to figure out our map location. We made radio contact with the fire direction center, but there was some confusion on both sides as to just where we were. We finally worked it out, and the first rounds were remarkably close to the target then, fire for effect, end of the barn. Fire direction center was really on the ball.

Fighting continued sporadically for a while as we advanced and by dark our battalion had established a defensive position just east of and partially into the Isar city of Landau. Along with the other two battalions to our right we were part of the regimental bridgehead dug in there about one and a half kilometers deep and about six kilometers wide, awaiting further orders to move east.

The following morning the battalion was essentially in reserve, conducting some mopping-up operations in the Landau area. During that time we heard that Hitler, along with Eva Braun, had committed suicide the day before, April 30, in his Berlin bunker. It occurred to me that this amazing month of April had seen the death of three quite different heads of major states: Mussolini, who had been in power from the early 1920s until deposed in July 1943; FDR and Hitler, both of whom had assumed their offices in early 1933.

By afternoon we were underway again. Enemy resistance was light and very scattered, with the regiment employing what is best described as leapfrog tactics. One or two battalions would move rapidly ahead with the transportation, bypassing resistance where possible. The remaining part of the regiment would move along on foot, mopping up the bypassed defenders; at some point they motored ahead to reverse roles with the other units.

As we were driving along that afternoon, Corporal Johnson, a live wire, wanted to know if I could remember the names of the various places we were passing through. When I stated that I didn't have a clue, he grinned and reached in his pocket to pull out a letter to the editor he had cut out of *Stars and Stripes*. Typical of GI humor at the time, it ran something like this: "After leaving where we were, we got here and not knowing where we were coming from there to here, we could not tell if we arrived here or not. Nevertheless, we are here and not there."

We covered seven miles that day, but at a battalion briefing that night the commander, Lieutenant Colonel Phil Brant, said that pressure was coming from higher echelons—I assumed he meant Patton-to accelerate our advance to the Inn River, some thirty-five miles ahead. Until 1938 the Inn had been the border between Germany and Austria.

Next day brought lousy weather—cold and overcast with two or three inches of snow on the ground. Just the same, we moved along rapidly and ignored, if possible, enemy strong points, leaving them for follow-up units. At that point we began to have to take into account the enemy prisoner problem. What had in recent days been an increasing number of enemy surrenders now became a torrent. All that could be done was to point them to the rear. Along with the gray-green uniforms of the German army, we now saw more and more troops in clothing the color of gunnysacks—Hungarians. Most of them had already been stripped of their arms by the fast retreating SS units. Their faces, though weary, wore faint smiles. We took this to mean that it was much better to be a prisoner of the Americans than of the Russians.

The 13th Armored Division working ahead of us had scouting parties at the Inn by early afternoon. Although the bridges had been blown, two large dams were still intact. The 5th and 66th infantries each sent a battalion ahead with the mission of capturing the dams before they could be destroyed. In each case a vicious battle occurred with the enemy units left behind to destroy the dams; but by midnight we had seized the dams and deactivated the demolition charges. Throughout the remainder of the night and into the morning our engineers labored to make the dams suitable for motor convoys. This they did with wooden planks perhaps slightly wider than eight feet. Troops crossed on foot; drivers of large vehicles were advised to drive slowly and to say a Hail Mary or something equivalent—the Inn was a long way down!

By the afternoon of May 3 the 71st became the first Allied force to enter Austria from the west. The 2d Battalion of the 14th continued on about six miles past the Inn to Freifing, where they prepared to continue attacking the following day. We had not fired any artillery all day, so Kortnik contacted fire direction to verify that they were still in supporting range. They were, in fact, only a short distance behind us.

That evening I looked up Lieutenant Ed Smith, the 2d Battalion operations officer, to get an idea of where from here. Although he did not yet have the detailed operation order for the next day, he knew that the regiment was to continue the attack at maximum speed. He said that the next day's goal was to capture the city of Wels some thirty-five miles distant, including bridges over the Traun River in that area. Presuming that was accomplished, the next goal would be the Enns River, the point at which we were supposed to link up with the Russians!

The movement forward the next day was at first unopposed, but by late morning the 2d Battalion, along with the remainder of the regiment, began to encounter enemy strong points, apparently set up rather hastily; the infantry platoon I was with that day ran into two of these. At the first the enemy defenders apparently had only small arms and were quickly run over by the infantry. The second was more formidable, armed with automatic weapons and mortars. Fortunately, I was able to bring in some artillery to support the infantry assault that overran the German position. Luckily, in neither case did the platoon suffer any casualties.

Don't be misled, though, we were still very much at war and not casualty-free. The previous afternoon we had lost two artillery officers from the 608th, Lieutenant Bill Tyson and Captain Henry Hudgens. Their light aircraft, while on an observation mission over enemy territory, crashed after being pursued by one of the few remaining Luftwaffe fighters. At about the same time as the actions I have been describing, Ed Christl, an artillery classmate, had been killed while serving as a forward observer with the 65th Infantry Division just to our north. Ed, who had been co-captain of the basketball team our first class year, was later awarded posthumously the Distinguished Service Cross for gallantry in action that day.

By early afternoon our column halted in a quiet area not far from the Wels-Lambach highway. I was talking to Kortnik and Johnson and eating a K ration when a puzzled-looking Captain Frank Langer, one of the 608th liaison officers, showed up with his jeep. He was searching for a place called Gunskirchen, which he could not find on his map. It was on mine, though, and only about five miles away. What was happening at Gunskirchen? Having heard on his radio that the 5th Infantry had found a concentration camp there, he wanted to see it. Would I like to go along? Indeed I would. Jumping in his jeep, I left Kortnik with mine. We would probably not need fire missions in our present location; but, if so, Ed was well qualified to handle them.

In about ten minutes we arrived at Gunskirchen Lager. Standing along the road were living skeletons begging for food. Near them were strewn bodies, some dead, some alive, who had tried to flee from the virtual hell they had been imprisoned in. Approaching the camp, we could hardly believe the stench. Inside the gates we walked to one of the nearby buildings which had dirt floors and three-decker bunks. Living and dead were mingled in with each other. Some, too weak to move, defecated where they lay. None of the inmates had had any food or water for several days. The former guards were gone. Troops from our division were trying to bring order and to help in any way possible.

It turned out that these were Hungarian Jews, perhaps fifteen to eighteen thousand, counting the living and dead there that day. Their captors had reduced them to animals. Unable to fathom what I was seeing, I looked over at Frank, who, like me, had tears in his eyes. There was nothing we could do. On the way back to the jeep we did not talk, each reflecting on the horror we had just witnessed. It was one thing to read about something like this, as we all had by now, but to see it—my God!

Sergeant Kortnik was still in the same location when Frank Langer dropped me off. Apparently, the units in front of us had run into a crust of resistance, but by sometime that evening the bridges over the Traun were in our possession. The division was now ready for the final thrust to the Enns about twenty-five miles away. The 5th Infantry set out on that task early on the 5th of May and reached its objective, the city of Steyr, with its bridge over the river, without firing a single shot!

Meanwhile, the other two regiments of the division were trying to get under control the thousands of prisoners who were moving west as rapidly as they could to avoid capture by the Russians. Both Germans and Hungarians, they were at this point equipped with everything from tanks to horses. In one area the division ended up with a full SS Panzer Division. Still with the 2d Battalion of the 14th as I observed this spectacle, I realized that I had probably fired my last artillery mission. There was one more fight; on May 6 the 5th Infantry seized a dam across the Enns and the high ground overlooking it on the east bank. The killed and wounded in that action turned out to be the last war casualties of the 71st Division.

On the 6th and 7th of May a rather remarkable incident ended the combat role of the 71st. General Wyman ordered the 71st Reconnaissance Troop to deploy its platoons east of the Enns River in order to contact the Russian forces. One of the platoons, headed by Lieutenant Ed Samuell, a West Point classmate, saw many German units heading west—but no Russians. Eventually, they ran low on gasoline and engaged in discussion with a German unit about procuring some of theirs. About that time a German major came along and offered to contact his headquarters for help. Eventually, Samuell ended up at what turned out to be the headquarters of German Army Group South, a huge force that included many SS divisions.

Samuell, now located some twenty miles past the Enns, did get the gasoline and a lot more. It seemed as though the Army Group Commander, Generaloberst Lothar von Rendulic, was considering surrendering to United States forces but had to think it over. During the night Admiral Doenitz (Hitler's successor as head of what was left of the Third Reich) ordered him to cease hostilities; thus ended the possibility of a redoubt strategy in the nearby Austrian Alps.

Later in the day a strange convoy wended its way back to Steyr. Ed's reconnaissance platoon escorted General von Rendulic (later tried as a war criminal) and his staff through enemy territory back to our own lines, where the official surrender took place. This is the stuff both of real courage and comic opera simultaneously, but it did happen on May 6 and 7, 1945. It also made certain what was later officially confirmed, that the 71st Division ended the war at "the easternmost point reached by American Ground Forces of any U.S. Army in the European Theater."

About midday on the 7th, division received a message from Eisenhower to all units stating that the German High Command had surrendered unconditionally and that all offensive operations would cease. A couple of hours later the 608th forward observer teams returned to their batteries. B Battery was located at Wolfern, Austria, where Jake had arranged billeting in some houses near the firing position. The two rooms occupied by the five officers even had a "liberated" radio.

The next day we heard Truman's announcement—that this was V-E Day—as well as broadcasts of the wild and spontaneous celebrations from New York, London, Paris, and Rome. Yet, after all the dreaming and wishing for this day that all of us had done, it seemed to come as an anticlimax. Our area had no celebrations. Was it that we couldn't grasp the news quite yet, or were we too tired? Or maybe in the back of our minds was the still-raging war with Japan and the question of what part, if any, we might play in that.

Of one thing, though, we were certain—we were a damn good division. As a historian put it many years later:

> The 71st Division in World War II covered 800 combat miles in a blazing 59 days—it fought hard, moved fast, and penetrated further east than any ground force in the European Theater—and never lost an engagement!

9. An End and a Beginning

The war in Europe, which had been going on for almost six years, was finally over but at a staggering price. Western Europe and the great sweep of Eurasia from the North German plain to Moscow and Stalingrad lay in ruins; the human costs had been even greater. For the 608th, though, that month of our great victory, May 1945, was spent away from the physical destruction. On May 10 our battalion moved to Losensteinleiten, a small village in the foothills of the Austrian Alps. Billeted in a castlelike complex, we remained there while higher levels decided on the disposition of the sixty-eight divisions in the three-million-American military force in Europe.

Meanwhile, the 71st became involved with the new tasks evolving from Germany's defeat. The most immediate was to care for and repatriate the hundreds of thousands of displaced persons (DPs)—former slave laborers, or wanderers, of every European nationality and age group—now in camps established in our division area. Simultaneously, the enormous defeated German military force had to be returned to civilian life. Our division area alone had some hundred thousand POWs to feed, screen and discharge. Some of these, the SS troops, we were not ready to release.

Deciding our own fate were the higher-ups, pushing around pieces of a large-scale realignment puzzle. Certain units were to be shipped to the Pacific war, either directly through the port of Marseilles or through the States; while others would be used in occupation duties in Germany. The thousands of soldiers with the longest time in service were to be returned home for discharge. In short, the American military force in Europe went in a few days from a single mission to myriad ones—a kaleidoscope that would keep changing in the months ahead.

My immediate world remained where it had been for the past seven months—B Battery. No longer concerned with artillery support, the battery now provided its vehicles and drivers to help relocate displaced persons or process German troops into civilian life. Our close-knit group remained the same with one exception, Jake. Transferred to battalion headquarters, he was replaced by their Captain Al Nottingham. The newcomer was an affable guy ("Call me Notty") who had graduated from Auburn in 1942; he had been with the battalion since its mule-pack days.

During our Austrian interlude the five battery officers lived in one large room. Not to worry, though; the fact that one could sleep on a mattress and in the same location for more than one night made it luxurious. Now everyone's first order of business was the mail. I had to catch up with three major correspondents: Aunt Annie, who had bombarded me with Paterson news; sister Daisy, the conduit for exchanging news with brothers Harry in Italy and Jim in the Pacific; and then, in a special category, Diana. That May she was excited about her forthcoming June graduation from Montclair High (a friend in Paterson promised to arrange for a dozen roses to be delivered with my love) and even more by her acceptance at Cooper Union for September.

Given our living arrangements, the battery officers had frequent bull sessions that often included discussions of postwar plans. Rudy Kehren wanted to get back home to Minnesota and into some aspect of agricultural work after a bit more schooling. Charlie Wheeler had one more year of law school at the University of Oklahoma and would then practice in that state. Norm Persson apparently was not going to take advantage of the G.I. Bill; instead, he would go directly into some aspect of banking. Notty wanted to try for the regular Army. Everyone assumed that I was a regular Army guy for life—didn't that go with West Point?—except me. I let it go at that, at least for discussion purposes, but the war had not changed my potential interest in academia or law as an alternative. Our discussions, usually while having a couple of drinks in the evening, were always qualified by a caveat "depending upon what happens in the Pacific."

Since leaving Fort Benning, we had pushed the Pacific war out of our consciousness, but now we were very interested in it. Old issues of *Time* that someone received in the mail, plus troop information kits, helped fill in the gaps. From our perspective the three most significant ground operations conducted by American forces during the past winter and this spring were the continuing campaign in the Philippines and two major island battles, Iwo Jima and Okinawa. Assaulting those two islands had a particular objective: to provide forward air bases for an intensified bombing campaign against the Japanese mainland.

The battle for Iwo, an eight-square-mile island seven hundred miles south of Tokyo, had turned out to be the bloodiest battle of the war in the Pacific. From February 19 to the end of fighting in late March, all but a handful of the 21,000 Japanese had been killed. For the Marines and Navy the cost was 6,800 killed and more than 18,000 wounded. As Admiral Nimitz was quoted as saying of the Americans who fought on Iwo Jima, "Their uncommon valor was a common virtue."

About 850 miles west of Iwo Jima lay the strategically well located island of Okinawa. Almost seventy miles long, it contained several airfields as well as about 75,000 Japanese troops. The 10th Army began its landings there in early April and at first was not heavily resisted. As the forces turned south, though, they ran into a series of defensive lines where the Japanese put up tough resistance. Simultaneously, hundreds of kamikazes attacked the large supporting fleet of American and British vessels. When the European war ended in May, the opposing forces on Okinawa were still pounding away at each other. Though there was little doubt in our minds what the outcome would be, the price in casualties was still to be determined. As any of us in Europe who had a map could see, the next major operation in the Pacific would be against Japan itself. What we did not know was what units or individuals now in Europe would be part of that assault.

Even in our remote area in Austria, routine military life was enlivened by occasional USO shows; and a Red Cross Clubmobile, complete with all the fixings including "Donut Dollies," made occasional visits. We also received announcements about recreation areas available to the troops. Some of these were nearby, such as the Ammer See resorts; others were distant trips to Paris, the Riviera, or Switzerland, all with quotas for both enlisted men and officers. When B Battery received its first quota for an officer to go to Paris in early June, Notty decided to hold a lottery. I won and could hardly wait.

In late May that frequently asked question, "What's next for the 71st?" was answered, at least temporarily. In the first days of June the division was to be moved into Germany as a part of the occupation force. We would be there until early February, at which time we would be redeployed—*where* was undecided at the moment. Division headquarters would be at one of Germany's oldest cities, Augsburg. Elements of the division would be spread around our area of responsibility, some 225 square miles north and west of Augsburg, terminating at the Danube. Once established there, we would take on policing and guard duties inherent in the task of an occupying force. At the same time we would begin a training program for "possible combat duties in the future."

The move out of Austria was quite different from our arrival over the dams a month before. This time we went by motor convoy, exiting the country just east of Salzburg. There we picked up the fabled four-lane German autobahn—one of Hitler's major projects of the 1930s—which presaged our own future interstate highway system. Numerous bridges on the autobahn had been blown earlier but only one south of Chiem See caused us to make a major detour.

There was compensation for the delay, however, as we passed numerous fräuleins walking along the local road who, as my driver opined, had that longing look. By the time the detour ended, I concluded that the nonfraternization policy would have a very short life span in the occupation zone of the 71st.

Before long we reached Munich, that "most German of cities." The name conjured up all kinds of images of the interwar years: the city that gave birth to the National Socialist Party; the scene of Hitler's failed 1923 "beer hall putsch"; and the place giving its name to that symbol of appeasement, the 1938 Munich agreement. That day, though, we saw a city in ruins. We had been told that one-half of Munich had been destroyed; it must have been the half that our convoy drove through.

As the convoy approached Augsburg, the 608th was routed northeast of the city on a rather narrow but paved road toward Pottmes. While the battalion continued ahead, B Battery was diverted off onto a one-lane dirt road ending in a small farming village named Schorn. This was to be our summer home. Waiting there to meet us were Notty and the section chiefs; they and the battery mess personnel had left several hours ahead of us; now with the arrival of B Battery the population of Schorn quadrupled. I barely had time to unpack and get some sleep before I was packing again, this time for Paris!

In that summer of 1945 the trip was neither fast nor easy, but that memory faded as we emerged from the dust-saturated Gare de l'Est into the City of Light. A waiting bus took our group of officers to a Red Cross hotel on the Rue Lafayette. Rooms with private baths, a shave by the barber in the mezzanine, and a string trio at lunch completed our transformation from soldiers to potential boulevardiers, and several of us were off by afternoon to the Champs-Elysées.

Sipping wine at a sidewalk café on the Champs, we made our evening plans; all the world seemed wonderful. For the first time I saw the Arch of Triumph, bulwarked against a blue sky. Commissioned by Napoleon to commemorate his victories, it later came to symbolize France's glory. I could not help but remember, though, a 1940 newsreel of Frenchmen openly weeping as Nazi storm troopers goose-stepped down the Champs-Elysées with the Arch of Triumph in the background.

On this beautiful June day, though, the world-famous boulevard was filled with French autos and an occasional carriage. The café patrons and pedestrians were both American military and Parisians, old and young. It was my first opportunity to observe the residents close up, and they all seemed to be talking and gesticulating at the same time exuding a certain degree of flippancy and warmth. Not far from where we sat was an austere and functional bit of architecture known as a vespasienne, or perhaps more descriptively as a pissotière, into which some men drifted as they passed—their legs remaining visible during their stay inside. Occasionally, as a man entered and his female companion waited at the other end, he would, on emerging, resume the conversation seemingly where they had left off. That, I thought, was savoir-faire.

After dinner at our hotel (the price of meals in Parisian restaurants that spring was exorbitant) three of us set out by Metro for an evening in Paris. Disembarking at Place Pigalle we headed for the Folies-Bergère. There was no longer a nude Josephine Baker throwing bananas into the audience; but the show, combining the erotic with banter from comédienns, was great entertainment for American servicemen. When the high-kicking cancan dancers, complete with sequins, feathers, and pompons had finished their routine, they received raucous applause and shouts from a standing audience.

From the Folies to the Bal Tabarine was only a few minutes' walk; Herb, one of my two infantry lieutenant companions, said that it was a must. We lucked into a good table, and after a couple of cognacs Herb began shouting "Allô, bébé" every time one of the lightly clad dancers went by. It was, said Fred, the third member of our group, time to get Herb out of the Pigalle "danger zone." The Metro closed at eleven, so we took one of the expensive (after Metro hours) taxis about halfway to the hotel and then set out on foot. As we approached our hotel, there they were as advertised: a long line of Parisian ladies of the night—price 1000 francs for officers; 700 for enlisted men, according to the conventional wisdom. "Bébé you and me" was a frequent invitation by the women or, alternatively, they took you by the arm and whispered some sweet little thing in your ear that might have come out of a *True Confessions* circa 1929. With one of us on each side of him Fred and I got Herb to his room for the night—I think.

The next morning two dozen of us boarded a bus in front of our hotel for a day of touring. M. Mirabelle, our dapper guide—bow tie, double-breasted suit, fedora, and unlit cigar in right hand—introduced himself and announced that our first stop would be at the Trocadero. Upon dismounting we posed for a group photo taken in front of the new Palais de Chaillot, built for the 1937 International Exposition. The photo is the only tangible evidence I have of that long-ago trip to Paris. On the right stands our guide, looking like a professor escorting a group of slightly unruly students; on the left stands Herb, my companion of the previous night, looking like someone at a New Year's morning reception wondering how soon he can return to bed. Our group displayed every possible nonregulation combination of service uniforms—the Air Force officers outdoing the Army, with the Navy in third place.

After the photo we walked to the top of the Palais and found ourselves on an enormous terrace, which Mirabelle called the "Mussolinian." The view was great—a real ooh and ah location—but the focus of the guide's discussion was directly ahead of us, the Eiffel Tower. He cited many statistics relating to this famous monument, but the only one I remember now was that someone at the top could see for forty miles on those rare occasions when the Paris weather permitted.

Heading back to the bus, M. Mirabelle commented that we would pause at many well-known landmarks, but that there was time to visit only three. The first was to Napoleon's Tomb, a truly impressive monument in the center of the Church of the Dôme. Monsieur's most memorable statistic was that the emperor's body was placed inside six coffins. The second stop turned out to be Notre Dame and the surrounding area on the Île de la Cité; the final stop was at the Louvre. The Cathedral and the Île interested me, but the nearby Left

Bank even more so. I decided to return there, perhaps the next day. At the Louvre we tourists were hustled through for a quick look at its two most famous holdings: the Mona Lisa and the armless Venus de Milo. As we stood admiring the goddess, she seemed to be looking down on us in amusement in recognition of the brief visit we were making for the record.

My seat mate on the bus that day was Tom, a Signal Corps officer from New York City. An opera buff, Tom wondered if I'd like to try with him for tickets that night to the Paris Opera. Never having been to an opera, I agreed, but after he described that evening's performance, *Faust*, I began to have reservations. Just the same, after dinner I joined him in the very long line of servicemen hoping for tickets. The interior of the building was impressive, particularly the lavish use of so many colors of marble in the grand foyer and staircase. Standing in line and contemplating my relatively brief stay in Paris, I decided that *Faust* could wait. Wishing Tom luck in his ticket quest, I headed out to Boulevard Haussmann, at the rear of the Opera.

I knew what drew me away from *Faust* and out into the streets. All that day riding the bus and viewing the kaleidoscope of Parisian architecture and activity, I began to realize that the landmark most worth seeing was Paris itself—and Parisians. The architecture was a mixture of decades of style. I was struck by the old apartment buildings with their wrought-iron balconies and the Metro stations with their fin-de-siècle signs "Metropolitan." How can one write about a first trip to Paris without sounding ingenuous? In only two days I had found the city of my dreams; it was already Mon Paris, even though I could only speak a few words of menu French!

While getting dressed the next morning I reflected on my self-guided walking tour of the previous evening. Boulevard Haussmann and the many side streets of my wanderings were the chic Right Bank of Paris, and the war had not changed that. The elegance of the apartments, the homes, and the shops themselves remained, from the enormous department store Galeries Lafayette, to the tiny boutiques and art galleries. But the part of Paris I wanted to see today was the Left Bank, glimpsed only briefly on yesterday's tour. First, though, would come a tour to the Palace of Versailles for which I had signed up earlier.

At breakfast I saw a familiar face. Lt. Deward Sims, 71st Division Artillery, had apparently arrived the night before. Since he, too, was taking the Versailles trip, we teamed up—a bonus for me as he spoke passable French. While we had expected Versailles to be large and impressive, we were overwhelmed by the palace and its surrounding grounds, which included the Trianon palaces. Equally striking was the artistry in the three areas of the interior through which we were guided: the Royal Chapel, the apartments of the king and queen, and the Hall of Mirrors. As soon as I entered the Hall of Mirrors I pictured the signing of the Versailles treaty on a June day twenty-six years before. The treaty that was described so memorably and in my opinion accurately, by John Maynard Keynes "without nobility, without morality, without intellect." Of the many statistics flowing from the guide during our tour the only one I now remember was the size of the kitchen staff during the hundred years that the palace housed the royal entourages—two thousand!

Deward, who had attended Emory and Georgia Tech before being drafted, was a good conversationalist with a great sense of humor. On the return trip to Paris our discussion inevitably turned to the division's future. He told me one rumor from Division Artillery headquarters that topped anything I had heard to date. The division was to be moved through Marseilles and the Suez Canal to Australia. There it would be fitted to become part of an American landing force on the Chinese mainland south of Canton. I was skeptical, but he insisted that this option had a basis in fact. All the more reason, I suggested, for him to enjoy the moment and accompany me to the Left Bank later that afternoon. Pretending to accept the logic of this glaring non sequitur, he agreed.

The narrow streets of the Left Bank, with their odd names like Parcheminerie, were filled with American servicemen in that late spring of 1945. By unspoken agreement soldiers and officers did not exchange salutes in this part of Paris; for a few hours we would all be Parisians. Eventually, Deward's and my wanderings took us into an area of cafés with fake marble-top tables and wicker chairs along the sidewalks. Occasionally we stopped for a glass of wine at places featuring music. Time seemed no longer to matter, and I felt not the slightest bit of guilt for not having returned to the Louvre or headed for the elevator to the top of the Eiffel Tower.

We found ourselves on the Boulevard Saint Germain as the bright blue afternoon sky faded into dusk, and we began to pick up the smell of French cooking. The hell with the cost (four or five times as much as at our Red Cross hotel!)—we settled on a small restaurant where an older man sang and a younger one accompanied him with a guitar. From there more walking, then the Metro back to reality and walking successfully past the "Bébé, you and me" crowd lined up outside of our hotel.

My final morning in Paris was dedicated to finding gifts for home. As the Paris branch of the Post Exchange was rumored to have low prices on good perfume, I began my search there. Making purchases, I noticed a large crowd of servicemen clustered around a counter at the far end of the store—a bargain perhaps. The "bargain" was sitting on the counter, legs crossed provocatively, joking with the troops. It was forty-something Marlene Dietrich exuding the sexual mystique that characterized her films of the 1930s beginning with *The Blue Angel*.

In early afternoon I boarded the Luxembourg train for the long, dusty return trip. The last three days already seemed like a dream—but what a wonderful one. I was determined that some day I would return, but whether I did or not I would always remember this gay, inflation-mad, G.I.-filled, beautiful city as it had been ten months after its liberation. Au revoir, Mon Paris!

That summer in Schorn was a strange interlude for us—neither a time of war nor a time of peace. We had finished one war, but would we be going to another? If so, when? Meanwhile, we continued on our daily tasks as part of the occupation forces. Our daily routine reflected that ambivalence. We resumed artillery training on a part-time basis, not knowing if B Battery would ever fight again as an artillery unit and, if so, in what kind of situation? American air and submarine attacks had cut Japan off from outside resources, and the B-29s were pulverizing her cities and factories; hence, in a strategic sense Japan was a defeated nation though it still showed no desire to surrender. The Japanese had substantial reserves of ammunition and over two million troopa in the home islands, whose defeat would require us to invade. As we discovered later, the first phase of the planned U.S. invasion was set for November against the island of Kyushu. The second phase, against Honshu, was tentatively scheduled for March 1946; this assault might involve many of us in the battery. We could be part of the 608th or, as individual replacements, be sent to other divisions if the 71st was not deployed to the Pacific.

Our occupation duties in B Battery usually meant that small groups of men were scattered over a wide area functioning as gendarmes on road patrols and at checkpoints. We also guarded installations such as hospitals, factories, and (the most sought-after of all) breweries. We also participated in a large-scale operation named "Tallyho," which took place throughout the U.S. occupation zone on a weekend in July. Its purpose was to check all persons for proper credentials and all properties for firearms, explosives, and illegal items of any type.

We found many civilians without proper identification in our area, most not even knowing they needed credentials. (I noticed that checking credentials of females from about seventeen to twenty took much longer than the checks of all other age groups.) In the search for contraband we found no firearms but did turn up many American supplies of food, cigarettes, and the like. The source was fairly obvious, notwithstanding the nonfraternization policy forbidding our dealing with Germans except in official matters. Anyone violating it paid a fine of $65 and lost one grade in rank for the first offense. This made sense before V-E Day, but by summer how could it work? Units, including our own, that employed Germans as cooks, housekeepers, and the like rarely filled the positions based on culinary or cleaning skills. In B Battery no one was ever fined for fraternization, perhaps heeding the biblical injunction in John 8:7, "Let him who is without sin cast the first stone." In any event this "look-but-do-not-touch" policy was quietly set aside as the summer progressed.

We all knew that the Schorn summer was a holding pattern for us as a unit and as individuals. This uncertainty, combined with our isolated location, made nonduty activities a top priority in maintaining morale. We had athletics and some practical personal training such as automotive repair, as well as travel opportunities. Sometimes that meant Paris or London; more often the troops took one-day local excursions, such as to Oberammergau, site of the Passion Play every tenth year, and to Hitler's lair at Berchtesgaden. One trip of a different sort—which no visitor could ever forget—was to Dachau.

To get a taste of the States each day, we needed no travel, just a flip of the switch on our liberated radios. Armed Forces Network (AFN) Munich came in loud and clear from early morning to late night. The station carried news, of course, but also music shows with such names as Morning Report, Luncheon in München, and Bouncing in Bavaria. New and old tunes frequently played that summer included "My Dream is Getting Better All the Time," "Paper Moon," "Oklahoma Hills," and, at least twice a day Spike Jones's "Cocktails for Two." A couple of times a week we had a movie in a big barn at Schorn, usually an oldie but sometimes one just out, such as "The Story of G.I. Joe."

Another outlet for us was a battalion newspaper, *The Whirlpool Observer*, on which I served as editor in chief. Milt Small, the battalion operations sergeant, was managing editor and the real ramrod in organizing the reporters from each battery. A great hit with the troops, the newspaper inevitably spawned many letters to the editor with gripes that we published: Why no liquor ration for lower ranks? How come the senior enlisted get all the good furloughs such as to London? While I thought it healthy to publish these, Division Artillery Headquarters deemed otherwise: "Stop publishing the letters or close down." We closed down.

Twenty-four hours after V-E Day came the program established to reduce worldwide U.S. forces by discharging individuals based on a system called the Adjusted Service Rating (ASR). Those with the highest ASR scores would be the first sent home for discharge. A person's score was based on length of service, time overseas, combat decorations, and number of children under eighteen. The magic number for discharge in July, a score of 85 or higher, enabled five enlisted members of B Battery to go home under that criteria. An individual's score could, though, change; for example, in July Rudy was awarded a Silver Star for a combat action north of Bayreuth in April; and Charlie, Norm, and I each received the Bronze Star for heroic achievement in combat actions as forward observers. We thus increased our ASR by five points each—academic in my case since regular officers were not eligible for discharge. For many reasons inequities in the ASR system were inevitable, and aggrieved soldiers lost no time in making them known, usually via Congress. Almost daily that summer *Stars and Stripes* carried an article about some aspect of the ASR system, sometimes prognosticating future changes in score requirements for discharge.

The first floor of the largest house in Schorn served as battery headquarters; the second floor as officer billets. The four lieutenants' billets were two large connecting rooms. Here we slept, stored our gear, and in the evenings read, wrote letters, and played games (Monopoly, for example) that Norm Persson could re-create from memory. The pristine appearance of our rooms when we first moved in soon changed, and they began to exude the ambiance of a Bedouin goat camp.

The Schorn summer provided me with the first opportunity to read in a long time, though books were hard to come by. I began with A.J. Cronin's *The Green Years*, found in one of my bags, apparently a gift of the Red Cross when I had boarded the *Christobal* in January. Very shortly into the book I could identify with the chief protagonist: eight-year-old Robert Shannon, recently orphaned in Roman Catholic Dublin, and sent to live with his mother's family in a small, defiantly Protestant town on the Clyde in Scotland. The plot covered the ten-year struggle (1902-1912) of a youth coming to maturity with its accompanying disillusionment, pain and sometimes joy. Cronin's cast of characters took me back to my Paterson experience beginning with the day of the taxi. This book and perhaps the confidence gained from my war experience enabled me to look back at the Paterson years for the first time with a sense both of detachment and humor.

But the major off-duty enterprise of all of us that summer was letter writing, both to catch up with our other worlds and to stimulate the more exciting corollary: receiving letters with news of home. In my case from Aunt Annie came family news plus word on St. Joe's friends, some of whom had already been discharged; from sister Daisy word that Harry and Jim had enough ASR points to be home and discharged by late fall; and from Lee Lauterbur the announcement that she and George Daoust, my area walking colleague, had become engaged engaged on June 5, the day his class graduated.

Consuming most of my letter writing energies, though, was the correspondence with Diana, who was spending the summer in Vermont. With her graduation photo in front of me, I shifted from my commentary on current events and plans to my hopes for the future. I quoted poetry from, say, Elizabeth Barrett Browning. Then one evening the movie at Schorn was *Hollywood Canteen* directed toward lonely servicemen everywhere and featuring a galaxy of Warner Brothers stars. In the lead role was that hazel-eyed, freckle-faced girl next door, Joan Leslie, whose facial features were remarkably similar to Diana's. As she sang to her serviceman date, Robert Hutton, "Good Night, Sweet Dreams, Sweetheart," I went over the brink. Back in my billet I wrote Diana a love letter of sorts. Reading it the next morning I debated whether to send it. What the hell, off it went! As Cicero, that greatest of Roman orators, wrote over two thousand years before, "A letter does not blush."

From mid-July until early August *Stars and Stripes* featured articles on the summit conference of the Big Three at Potsdam. Truman had, of course, replaced FDR, and in the middle of the conference Clement Attlee replaced Churchill, whose party was defeated in the British election. But Stalin remained, along with his insistence that the Soviet Union dominate Eastern Europe—a *fait accompli* that the conference confirmed. Among the issues considered at the meeting the one that interested us most was the ultimatum sent to Japan demanding its immediate surrender; otherwise, they would face "complete and utter destruction."

The conference recessed for a few days so that Churchill could return home to get the election results, and the senior participants went in several directions. The 71st was tasked with conducting a review for an unnamed dignitary on the afternoon of July 27 at the Munich airport. Though our unit was not involved, Charlie Wheeler and I decided to jeep down and observe the event. From where we stood, we could not see the plane unload its passengers, but by counting the number of rounds fired in the salute we could tell who the dignitary was. The number reached nineteen ("at least Secretary of War Stimson"); twenty; then the maximum possible, twenty-one ("It's President Truman"). Then twenty-two, "What the hell!" From out of the silent crowd came the loud voice of a G.I.: "Jesus Christ, it's Joseph Stalin!" Some red-faced cannoneers had fired three rounds too many; it was Mr. Stimson after all.

Each day in late July and early August brought news of the continuing destruction of Japan by our bombers. Most of the major cities had been essentially destroyed; Tokyo alone had over three million homeless. Still the bombing went on, eight hundred planes at a time, night and day, hitting smaller cities and other targets.

Around midday on August 6, Notty, Charlie, and I were sitting in our small dining room waiting for lunch and listening to AFN Munich. Breaking into the normal program came a bulletin: we had just dropped a single bomb of unprecedented power on Hiroshima; most of the city, including its inhabitants, had disappeared. It took a moment for this to sink in, and we stared at one another in puzzlement. Then someone in Washington read a previously prepared statement from President Truman (he was still on the *Augusta* en route home from Potsdam). The Commander in Chief described the bomb as a scientific achievement based on the release of atomic energy. He went on to warn the Japanese to surrender or to face complete destruction. We did not grasp the full implications of what we were hearing, but one thing we did understand immediately: our war was over, there would be no assault landing on Japan. Looking at each other with smiles reflecting enormous relief, each of us was thinking in his own way, "Let the good years begin."

> Symphonie, symphonie d'un jour
> Qui chante toujours . . .

I was in the dining room of the Hotel Martinez on the waterfront in Cannes; the vocalist, accompanied by piano and some strings, was singing with intensity. Though the food was Army issue, the service and the ambiance were elegant. It was midday on September 4, and I had just arrived at the Riviera on a one-week leave.

Earlier, disembarking at the *gare* with the other officers (the enlisted men continued on to Nice) after a tortuous two-day trip from Augsburg, we were welcomed by the colonel commanding the "Riviera Recreation Area." Standing on a box he delivered a very brief message: "When you get drunk, don't lean on the balcony railings in your hotel; they are quite old. Two officers were killed last month when their railing collapsed. Have a good time."

We stood in line at the hotel registration, where two officers at a time were assigned to a room—in my case with an Air Force captain. Upstairs he asked if I minded if he showered first. Then, afterward, dressed, and with a small tote bag he headed out of the room with, "Don't worry if you don't see me for a while."

During lunch I reflected how much had happened in the month since the Bomb was dropped on Hiroshima. On August 8 the Soviets declared war on Japan and moved their armies into Manchuria. The following day came our second atomic bomb, this time on Nagasaki. That was enough. On August 10 the Japanese offered to surrender, and by the 14th the final terms were worked out; meanwhile, the Soviets invaded Korea, and on the 26th our own troops arrived in Japan. Then, September 2, while I was en route to the Riviera, the formal surrender ceremony took place on the battleship *Missouri* in Tokyo Bay, where the U.S. fleet was anchored. The most destructive war in human history was over.

After lunch, and into swimming trunks, I headed out across Boulevard de la Croisette and onto the beach with its arresting display of scantily clad French womanhood. Finding a spot on the sand to take in all of this, I ended up next to an officer who seemed to be asleep.

Settling in, I noticed a book face down between us, opened apparently where he had been reading. Happy to find anything to read at that point, I picked it up and started in where he had left off on the first page of Chapter 18.

> . . . to live in the world at all is to be committed to some kind of a journey.
>
> If you are ready to go and cannot, either because you are not free or because you have no one to travel with—or if you have arbitrarily set a date for your departure and dare not go until that day arrives, you still have no cause for concern. Without knowing it, you have actually started. On a turning earth, in a mechanically revolving universe, there is no place to stand still.

Wow—powerful! The author was William Maxwell and the book *The Folded Leaf.* The title intrigued me. Looking back at the front materials, I found its origin—Tennyson's "The Lotus Eaters" ("Lo! In the middle of the wood, the folded leaf is woo'd out from the bud")—though not yet its relevance to the novel. About the time I finished the four or five pages of the chapter, the book's owner awakened and held out his hand. "I'm Ed Morris." A lieutenant in the Transportation Corps, Ed had been in Europe since just after D-Day and now had enough points to anticipate heading home to Virginia in October. He had arrived in Cannes the day before. A friendly guy, Ed was well versed on the various tour possibilities, although he had not yet taken any. He mentioned Grasse with its perfume industry; a bus tour to the east through Nice and along the Grande Corniche overlooking among other places, Monaco; and the island of Sainte-Marguerite in the bay in front of us. I expressed an interest in the last two, and we decided to do those together during the next couple of days.

Unlike Paris, where leave groups went in every direction when not on tours, activity on the Riviera focused on the Recreation Area hotels, including the Carlton to the east of the Martinez and the Majestic a few blocks in the other direction. Each had a bar, and in the evenings a full orchestra played. Tables lined the front all along that elegant promenade, La Croisette, bordered with palm trees and small gardens.

The evenings provided a great opportunity to meet officers from many different divisions. At the Carlton the first night I sat with a couple of lieutenants from the 9th Division. That division had fought in North Africa in the fall of 1942, Sicily in July 1943, and northern Europe since June 1944. Most of the original officers had, however, long since disappeared, one way or another. My companions—typically for that time frame—joined their units during the last phase of combat.

The few women we saw at the bar were mainly nurses and WAC officers bussed over from the hotel for women officers at Juan-les-Pins. The females who caught my attention were the French mademoiselles strolling along La Croisette.

The hotel bars closed in sequence: the Carlton at 12:30 A.M., the Martinez at 1:00 A.M., and the Majestic at 1:30 A.M. Reaching the Majestic that first night, I sat down with a group of lieutenants from the 3d Armored Division, a unit that had arrived in France two weeks after D-Day. By the time I joined the group it was after midnight and they had reached the singing stage. At one point the song was "Lili Marlene," that nostalgic German melody picked up by Americans from the Afrika Korps during the winter of 1942-43. Wait a minute. Though the tune was "Lili Marlene," the words were different. Because they so depict what was on the mind of most Americans in Europe that September and since I never heard the words again, I repeat them here.

Please Mr. Truman,
Won't you send us home?
We have fought at Aachen and we fought at Cologne.
We have defeated the Master Race,
We know you've got the shipping space,
So why can't we go home?
So why can't we go home?

Our bus tour the next day covered in a general way much of the French Riviera, that is, the Mediterranean coast between Cannes and Menton near the Italian border. After cutting through a portion of Nice along the waterfront, the bus headed up to the Grand Corniche with its superb view. At the many stops the guide discussed the towns and areas below. He timed the stop for box lunches to give us an eagle's view of that Grimaldi family preserve—Monaco.

Unlike officers' drinking-time discussions, which tended to feature war stories, the talk on this trip was mostly about where from here in personal lives. Almost all planned to take advantage of the G.I. Bill; beyond that, interests ranged over a wide spectrum of careers, sometimes more than one career by the same person. I began to envy the open road ahead that most had, or felt they had. I was obligated to the Army until the summer of 1947.

As we discovered that there was no tour to Sainte-Marguerite, the following morning Ed and I rented a pédalo—a kind of bike boat—and pedaled the half-mile or so out to the island. A national prison in the seventeenth century, it is best known as the place where the "man in the iron mask" was incarcerated from 1687 to 1698. What I knew of that episode came from a 1939 movie roughly adapted from the Dumas classic. After a long, frustrating conversation with the French caretaker, which did little to clarify the identity of the prisoner, I regretted having raised the topic. He was still talking as we headed back to the pédalo.

Sometime in the course of the week in Cannes I decided that this was the time and place to get rid of one bugaboo—my virginity. Although I had desired women for many years and had long since learned the pleasure of encircling a woman's waist while running a hand along her leg or feeling a breast, I had not yet done what I really wanted to do—go all the way. I am uncertain what caused this undue reticence. I suspect that it had to do in part with my being brought up by three older women with no siblings around. Perhaps even more controlling were the nuns and priests of St. Joe's with their discussion of mortal sin and how it flowed from violations of the sixth commandment. Whatever the cause, it was time for this rite of passage.

On Saturday evening I was sitting in front of the Carlton with one of my 9th Division acquaintances while we both observed the mademoiselles as they passed. In a vague way I had communicated my objective to him. After a while an attractive girl in shorts stopped near us and was taking in the hotel orchestra. My friend said, "Let's go." There followed some brief greetings in a French/English melange, and shortly the three of us were sitting on the wall overlooking the beach. Before long he glanced in my direction. I nodded, and he handed me a condom behind her back as he excused himself.

The two of us headed down the beach; without any preliminaries she lay down, proceeding to give me some lessons on what it was all about. We were there a long time, and gradually each of the orchestras at the three hotels finished playing. About two A.M., when she decided it was time to leave, I walked her home, a nice house surrounded by a large fence. As we parted, I asked if she wanted to get together later that day. She said no. Apparently, each of us had accomplished our goals that night—she as teacher, I as pupil.

The next morning I saw Ed off on his return trip to his unit located somewhere near Le Havre. He promised to send me his copy of *The Folded Leaf* before leaving for home in October. On returning to the hotel room, I found my roommate, whom I had not seen since our arrival the previous Tuesday morning. He looked absolutely exhausted, stating only that he wanted to rest before his trip back to Germany. It dawned on me that five days dedicated to the type of activity I had experienced for a few hours the night before would indeed be debilitating. A verse of Robert Frost's from his poem "After Apple-Picking" came to mind:

> For I have had too much
> Of apple-picking: I am overtired
> Of the great harvest I myself desired.

I began at that point to think about my own trip back to the 71st starting the next day when I would be facing a return to a new situation. The war's end had accelerated the deployment process both of units and of individuals; it also set up many transfers for those remaining. Charlie Wheeler had already transferred to an activity near Nuremberg, and Rudy Kehren had gone to Battalion Headquarters. Just before I left for the Riviera, Notty had informed me that both of us would also be going to Battalion Headquarters when I returned. He would be Executive Officer; I would be Adjutant. Later in the fall I would take over as Headquarters Battery Commander. Moreover, sometime in September the 608th would be taking over a larger occupation area with the headquarters to be located at Dillingen on the Danube River.

Dillingen an der Do-Nau, a Bavarian town with a population of about twelve thousand and a history going back to the thirteenth century, became the home of the 608th during that fall and into the first part of winter. The 12th Armored Division had captured the town in April; and since our division's return to Germany from Austria our 66th Infantry Regiment occupied it. As a result of the regiment's life style we inherited first rate facilities: good billets, our own movie theater, a well-equipped gymnasium, and a Red Cross coffee shop complete with "Donut Dollies." We also inherited a large displaced persons (DPs) camp, Leopold Kaserne, whose occupants were mostly from Poland and the Baltic states.

Though each division had unique experiences in the occupation, three major realities affected the way our forces as a whole went about their tasks during the first year after the war. The realities were Germany's physical destruction and its resultant inability to produce and distribute food and other necessities of life; the plight of displaced persons, particularly those from Eastern Europe wandering around the devastated landscape; and the disintegration of the American Army in Europe in the fall of 1945.

Bombed around the clock for months, its ancient and beautiful cities incinerated, and invaded by armies from east and west, Germany was in those days a desolate place. Almost all food supplies had to be brought in from the outside and thousands more would die as famine and disease swept through the country that fall and winter. The deprivations affected all age groups and classes of Germans; in the streets of the major urban areas homeless children wandered, frequently without shoes or adequate clothing. With industry at a standstill, few jobs existed other than clearing rubble. The black market flourished, as treasured Leica cameras and other personal effects were traded for food. Cigarettes from the American post exchanges replaced the mark as the coin of the realm. (It should be added parenthetically that Eastern Europe, thanks to the German war machine, suffered even more.)

Across this ravished landscape moved millions of DPs, trying first of all to find something to eat and then to get home, if they still had one. These people, representing practically every nation in Europe, had been taken to Germany to labor for the Third Reich's war effort. In the month that the war ended, the Third Army area alone had over 900,000 DPs. The number gradually decreased over the summer and into the fall, then stabilized at approximately 400,000, even with the repatriation of thousands each month to Eastern and Southeastern Europe. It was not difficult to figure out the reason for the continued arrivals into the American zone, when one considers the options. Maintaining the camps and feeding the DPs remained a major problem for the occupation forces. The camps themselves were administered by an agency with the cumbersome name of the United Nations Relief and Rehabilitation Administration (UNRRA), established by some forty-four nations in the late fall of 1943.

Shortly after V-E Day, American military personnel started to be redeployed for manpower needs in the Pacific war. Then, with Japan's surrender, the main goal became simply to return individuals to the United States for discharge as rapidly as possible. The pace of return exceeded all earlier estimates; combined with a halting flow of new replacements, occupation units became short both in numbers and quality of manpower. For an idea of the numbers involved, consider the following: On V-E Day the strength of American armed forces in Europe was three million; by November it was one million; by January 1946, 600,000.

Stars and Stripes carried daily articles on the rising demand at home for rapid demobilization and, in time, of demonstrations by members of the armed forces, at first in the Pacific, then in Europe, mostly in Paris and Frankfurt. The net result was that many units, perilously degraded, were unable to carry out their occupation mission; and frequently, too, their discipline broke down. In November, a few days before he left Europe to assume his duties as Army Chief of Staff, Eisenhower addressed this matter. In a letter to all unit commanders he said that U.S. forces were acquiring "a bad reputation that will take our country a long time to overcome." By mid-January the protests and overt breakdowns in discipline in Europe ended, thanks to the firm approach ordered by General Joseph McNarney, Ike's successor as American commander. Still, many months would pass before many units could perform their mission adequately.

In the 608th we felt the impact of these problems only indirectly. To begin with, Dillingen was neither urban nor destroyed. In addition the DP camp at Leopold Kaserne was fairly stable and its problems not unusual. Finally, our personnel distribution was such that those heading home for discharge left gradually throughout the fall and early winter. For this reason the 71st was among the final half-dozen divisions designated to remain in the occupation, at least for the time being. With this status came a real morale builder: members of the division were still eligible for promotion.

Our living arrangements were the best to date. We company grade officers had a small house with our own dining room and frauleins to handle the cooking and housekeeping. Opposite our quarters was a convent in which Headquarters Battery was billeted on the first floor. On our other side was a small park, near which Collier, now a lieutenant colonel, and Notty, soon to be a major, had their quarters in a large house. About once a week we were all invited for a social evening there.

Our occupation duties that fall were fairly routine, usually requiring small groups of soldiers for guard duty, road patrols, and logistical support of the DP camp, or for providing drivers and trucks for moving personnel or supplies. My own work in the headquarters was handling personnel matters or acting as the liaison officer with that great rumor factory, Division Headquarters, in Augsburg, about thirty miles away by jeep. In short, this was a good time to relax, to write letters, to begin thinking about the future, and to do some reading. One welcome book, *The Folded Leaf*, arrived in the mail from Ed Morris just as he left for home. Although the title page had a nice note, there was no forwarding address and hence no further contact.

Letters that fall increasingly brought news of my two brothers and old friends being discharged and resuming their lives in one fashion or another, many using the GI Bill. My main correspondent was still Diana, though understandably her letters became less frequent as she was now a freshman at Cooper Union Art School and commuting daily from Montclair. Her letters told of new experiences and new friends, and I realized that I would have some competition, especially as veterans returned to school. I did ask Lee Lauterbur to contact Diana, and they got together in New York a couple of times, once backstage when Lee was still dancing in *Carousel*. Beyond that, my romance was mostly in fantasy land, at least until that day I could arrange to get myself back to the States. Perhaps not surprisingly, one of my favorite songs that fall was a new one, "Love Letters":

> "Love letters straight from your heart
> Keep us so near while apart . . . ."

A major program in Europe that fall boosted the quality of troops' off-duty time. Special Services sponsored, among other things, division-level sports competition, USO-sponsored performances by star performers, and Broadway plays. Listings in the division weekly newspaper, the *Red Circle News*, that fall included such announcements for topnotch entertainment as the Jack Benny show, singer Paul Robeson, the Radio City Rockettes, and plays such as "Blithe Spirit," and "Night Must Fall."

The troops were especially enthusiastic about the division baseball and football teams; they listened to the games on AFN Munich or attended in person. By early fall the 71st Nine, with aces like pitcher Ewell Blackwell (who later starred for Cincinnati), and playing before audiences of fifty thousand soldiers won the Third Army Championship. The team went on to be runner-up for the all-Europe crown. Football was equally or even more spectacular for us. Coached by Captain Sam Bartholomew and with a back like Monk Gafford (both had been All-Americans at Tennessee and Auburn respectively), the team won the European championship. All of this was a welcome diversion for most of the former warriors whose main Christmas wish was "Please Mr. Truman, Won't you send us home?"

For a time that fall the European news spotlight shone on Nuremberg, site of a legal proceeding without precedent. On November 20 there began the trial of Hermann Göring and twenty other ranking officials of the Third Reich for "crimes against humanity" and for waging aggressive war. On the evening of the second day as we listened to AFN Munich reporting on the proceedings, I was particularly impressed with the eloquence and, at times, Victorian style of the chief U.S. prosecutor, Robert H. Jackson, on leave from the Supreme Court. He emphasized the legitimacy of the court: to establish for the record that it was not a proceeding controlled by victors' vengeance but rather a legitimate pursuit of justice—"to put the chalice to their lips would be to put it to our own as well."

Later, after discussing the broadcast, Rudy and I decided we would like to visit the trial. A call to our former B Battery colleague, Charles Wheeler in Nuremberg, soon led to word that he had two courtroom passes for us on the morning of November 27, and that we could spend the preceding night with him. Charlie was assigned to a Transportation Corps unit with his office and quarters in a railroad station called Nuremberg Dutzendteich.

We had a fun reunion at his quarters on the night of the 26th. It turned out that the station was close to Dutzendteich Park, site of the huge Nazi Party conventions from 1933 to 1938. We headed there early next morning to find a huge, desolate field. Still standing were the poles that once carried enormous banners and, up high, the massive marble platform from which Hitler addressed the throngs. Closing my eyes, I was back in a Paterson theater in the 1930s looking at a newsreel—a Wagnerian spectacle with torchlights, martial music, little blond boys beating drums, Hitler in a tirade, and afterward the mass of people shouting *Sieg Heil!* I opened my eyes; it was all gone. Time to head out to view the remnants of Hitler's Nazi leadership on trial for their lives.

Crossing Nuremberg to get to the trial, Rudy and I were astonished at the city's destruction, far worse than we had seen in Munich. The city had been bombed eleven times and finished off by the artillery of our 3d and 45th divisions in five days of house-to-house fighting. We found out later that less than 15 percent of the buildings and only 35 percent of the population remained. As we headed toward the entrance of the Palace of Justice, we noticed two British soldiers in dress uniforms, busbies on their heads, standing guard at the entrance. On our approach they came to Present Arms with much eclat, and we stood aside for whatever dignitary was behind us. To our surprise, there was no one; so—two sheepish lieutenants in field uniforms—we returned the salute and headed inside.

Our seats, slightly elevated, gave us a good view of the crowded courtroom. When the trial resumed, we noted the twenty-one defendants to our left front with their defense counsels. On the opposite side of the courtroom sat the justices of the four nations: Britain, France, the Soviet Union, and the United States. Directly in front of us was the prosecution staff. That morning was taken up by an assistant U.S. prosecutor droning on as he introduced a series of documents, not by reading them but by simply identifying each. Before long I tuned him out and began studying the personalities in the courtroom. I noticed that one of the American MPs was a lieutenant who looked familiar. Could it be Dick Nalle, a G-2 classmate?

At the break I headed down the steps to the gate leading into the main courtroom and asked to see the lieutenant. Yes, it was Dick. Would we like to walk through the main courtroom? Indeed we would. In a moment we were walking in front of the defendants, who were talking to one another or to their counsel, except for Rudolf Hess, who remained seated, looking straight ahead. Göring was easy to recognize even though he had lost, Dick said, 120 lbs. and his uniform coat was stripped of all but buttons. Of the others I recognized only Hess, von Ribbentrop, Keitel, Jodl, Raeder, and Dönitz. When the court reconvened, Rudy and I left to head back to Dillingen. The trial's outcome would be months away, and appreciating its legacy would take years; but as we drove away we were convinced we had viewed, however briefly, an event of historic importance.

By early December I was in command of Headquarters Battery, finding it quite a different experience from a firing battery and much more banal. We rarely functioned as a unit, as the troops were spread out on a variety of tasks such as manning the battalion staff, repairing telephone lines, helping out at the DP Kaserne, and driving our trucks for everything from hauling people to disposing of excess property. We did have one experience as a unit that month, beginning one Monday morning with a 3:00 A.M. reveille and, an hour later, an unannounced inspection of the DP camp. We were looking for contraband. After surrounding the Kaserne, we sent a team into each of the barracks, where they seized a significant number of verboten items, mainly pistols and knives. There was another discovery: One of our corporals, missing at the early reveille, was awakened to look not into the gentle features of his female companion next to him but at the scowling visage of the first sergeant. Oh well, privates rotated back to the States on the same schedule as corporals did.

Our work in Dillingen brought us into official contact with nondivisional agencies such as the local military government detachment and, in particular, UNRRA, which administered the DP camp. We also had personal contact with some of the local UNRRA officials, since three of them were attached to our mess—Bill Cullimore, a former British major; Jim Davis, an American; and Connie, also an American, a good-looking redhead about my age. We soon discovered that Connie was a lot more fun when Bill was tied up elsewhere for the evening. On such nights the après dinner period became the highlight, at least for a couple of us, but the situation did not lend itself to developing what was on our minds, including, I suspect, hers.

Perhaps the most memorable character I got to know in the Dillingen days was the battalion personnel sergeant, Robert Holmes Beck. The Holmes, it turned out, came from his mother, a distant relative of Oliver Wendell Holmes. On meeting Bob my first day in the headquarters, I found him interesting, witty, and very personable. One day when I asked him where he had gone to school, he told me about his undergraduate degree at Harvard and Ph.D. in history from Yale; he was just into his teaching career when drafted. "Why are you still an enlisted man?" I asked. Smiling, he answered, "Just lucky, I guess." He left for home when I was battery commander and stopped by for a final chat. Assuming that I was going to make the Army my career, he gave me a final word of advice, rendered in, of course, Latin: "Don't let the bastards grind you down."

George Patton, our Army commander (by now an American folk hero second only to Ike in popularity among the U.S. generals of the European war) dominated the news on two occasions that fall. The first event was probably inevitable at some point, given the old warrior's personality; the second was tragic.

On September 22 at an informal press conference Patton was faced with a loaded question: why were there Nazis still in government positions in Bavaria? His answer was reasonable except for one sentence that, taken out of context, became a political bombshell: "The way I see it, this Nazi question is very much like a Democratic and Republican election fight." Naturally, the story made many stateside papers as well as our own *Stars and Stripes*. On September 28 came the main fallout of the story. Ike gave Patton a new assignment: leaving his beloved Third Army, he would take over the Fifteenth Army, a small headquarters with the mission of preparing a history of the European war. The story broke in the *Stars and Stripes* on October 2 with the headline "Patton Fired." On October 8 Patton turned over his command to Lieutenant General Lucian Truscott, who had most recently commanded the Fifth Army in Italy.

On December 9 Patton reappeared in the news, this time as a victim of an auto accident near the city of Mannheim. His injuries, involving the spinal cord, were critical. For the next twelve days we heard occasional reports on his condition from the 130th Station Hospital near Heidelberg, then the announcement of his death on the evening of Friday, December 21. On the 24th Patton was buried in the American military cemetery in Hamm near Luxembourg City. He would be near the soldiers of his beloved Third Army who had fallen in the Battle of the Bulge. Although he was a controversial figure, many considered General Patton the greatest American combat commander of the twentieth century.

Even though we were far from home, most of us had our best holiday season in years. Bavaria is the Germany of oom-pah-pah bands, lederhosen, fairy tales, and long Christmas seasons. Despite the shortages of goods and transportation, all of us in Dillingen tried hard to make this a happy holiday. Through military government we were invited to many German and UNRRA events, especially concerts and recitals in the Studienkirche (academic church). We also assisted UNRRA in their sponsorship of several parties for displaced persons and, of course, had our own events in the 608th. The most fun were the jointly sponsored parties for German and displaced children. Here we all pitched in, particularly the Army chaplains, who throughout the year spent much time in guiding and assisting children.

The final event of the season was a New Year's Eve party for the 608th officers, hosted by Notty, the Battalion Commander since Collier had left for home. Returning to my quarters and getting ready to turn in, I found captain's bars sewn on my pajamas, thanks to our frauleins. What characters! They had discovered my promotion, effective January 1. Private Jack Mills had pinned on my first lieutenant bars during the Battle of Bitche, and now some housekeepers had presided at my promotion to captain. I wondered if I stayed around long enough to become a major what high-ranking official would handle that.

As January moved along, more and more of my old friends, including Rudy, left the division. I was the last of the old B-Battery group from the Benning days. Finally, in late January I received orders to the 9th Division Artillery, effective early February. I was not overly excited about that, as they would be doing the same mundane chores that we were handling in Dillingen. Then one evening a call came from Harry Grace, recently assigned to Third Army Headquarters. They had a job there in G-1 (Personnel). Would I be interested? Indeed I would.

On February 7 I set out by jeep for my new assignment after a short visit with Notty. He was taking the battalion home, where in early March it would be inactivated along with the division. I asked him what general was going to take the division home. None, he replied; it would be a colonel from the 9th Division that neither of us had ever heard of—William Westmoreland. As we headed down the autobahn to Munich, before turning south to Bäd Tolz, it occurred to me that the real 71st had already left, one soldier at a time. In another sense, though, my sixteen months in the division would always be with me. Even when the battles faded from memory, I would always remember the names and faces of the soldiers as they were in 1944-1945.

Third Army headquarters blended with the foothills of the Bavarian Alps, near the village of Bäd Tolz about twenty miles south of Munich. The headquarters complex occupied some forty acres in what had been a school for Himmler's SS. The main building comprised about nine hundred rooms; besides the offices it contained dining rooms, a swimming pool, a gymnasium, a movie theater, and a library. Third Army lived well.

Upon checking in I was told that, beginning next morning, I was assigned to the Strength Control Branch of G-1. I headed for the village to arrange a billet in one of the hotels that Third Army controlled. When my driver left me off, I had a final look at the jeep with Diana's name painted on the front. No doubt by that night it would be renamed Maisie or Wilma or something else by *droit de seigneur*.

Strength Control took up two adjoining offices. When I walked in next morning, all of its many telephones seemed to be busy or ringing. The branch chief, Major Orwin Talbott, began by introducing me to my colleagues: Captain Cunningham, Lieutenant Scoville, and Mr. de Coursey, a civilian. Talbott had been with the 90th Division from Normandy until it returned home in November; the others, including then-Sergeant de Coursey, came from various units, all now inactivated, just as the 71st would be in another month.

I learned that Strength Control, military jargon for manpower allocation, was at that point responsible for two major programs. The first was to reassign soldiers with enough discharge points to units returning to the States (such as the soon-to-depart 71st). For Third Army this meant about twenty thousand soldiers a month for the next six months. The other program, a new one to me, assigned replacements to an organization called the U.S. Constabulary, which would become active throughout the American occupation zone on July 1.

Planned as a corps-sized force of about 31,000 officers and men, the Constabulary was charged with maintaining security in the U.S. occupation zone. This entailed active patrols, checkpoints and road blocks, and border control posts. The new organization was being created largely out of existing units, which we would then bring up to an authorized strength. Its designated commander, Major General Ernie Harmon, a protégé of Patton's, had a reputation for ferocious speeches loaded with every known profanity as well as some that he invented. To fill this force we needed all the manpower we could get our hands on. When the Constabulary was fully manned, remaining troops would be able to support only one of the three American divisions then in Europe. Well, there were no more enemies to fight, right?

After giving me a general description of branch activities, Talbott asked that I begin by developing what he called a policy file. As source material someone had dumped a pile of messages, letters, and miscellany on my desk. Though this seemed a strange way to begin, I assumed that he considered it the best way to get me involved. In any case, the project took until the following afternoon, a Saturday. After discussing and clarifying some of the more anomalous policies, especially about redeployment, we called it a day and headed out until Monday morning.

That evening Harry Grace took me on a tour of the four or five hotels occupied by Third Army officers. Each had a fairly elegant dining room and a well-appointed bar. Life in Bäd Tolz, though not quite *la dolce vita*, appeared luxurious compared to anything I had experienced. On our tour I was struck by the large number of majors and lieutenant colonels and by the relatively few company grade officers. Harry, who was in the officer assignment business, said that this was true of higher echelons generally. He also pointed out that many of these officers were only two or three years older than we were; this discrepancy in rank was based on the date of entry into the wartime military. The gap was, however, going to remain that way for many years now that wartime promotions had ended. Something to think about when one began to make decisions about one's future.

Back at the office on Monday morning I found everyone grouped around Major Talbott, who was dressed in pinks and greens. "Going on a trip?" I asked. "Going home; came up rather suddenly," he replied. After his quick departure I began to understand the rationale for my hurry-up project on the policy file. I soon saw the real reason. Sitting down next to Cunningham I indicated my willingness to help him in every way but mentioned that I needed a bit of time to get a feel for the operation. He smiled as he asked if I had looked at the dates of rank. When I looked puzzled, he added, "You rank me by a week." Just then I was summoned to report to the G-1 Colonel Nelson Dingley III. After a ten-minute homily he told me that I would be the branch chief since, as of now, he had no senior officer he wished to put in the job. He went on to remind me that it was a lieutenant colonel's job; thus, I might be replaced at any time. *Couldn't come soon enough*, I said to myself on leaving his office.

Actually, it worked out fine. De Coursey, a hard worker, really knew the ins and outs of redeployment, and the other two were into the problem of manning the Constabulary. I jumped back and forth until I felt at home in both areas, but my major function was working with the other agencies. Much of this was by telephone to the U.S. Forces headquarters in Frankfurt or to the divisions and the embryonic Constabulary headquarters in Bamberg. Within our headquarters I represented G-1 at staff meetings when the issues related to Strength control. Afterward, I would debrief Dingley the Third when a decision was needed at his level. On occasion he disagreed with my recommendation on a course of action. When I felt that logic was not on his side and continued the discussion, he always ended such sessions with, "Well, that's the way the great white father wants it." The first couple of times I assumed that he meant General Truscott, the Army commander. Later it dawned on me that Dingley was the great white father and was using a dialectical stratagem to avoid offending this young and inexperienced staff officer.

Since most of the officers on the Third Army staff did not have personal transportation, our lives off-duty centered around the headquarters Kaserne or the village hotels. Many used the gym and pool routinely; others, including myself, who had had enough of that for a while, were more likely to be found in the well-stocked special services library. One interesting by-product of village life was the chance to meet more senior officers on an informal basis, usually at cocktail time on weekends. One bar buddy, a lieutenant colonel that Harry and I became acquainted with, had been a tactical officer in our cadet days; our class had called him Dusty Joe for the abundance of demerits he assigned us for dusty shoes. I had to struggle to keep from inspecting his own shoes as he sat on the bar stool telling us war stories.

With the weeks going by rapidly that winter, I began to think actively about something that had been on my mind for some time. Each of us who had been in combat and who were required to remain in Europe were authorized a forty-five-day home leave known as R and R. Ordinarily, I might have passed it up until my transfer back to the States scheduled for summer 1947; however, it was, I felt, time to return home to see Diana. Though we had been corresponding intensely for a long time, we had not seen each other since that last dance of June Week 1943. She was no longer a high school girl, nor I a boy cadet. We knew the "letter us" very well, but it was time for the real Diana and Doug to stand up. On the ides of March, my application for R and R was approved, beginning June 30. Colonel Dingley attached a note that I would remain branch chief until my departure on leave.

An official announcement that same month of March contained news not only significant to the Army but also exciting to me personally. The U.S. Occupation Zone in Germany, which had been divided between the Third and Seventh Armies, was to be consolidated into a single jurisdiction under Third Army. Then the exciting part: On April 1 we would move to Heidelberg, where Seventh Army headquarters had been.

Heidelberg conjured up lingering childhood images first implanted by Mark Twain's *A Tramp Abroad*, chanced on in Paterson's Danforth Library. I still recall vividly how Twain described the beautiful old city, its backdrop the hills of the Neckar River valley, and I could visualize the huge, dominating ruins of Heidelberg Schloss (castle). But what had really intrigued me was his description of life at the University, circa 1880, with its student corps, duels, beer drinking, student prison, and the age-old hymn "Gaudeamus Igitur." Later, I became aware of Sigmund Romberg's music from *The Student Prince* with its "Golden Days" and "Drinking Song" portraying a fantasy of nineteenth-century student life. Heidelberg was one of the places in Europe I had most wanted to visit—and now I was going to live there!

On April 1, moving day, the drive was all autobahn past Munich except for the remaining wartime-inflicted detours. On arrival I was billeted in the midtown Hotel Victoria, an aging but comfortable three-story building with its own dining room. Early next morning I headed out to the new headquarters location. Gone were all the goodies of the Bäd Tolz SS Kaserne; this one was very plain, a series of barracks buildings with a parade ground in the middle. But with Heidelberg at hand for off-duty activities, who cared what the offices were like?

Except for their scope, branch activities remained the same. We had inherited a couple of soldiers, including one WAC, to help out with the increased load. One other change, though, brought no additional help. On April 1 not only had the Army Headquarters in Europe (USFET) lost Seventh Army, it had also lost its responsibility for military government in Germany. We became the only kid on the block. USFET officers were on the phone to our branch at all times; soon we began to get summoned to attend meetings at their Frankfurt headquarters, frequently on matters of marginal significance. This was my first experience with a bureaucracy's ability to fill a void with nonsense material. Driving through Frankfurt we saw the vast destruction of the city. Thousands of *Trümmerfrauen* (rubble women) were at work clearing the mess, a necessity before reconstruction could begin. In the ruins' midst stood the untouched I.G. Farben building, now the U.S. Headquarters. Its survival could not have been an accident. One could almost visualize the restraining arm of Ike on many Air Force bombardiers protecting his future headquarters.

The actual reconstruction of Frankfurt and other German cities was still in the future; for now other concerns were more pressing, especially getting enough to eat. Since Germany had imported food during the best of times, the challenge was to restore industrial production to pay for importing enough food to sustain life. In that spring of 1946 the United States could not maintain its goal of a 1,500-calorie daily ration for the German population; it was reduced to the 1,250-calorie range. By way of comparison the British and French zones were on a 1,000-calorie daily ration.

Meanwhile, adding to the half-million DPs being supported in the American zone, came a flow of Germans being expelled by the Soviets from the Russian zone. Averaging almost fifty thousand per week, this group expanded to almost a million by the end of spring. Most were women and children, and many of the expelled men were old or incapacitated.

These problems and many others, such as housing, required

finding a balance between a victorious army living in a conquered nation and an army increasingly concerned for the welfare of its former enemy. I raise these issues not because they affected most of us in places like Heidelberg but rather to show the condition of the former "master race" in that spring of 1946.

Life in Heidelberg was the closest to normal that many of us had experienced for a long time. Our work rarely extended into the evening or past noon on Saturdays, and afterward we were able to enjoy life in downtown Heidelberg, one of the very few German cities that had not been bombed. Next to the Victoria was a small park with a tearoom, and across the street a first-class hotel, Der Europaische Hof (the Europa). Only higher-ranking officers were billeted there, but the dining room and lounge were open to all of us. The lounge, and especially its outside terrace, was a favorite gathering place for junior officers on weekend evenings. At nightfall came the inevitable group singing, a favorite being a mid-1920s German melody, "Ich hab mein Herz in Heidelberg verloren." We all had memorized the German words, which tell of a love found and forever lost one lovely summer night in Heidelberg.

There were many interesting areas within walking distance of the Victoria, including Hauptstrasse in the heart of the city. Its many shops would have been fascinating but, unfortunately, they had nothing left to sell unless we wanted to get into the black market. The student pubs, with initials carved into the tables and walls, were an exception; there we could get a beer. Up above the city were the still impressive remains of the Heidelberg Schloss, providing a great view of the gabled buildings and hodge-podge of Heidelberg's streets.

My favorite evening stroll was to the center of the old university, Universitätsplatz, with its old buildings and lecture halls. The Special Services library occupied a building there; its supply of current periodicals and journals drew me there about twice a week. On one visit I chanced on the nearby old student prison; until 1914 it had been used to punish students (then exempt from civil prosecution except by the university faculty).

Another frequent user of the library was a German-speaking

Engineer captain named Hans; like me he was billeted at the Victoria. Having learned a good deal about the university, he gave me a tour one Saturday afternoon. More interesting to me than the old structures was how he characterized the nature of the university: almost no administrators, no student dormitories, the centrality of the lecture, and the heavy reading schedule of most students. Standing in a lecture hall, Hans described the entrance of the professor, greeted by the students with knuckle rapping. By the time he reached his lectern he had started talking and would continue throughout the period. Students chose what lectures (or seminars) they wished to attend as supplements to their reading program. They also were responsible for passing the examinations at the end of their student years. I marveled at this mature approach as contrasted to, say, my own spoon-fed college experience.

Since the past winter, articles and commentary in news magazines had been addressing increasing tensions between the West and the Soviet Union, reinforced on several occasions by official speeches. On February 9, in one of his rare public pronouncements, Stalin implied that future wars were inevitable until Communism replaced capitalism as the basis of world economic organization. Our reply came on February 28 in a speech by Secretary of State James Byrnes: we would not allow "force or the threat of force" to be used contrary to the principles of the United Nations. Then came that blockbuster, Winston Churchill's "Iron Curtain" speech at Fulton, Missouri, on March 5. In the West reaction to Churchill's powerful message was mixed, but Stalin's brutal reply compared Churchill to Hitler. None of this, though, had prepared me for a required briefing that I and the other branch chiefs attended in early June at Third Army headquarters.

The briefer, a colonel from the headquarters in Frankfurt, began by stating that no notes would be taken. The content was not to be discussed beyond the meeting, except as part of our work. Beginning the substantive part of his talk, he discussed the capabilities of the Soviet ground forces. Then, without developing any motivation for their action, he hypothesized a Soviet attack on the West. From there—and this was the main part of his talk—he outlined a planning concept for our response. Since our forces were now inadequate either to counterattack, or even to establish a defensive line, we would fight a delaying action while retreating to the west. Military dependents (now beginning to arrive in Europe) and our civilian employees would be evacuated behind our shield. Our forces would gradually withdraw toward the Schelde estuary in the Antwerp vicinity. From there we would be evacuated from the European continent. All this, he added, was a preliminary concept, depending on developments; we would get detailed planning instructions later, if required. Astonished, I felt that the entire briefing was something out of *Alice in Wonderland*. I never heard anything more on the subject prior to R and R—but this briefing did happen in June 1946 as I have described.

Between work and off-hours life in Heidelberg, the days before departure sped by. By June many of my new friends were removed from the bachelor social life as their dependents started arriving in Europe. By the time I returned from leave, the Victoria would be a bachelor officers' quarters. To fulfill the final prerequisite for departure, I secured newly arrived Captain Jack Gibson as my replacement, at least until Talbott's return later in the summer. On June 30 De Coursey drove me to Frankfurt to begin the long journey home. No doubt when I reached Le Havre I would board one of Henry Kaiser's Victory ships, the seagoing equivalent of the "Puka Dive Bomber" of cadet days. Looking ahead to my home leave, I wavered between optimism and apprehension. How would I find life in postwar America, particularly Paterson, after a six-year absence? And, most of all, what would it be like on my visit in Vermont with the real Diana?

10. The Best Years of Our Lives

". . . Faith of our Fathers, Holy Faith, We will be true to thee till death." It was Sunday, July 14, and I was singing the old hymns again at Mass in St. Joe's, having arrived in Paterson the evening before. As Aunt Annie and I left after the service, she pointed out the new bronze plaque listing all the St. Joe's boys who had served during the war. It contained the names of almost all thirty-five of us from the grammar school class of 1935. Outside church I greeted many old friends and acquaintances. Since I was in uniform, several asked a variant of "What are you going to do now that the war is over?" The best I could come up with was "Good question."

That afternoon I plowed through the last week's collection of local papers that Annie had saved for me. Some representative items: my Eastside High Class of June 1939 was planning its first alumni dance for October; the Paterson Panthers professional football team, terminated in 1942 because of the war, would resume play on September 15; in the two weeks since the OPA lifted controls, prices had risen 22 percent; the American Rocket Society wants the U.S. to become the first nation to put a man on the moon and says it could be done by 1949, using atomic power; the worst polio epidemic in twelve years is headed this way from the Midwest.

For our late afternoon dinner that day Annie had invited Walt and Irene, along with Toots and, of course Johnny Bustard. Each had ideas of things for me to do, and Irene wanted me to spend the next weekend with them in West Orange. All the ideas, plus my own plans, made for about a two-week agenda. That night I called Diana in Vermont; during our long conversation we decided that I would arrive there on Monday the 29th for about a week's stay. She sounded great. On one pretense or another—such as how one got to her place by train—I called about every second or third day, usually on someone's phone other than Annie's. Following Irene's advice I had explained to Annie that my interest in Vermont was to visit a friend—gender not stated—from the West Point days.

The physical Paterson seemed remarkably unchanged. The St. Joe's complex and Sandy Hill Park directly opposite Aunt Annie's were exactly like my 1930s haunts. In downtown Paterson the major department stores such as Myer Brothers still had pneumatic tubes whirring overhead with bills and change, and the theaters seemed just as they had before on so many Saturday afternoons.

What *had* changed, I realized, were the people and not just because of the six-year interval. The way we had been was now only a memory. Among my friends, Jim Farrell and Walt Kennedy were fairly typical. Both were now married and using the G.I. Bill. Jim would soon be heading for a job in hospital administration in Toledo, his wife's home town. Walt, still in law school, was looking forward to a job after graduation in Congressman Gordon Canfield's Washington office. Many were hoping for work in New York City, while some of the less focused were members of the "52-20" club, a veterans' program paying $20 a week for fifty-two weeks for those unemployed or earning less than $100 a month.

Though the war had ended a year before, shortages, such as transportation and housing, still existed and no doubt would be around for a while. Gas rationing was a thing of the past, but my friends who owned cars were stuck with clunkers. New cars were few and far between unless one had a hefty bankroll to pay "under the table" for the privilege of buying a new one. Fortunately, for those in good rental housing, price controls were still in effect; otherwise, rents would have gone out of sight. After observing all this for a while, I concluded that the earlier aura surrounding war veterans was gone. We were no longer anything special, but that was fine. Most vets were focused on the future, not the past. The summer of 1946 was a time of rapid change in attitudes as well as in events.

For others, like Aunt Annie, lifestyles had not changed a great deal. She no longer took boarders, except for Johnny Bustard, but did rent her top floor, which had a private entrance, to male roomers. Annie still spent several hours each afternoon listening to the radio "soaps." Besides her old favorites, such as "Just Plain Bill" (the barber who spent more time solving people's problems than cutting hair), she now followed some new serials. "Our Gal Sunday" asked—but never quite got around to answering—whether this orphan girl from a little mining town in Colorado could find happiness as the wife of a wealthy and titled Englishman.

The long weekend in West Orange included a couple of dinner parties and took me into a different world. Walt, Irene, and their friends had now become a conservative generation and were more focused on the present than on the future. Many of them worked for corporations based in Manhattan; they naturally viewed the world from that perspective, especially regarding the current warfare between management and labor. After years of wage controls, almost all major unions had struck for higher pay. The discussions between Walt and his friends were, to put it mildly, distinctly anti-labor. President Truman was one of their villains and frequently the butt of their wisecracks or jokes: "To err is Truman"; "Washington couldn't tell a lie, Roosevelt couldn't tell the truth, and Truman can't tell the difference."

I planned on seeing my own dispersed family in August after returning from Vermont, but meanwhile sister Daisy brought Harry, Jim, and me together for an evening. Neither was married, and I doubted that Jim, the ladies' man, now thirty-nine (an age at which he remained for a decade), ever would be. He was into the landscaping business in northwest New Jersey's Sussex County, and Harry had started his own home construction business in the same area. During the course of the evening Daisy asked if I had called Lee Lauterbur, whom she had gotten to know. The answer was no, since I had assumed that she had married George Daoust and left the area. Daisy looked at me a bit quizzically; giving me Lee's new New York telephone number, she suggested that I call her. It turned out that she and George had gone their own ways, but she was to be married in the fall anyway—to my classmate Phil Toon, who was stationed in Tokyo. Rather than trying to unravel all that on the telephone, I made a date for Sunday, since I planned on being in New York the day before the Vermont trip.

From a crowded early morning Grand Central to my bucolic Vermont destination was a three-train journey. The first, to Springfield, Massachusetts, took most of the morning and provided a good opportunity to rest after a Sunday with Lee. We had taken a long afternoon walk; had drinks at the apartment she shared with an airline stewardess; and ended up at the nightclub El Morocco, her choice. Lee had recently left *Carousel*, and was preparing for her early fall wedding to Phil, now back in Japan after his (or was it hers, I wondered) blitzkrieg courtship, a subject we did not discuss extensively. Lee gave me the impression of having misgivings about the future. For one thing, she was not happy about giving up dancing and hoped that in the future, when they returned to the States, she could open a small dance studio, depending on where Phil was stationed. When we parted, I too had misgivings that I did not express. Lee would, I felt, have had a successful dancing career in New York at least for a while. In marrying an Army officer she was expected to be a pro bono employee of the Army. When they returned from Tokyo, she would probably end up, not in a dance studio, but rather as a "volunteer" in the thrift shop at Fort Somewhere.

The second train, a local, proceeded up the Connecticut River Valley. I swung down at Bellows Falls, Vermont, a junction for boarding what Diana called the Rutland Rocket. The "rocket" turned out to be two antique wooden cars pulled by an engine that looked as if it had been recalled from retirement to help during the war—and might decide at any moment to retire again. It did get me to my final rail destination, Proctorsville, while chugging along at a speed that allowed plenty of time to take in the Vermont scenery. On arrival I was relieved to see an old car parked nearby, evidently the local taxi. The driver sent to meet me waved me in without a word (few captains in uniform arrived in Proctorsville); off we went from paved to unpaved roads and finally onto what was almost a trail, halting in front of a farmhouse.

Heading toward me was a much more mature-looking Diana than my June Week date of three years before, but just as beautiful. As we exchanged greetings and headed for the house, her mother and a girl about Diana's age appeared on the porch. Constance Hamilton looked as if she were in her early fifties and was both warm and personable in her greeting. The other girl was Joan Traendly, a Montclair friend of Diana's.

The farmhouse, in good condition, seemed to be to go back to the previous century and, except for the kitchen and plumbing, did not appear to have been remodeled. Constance took over that evening, leading long conversations during and after dinner on such matters as life in Heidelberg, Diana's work in graphic arts at Cooper Union, and the Cavendish area, where the farm was located. She then decided that we should play bridge. Never mind that I had never played before; she would teach me. Constance was a good conversationalist, and I felt an immediate rapport with her; however, since my time in Vermont was limited, I hoped that by the following evening Diana and I could begin our ballet.

The next day, dedicated to touring the local area with its scenic back roads, took us along valley streams and through quiet villages. I could see why so many flatlanders were becoming summer residents of this beautiful state, whose population was still well under a half-million. One stop was at a museum in a school building connected with a boys' academy in Ludlow; Calvin Coolidge had graduated from there in 1890. The guide, perhaps emulating the thirtieth

President, exuded the wary, taciturn personality frequently characterized as the Vermont Yankee in books and films. One interesting historical fact I gleaned from the guide's answer to a question was that Vermont, before joining the Union in 1791, was one of only two states that had been a sovereign country.

That evening Constance and Joan headed out after dinner to play cards at a neighbor's, while Diana and I picked up the dinner things. Afterward, sitting on a divan and sipping the rest of the dinner wine, we engaged in a long conversation. I think we had the same goal: to see what the person not in the letters was really like—our interests, our dreams, our personalities. Things went so well that after the wine was finished, I suggested relocating to the front steps and the moonlight. Almost immediately we started kissing, at first in a restrained way, then gradually moved into a necking session. (If this pace seems unduly slow to a reader of a later generation, remember that we are all children of our own time, and both Diana and I had reached our emotional maturity in the mid-1940s. It was a period when serious relationships between people of our ages began with a combination of flirting and kissing and then tried to find a balance between intense desire and intense frustration.) On that evening as we were having a mutually exciting experience, the headlights from the Hamiltons' car suddenly lit up the driveway.

Deciding the following day that it was time to put this able-bodied war vet to work, Constance assigned me the task of laying out a badminton court behind the house. Sometime in the course of my digging and leveling project she came across *The Folded Leaf* that I had brought along for Diana to read. Mrs. H. wanted to borrow it; it turned out that at one time she had worked in Brentano's in New York and was an avid reader. Great, I thought; maybe that will keep her busy tonight.

That evening after a short bridge session Constance announced that she was heading for her room to read my book, and Joan disappeared upstairs to write letters. Diana and I thus had a clear stage for the next act of our ballet. We needed no wine this time to be kindred spirits with lots to talk about. I mentioned that Mrs. H. had invited me to stay another week if I wished; but, as much as I wanted to, I felt that I really should get home as planned. Was it possible, though, that she could get down to New Jersey for a while during August? She promised to check it out.

After this conversing on the front steps, we resumed the activity that the headlights had interrupted the night before. Ending up in the wrestling mode on the lawn, we were no longer imaginary personalities in letters; this was real. Coming up for air, Diana said that there was something we should talk about, and we moved back to the steps. During the past semester, she said, she had been dating and was attracted to a veteran who had resumed his engineering studies at Cooper Union. She had waited to tell me this, to be certain that we two were serious—which we both agreed we were—but the message was that she also felt this way about the other guy.

Though disappointed, I was not surprised; she was an attractive girl, and there were lots of vets. My response was that this was unfair competition: *he* would be on the scene while I would be in Europe for another year. Meanwhile, though, let's not waste time—"How about another kiss?" She smiled and complied. By now I thought I knew my long-range goal, even though Diana was not certain of hers. How best to accomplish it would require a lot of thought, given all the variables.

The following afternoon Diana's father arrived from New Jersey, bringing along her cousin David from New Haven. Richard Hamilton appeared to be in his mid-to late fifties, a likable, gregarious guy in the real estate business. Their arrival meant another car and a date for Joan—good news for me on both counts. With all the conversation that night, though, Diana and I had no chance for a tête-à-tête. Constance looked sympathetic, but Mr. H., a World War I veteran, was much interested in talking about my European experiences, and this was a good way of getting acquainted.

The next day we all headed for Ascutney, a tiny Vermont village on the Connecticut River. We stopped first at a small, peaceful, typical New England cemetery where Diana's brother was buried. Dick was one of the more than 400,000 of our World War II generation who were killed in action or died as a result of a combat action or in training and now "all, all, all were sleeping, sleeping, sleeping on the hill."

From there we drove up Mount Ascutney, parking below the summit, where we enjoyed fabulous views of New Hampshire and Vermont. Coming down the mountain I became convinced of something I had shrugged off on the way up: Mr. H. was an awful driver. This was of more than academic interest, since I had accepted his offer of a ride back to New Jersey beginning late Sunday afternoon. We made one more stop in Ascutney at a house—a sometime home—owned by Connie, Diana's oldest sister, and her husband Norman Hudson, who were both fun. Norm, a sales representative in New Jersey, struck me as a real character who would be interesting to get to know.

Saturday night featured dancing and lots of conversation, along with rum and Cokes, at a roadhouse near Ludlow for four of us—Dave and Joan, Diana and me. A combo played good dancing music all the way from "Sioux City Sue" to "They Say That Falling in Love Is Wonderful." When they got to "The Girl That I Marry," I could not resist stealing a kiss, this time without resistance, unlike the rebuff I had received at the graduation hop in 1943. Afterward, though, she looked at me as though I were being sophomoric, which I was.

It was Sunday, August 4, the last day of my visit; Congregationalist Diana was sitting next to me at Mass in St. Mary's Church in Springfield. She was making a major concession to a visitor, and I carefully avoided any discussion or even allusion to the complications involved when a non-Catholic married a Catholic. This would be a divisive issue at best and should be postponed until, say, "mañana." On the drive back to the farm she gave me the good news that her parents had agreed to her coming down to New Jersey at the end of August for the last week of my leave. She would be staying with Joan Traendly's mother, while Joan remained at the farm.

The remainder of the morning, leading up to Sunday afternoon dinner, was for reading papers and playing badminton. At this point I really felt at home. Mid-afternoon all of us, along with Connie and

Norman, went swimming in a pool formed by one of the mountain streams. I enjoyed the swimming but not as much as watching Diana in a bathing suit for the first time. Afterward, upstairs at Connie's, having completed dressing for the trip back I stopped to study some family pictures on the wall. At one point I felt a pressure behind me—it was Diana. On this, our last chance to talk, we focused on our August plans for her visit and said our private good-byes. Back at the farm, with the car loaded, I had two reasons to regret not having accepted Constance's invitation to stay another week. The first, obviously, was leaving Diana. The other struck me when I saw that Mr. H., not David, was the driver. Where was my St. Christopher's medal!

Not long after our departure Mr. H. wondered if either of us wanted to drive. By all means, David and I were delighted to share that chore all the way to New Haven, where we spent the night with his folks, John and Bonnie Hamilton. The next morning as Dick Hamilton and I headed for West Orange with him driving, I assumed that my chances of reaching 69 Edgewood Avenue intact were about on a par with a copilot making it back from a bombing run over Germany. What the hell, there was nothing to do but relax and enjoy the conversation.

Arriving about noon, we found that Irene, previously alerted, had lunch waiting for the three of us. As Mr. H. left to head for his office, I walked him to the car and mentioned how much I was looking forward to Diana's visit. He replied that she was, too; then after a pause he added, "Diana is not very sophisticated." I understood the words but not their intent. Was this a warning or an apology? Since some questions are best not asked or answered, I responded with a smile and something to the effect that she was sophisticated enough for me.

Irene, of course, wanted to know all about my Vermont visit and, in particular, my reaction to Diana. When I finished, we agreed that I could not do much that summer except to make the visit enjoyable for both of us. As I had to return to Europe, Irene felt that the best approach would be to play for time and then try to arrange for an assignment close to New York City after Europe. Agreeing, I thought of West Point as a good possibility. Meanwhile, Irene wanted to have Diana for dinner on the first night of her visit. She also posed a good question: How was I going to solve the car problem for that week?

The August days were a good opportunity to visit with my families and friends. During my overnight visit to sister Ruth's on Long Island, her husband Andy and I had lunch together in the course of which Andy asked what was happening in Paterson these days. I mentioned how the housing shortage was causing an exodus to nearby suburbs, such as Fairlawn, which had plenty of real estate for building. After lunch he decided to drive about fifteen miles to show me one approach to Long Island's housing shortage.

It turned out to be a massive assembly line for building houses: One group of workers set up foundation forms, followed by another group pouring concrete; then came carpenters with prebuilt house frames, and so on. All this was taking shape in the middle of large, empty fields. A builder named William Levitt had acquired the land and was putting up about one thousand essentially identical homes. Andy said that the rumored selling price was about $10,000 each. I asked if he were interested. "Hell, no," he replied. Andy admitted that these new houses would help the housing shortage but maintained that they would never become homes in the traditional sense. Rather, they would be more like automobiles, to be disposed of when one could afford a better model. At this early stage of postwar America neither of us could possibly have imagined that this development would eventually result in a city named Levittown with a population of more than fifty thousand.

In late August the newsstands in Paterson and elsewhere displayed what became, perhaps, the best-known issue of *The New Yorker* ever published. Containing only one article, "Hiroshima" by John Hersey, it described the experiences of a doctor, a tailor's widow, a German Jesuit, a young surgeon, a clerk, and a Methodist pastor beginning "At exactly fifteen minutes past eight in the morning, on August 6, 1945, Japanese time. . . ." The article drew public commentary almost immediately.

Most readers reacted to "Hiroshima" as a human-interest account of survivors' stories. A minority claimed that the bomb should not have been used, as the Japanese would have collapsed anyway. Try telling that to someone who would have participated in the invasion of Japan scheduled for fall 1945 or, like myself, who likely would have been in the main invasion planned for the following spring. I never questioned Truman's decision, the only one he could have made as Commander in Chief. Anyone looking for an example of unnecessary destruction should consider the pointless fire bombing of Dresden on February 13, 1945, which killed one-third more than did the bomb on Hiroshima. This seminal article though, helped sensitize most of us to the need for something that unfortunately never came about—the elimination of such weapons from the human inventory.

Three weeks after my return from Vermont Diana replicated the trip as Mr. H's copilot. We had worked out by telephone the details of our four-day date. The only missing ingredient was a car, not easy to come by in those days before readily available rentals. The loan of my father's 1939 Plymouth solved the problem, a one-time exception to my resolve never to ask the architect of "the day of the taxi" for anything.

In the weeks since Vermont I had thought about Diana a great deal, no longer as an image in letters but now a real person, warts and all (at least those you can see in the course of one week). I knew that I was in love with her. Before I could tell her, though, I wanted her to know more about me, in particular my Paterson background. That would have to await my return from Europe. In some ways I wished that she hadn't told me about the competition. My approach to her was bound to be inhibited by knowing that I was in a contest with someone who would have home-field advantage for a year while I was off in Heidelberg. In the meantime, enjoy the four-day date, Doug, and avoid getting serious with her. But would I, could I?

Approaching the Traendlys' front steps, I could see my candidate for Miss America, brunette hair down to her shoulders and now dressed like a city girl. She was sitting on the steps reading a newspaper so, approaching unobserved, I studied her profile, no longer Joan Leslie, now more like Ingrid Bergman. *Get a grip, Doug.* On hearing my step she turned toward me with that big smile and came to her feet with a greeting. Soon we were off to the Plymouth, heading toward West Orange.

That afternoon and evening were a mirror image of the first night at the farm, without the card game. Irene displayed her most gracious mode, and Walt, after arriving from New York, fixed cocktails in his usual friendly and gregarious style. When Irene disappeared to finish dinner preparation, Diana and Walt engaged in some interesting dialogues on topics big and small. Because Constance had dominated the conversation at the farm, this was my first opportunity to observe Diana in this role. Sitting quietly next to her on the divan, I began thinking about her personality, in particular her father's comment that she was unsophisticated. If he meant that she was ingenuous, I found that both refreshing and warm. I also sensed the emergence of a strong character; she was for sure going to be her own woman.

Dinner conversation was animated, but by nine or so it was time to head back to Montclair and to let Walt the commuter get ready for his morning trip to New York. Diana and I would be going there ourselves in a more leisurely way next day for dinner and to see *Carousel*. Arriving at Traendlys' I discovered that the front seat of the Plymouth, though a bit more cramped, would be substituting for moonlight in Vermont. The action picked up just about where it had left off three weeks before.

Strolling up Fifth Avenue on a late August day with your girl (at least for that week) next to you and an evening in New York ahead—it doesn't get much better than that. I felt especially comfortable in my first new civilian suit since 1940 and not just because it was well fitted. Since we had to wear uniforms in Germany, I had intended to wait until the following year to buy new clothes. What changed my mind was something I picked up—and others had confirmed—on recent trips to New York City. Some ex-GIs were openly antagonistic toward people wearing an officer's uniform. That was natural enough, I guess.

I had made reservations for dinner at the Algonquin's Rose Room. Like many people our age we had heard and read about the now-defunct Algonquin Round Table of the twenties and thirties and its well-known participants. During dinner we enjoyed talking about these writers, journalists, and artists, especially that caustic wit Dorothy Parker (Katharine Hepburn's acting ran "the whole gamut of emotions from A to B"). Some of her sardonic verse, not directed toward a particular person, could be vaguely disquieting, depending on one's circumstances. For example her *Comment:*

> Oh, life is a glorious cycle of song,
> A medley of extemporanea;
> And love is a thing that can never go wrong;
> And I am Marie of Rumania.

Carousel, a Rodgers and Hammerstein musical based on Ferenc Molnar's *Liliom*, was well into its second year on Broadway. I held up well until the song "If I Loved You" with its personally relevant lyrics: "Soon you'd leave me . . . never, never to know/How I love you . . ." cost me my cool. Had I been in uniform, I would have been guilty of "displaying affection in public." As it turned out, the only outside critique was the amusement and eye approval of two middle-aged women behind us.

At breakfast the next morning Aunt Annie had sad news, her brother Andrew had died of a heart attack while I was in New York. His wake was to be the following evening at his home, some distance from Paterson. She asked if I would take her and I, of course, agreed. As that same night, Thursday, was the last one of my leave, Diana and I had planned on dinner and dancing at Pal's Cabin in West Orange. Oh, well, there was still a day and a half before I turned back into a lover by mail.

That afternoon Diana and I headed for Daisy and Steve's apartment to meet them, along with Jim, Harry, and my sister Helen—lots of talkers in that group. Since they arrived incrementally, Diana was kept busy. As usual, Steve had made potent drinks, so after dinner I had no problem in talking everyone into going dancing.

At Jim's suggestion we ended up at Donohue's on Route 23 west of Clifton. It was a good choice. A small band played continuously, featuring many of the currently popular tunes: "Prisoner of Love," "South America, Take It Away," and, a bit too relevant that night, "Now Is the Hour." When we broke up about eleven, everyone was in a good mood, promising same time next year. Afterward, Diana and I parked for a long time in Montclair and, as we had the night before, eventually moved to the Traendlys' front hall. At one point she said, "I feel the way you did in Vermont." Nothing enigmatic about that, but what to do or say? I was so inexperienced and this meant so much to me. I knew what I wanted to ask, but that was crazy; she still had college ahead. And what about that other guy in New York? There was no easy way. Maybe by tomorrow I'd think of something other than playing for time; maybe not.

The final day of our golden week we took a picnic lunch to a spot Jim had suggested the night before, which turned out to be an extensive public area of woods, fields, and ponds. We brought along a couple of games, which we played for a while as we sipped wine. Eventually, that gave way to conversation about our own plans. She said that she had decided to live in New York during her second year at Cooper Union, rather than to commute. What was I going to do after Heidelberg? I mentioned the West Point idea, along with another one I had picked up from my correspondence with the Academy. During the next couple of years the Army apparently was going to be pushing graduate schooling; I might apply for that. Wouldn't it be great if I could attend a school near New York? She agreed. Had I ever thought of leaving the Army? Yes, and my interests then would be either law or college teaching, both requiring several more years in school. She did not comment and I could not articulate the question on my mind: If we were married, which of three careers would you prefer me to pursue? If I had had to guess, I would have said law.

I can still visualize how she looked that day sitting on my West Point blanket. Wearing a dress printed with blue flowers and buttoned down the front, she exuded a striking freshness. As I lay on the ground nearby, resting on my elbow and watching her, I realized that though first attracted by her beauty at that long-ago Christmas party, I now admired her for more than that. Over the course of this summer I had grown to know Diana herself, the person.

At one point she turned toward me rather suddenly and met my gaze with direct eye contact. Her cheeks flushed and we kissed, holding each other. How much I wanted to blurt out, "Come with your mother to Heidelberg this fall and marry me." No, that was crazy. She would not, probably could not, say yes to that. Then where would we be? Stop trying to possess her; it will all work out in time—let's hope.

All too soon we were back in Montclair; now it was time to say au revoir. Next day Diana would be returning to Vermont with her father and I would head to Fort Dix en route to Europe. That wonderful summer of '46 was over.

The trip back was delayed because of the Labor Day holiday and the threat of a major maritime strike. That possibility and its timing, as yet unknown when I reported in, woud affect our departure. As a result of these complications, our shipment group was told on Saturday to return Monday afternoon. If only I had known this in advance, I could have gone at least as far as New Haven with Diana. Who knows where that might have led?

Fortunately, two classmates, Tammy Flynn and Ed Millington, were stranded along with me. Tammy's suggestion that we go to New York seemed as good an idea as any, since each of us had said our good-byes for the next year. Before leaving on Saturday afternoon Tammy called ahead to arrange a date for himself on Sunday. His date, moreover, was bringing along two friends for Ed and me—a bonus neither of the recipients really wanted. My date, Karen Black, turned out to be an editorial assistant on *Time*. Though she was personable and an interesting conversationalist, my emotional reaction to her was about what it would have been to a younger sister. Late in the afternoon we ended up having dinner at the Monkey Bar on 54th Street, a favorite of Tammy's. He particularly wanted us to see the performance of two pianists playing simultaneously "like mad like mad." Depending on what one meant by that, he was right.

Back at Dix on Labor Day afternoon we learned that a bus would take us to Camp Kilmer for shipping out of New York Harbor as soon as possible. I did find time to dash off a short note to Diana, bringing her up to date. Next day at Kilmer we boarded our Victory ship with the goal of being at sea before midnight to escape the strike, later described by newspapers as "the most disastrous port strike in American history." We got out just under the wire.

By mid-September I was back in Heidelberg. After a two-and-a-half month absence, how beautiful this ancient city looked with its ambience of castle, river, and winding streets. And, for the first time since the war ended, many of its cafés and shops were reopening.

Returning to my work in G-1 Strength Control required little acclimation. Talbott was back as branch chief; Jake Gibson and de Coursey were still on board. Redeployment was now a minor part of our function, with less than ten thousand Third Army troops returning to the States each month. Our major problem was directing the incoming replacements to those units with the highest priority. All units were under strength and though many of the replacements coming from the States were of marginal quality, we had no choice except to assign the manpower provided. Only the U.S. Constabulary had an option to reject certain replacements: those who were illiterate or did not speak English or were outright undesirables. (So much for the plan to make the Constabulary an elite unit.)

Waiting on my calendar when I arrived at the office for work was a note to see Lt. Col. Wells in G-2 (intelligence) as soon as possible. His message came directly to the point: "I am 'debriefing' you on the meeting you attended in June concerning the Soviet threat and our concept for dealing with an attack on their part. Forget you attended the meeting and do not discuss it with anyone. Sign your name here indicating that I debriefed you." Since June I had wondered about that panicky session on two counts: Were the Soviets really in shape to make and sustain such an attack? If so, what would its purpose be? I was relieved to find out that we were not doing that kind of planning—at least as far as I knew.

The office environment had not changed perceptibly during my absence, but the same could not be said for the off-duty life of the American community. Over the summer the dependents of military personnel had arrived in large numbers (eventually reaching ninety thousand in Germany); accordingly, a new lifestyle developed for all of us, not just for the married men. As the Victoria Hotel had become bachelor officers' quarters, those of us who remained there had better accommodations. I now had a room with private bath and a balcony with a good view.

Off-duty life, though, except for an occasional dinner invitation by a married couple, was pretty much the same for me that fall. In my strolls I became increasingly fond of the city, and at least two nights a week browsed at the Special Services library, whose journal subscriptions had expanded over the summer. Sometimes on Saturdays a couple of us borrowed one of the G-1 controlled German cars. Since the gasoline ration was tight, we had to restrict our trips to nearby areas. Frequently, we followed the scenic Neckar Valley on what was called Castle Road to places like Neckarsteinach or Hirschhorn am Neckar with their ruined castles and lovely vistas. In town the Europa bar, with its drinking and singing, remained a favorite on Saturday and Sunday nights. Enlivening it still more were recently arrived female Army brats who dated some of my colleagues.

Outside the American enclaves that September the real Germany continued to be confronted by many serious problems, in particular a shortage of food, clothing, housing, and other basic necessities. These shortages, combined with an unstable currency, had resulted in a rampant black market. Some bright spots, though, were beginning to appear as agricultural and coal production increased and as state and local governments got back into operation.

At a higher political level, though, no progress was being made toward the establishment of a major American goal: a national German government. In addition, Allied cooperation with the Soviet government had come to a standstill on many German issues such as reparations. In light of these and other uncertainties, the United States felt compelled to make a public statement on its policies and to announce its intent to stay the course. Secretary of State James Byrnes accomplished this in his September 6 speech at Stuttgart to an audience of both American and German nationals. Byrnes's talk raised German problems to a national level and set forth American policies to meet them; at the same time he reaffirmed our intention to stay in Europe. This political commitment, well received by the German population and press in the American zone, seemed to mark a new phase of the occupation.

On the last Friday in September I returned to my office desk after a long afternoon meeting. Among mail from the States I found Diana's first letter since my return. About to leave for the Victoria, I tucked it in my pocket and decided to read it in a leisurely fashion en route at the Europa lounge. There I opened the long-awaited epistle. I couldn't believe my eyes. What I had expected to be a love letter—or at least an affectionate one—was not that at all. In a panic all I could think was, Oh, no! I don't believe it. Read it again. Jesus, it was a "Dear John" letter. What the hell, what had happened? When we parted a month ago, everything was great, or seemed to be. Another reading made clearer to me two reasons behind her decision, neither of which I found convincing. My weekend in New York, described briefly in my departure note, had upset her. I found that puzzling and, in any case, trivial. The other reason was her perception of differences in our personalities. These, she felt, would cause problems in the long run: she was artistic and I was pragmatic. My reaction was So what!

I must have been sitting there a long time thinking and probably looking stricken when I became aware of an Army-wife friend standing in front of me. "Are you all right, Doug?" I handed her the letter as she sat down. She read it all and was very sympathetic. Would I like to have dinner with her and her husband? I thanked her, but not tonight—I'd be lousy company. On leaving, she put her hand on my shoulder with a final word: "Don't worry, you'll get over it in a week, or two weeks, at most."

Back in my room at the Victoria I went through one hell of a night. The suddenness of this rejection, combined with my lack of even a remote awareness of any problems, left me stunned and desolate.

Best to put the letter away until morning and then take a fresh look. Perhaps then I could figure out what to do. But very little sleep came on that restless night. Though the situation was very different, my emotions were like those of the day of the taxi twenty years before, essentially a feeling of being abandoned.

Saturday morning after a walk around town I settled down in my room to reflect on the situation. To begin with, my feelings toward Diana had not changed. I was in love with her, but what, if anything, could I do about her decision? Although I still found her reasons for the breakup unconvincing, I knew her well enough to assure myself that the letter was not a ploy. She really did want to break off the relationship. Perhaps she herself did not know the real reason for her decision—maybe it was unknowable.

Well, what could I do now that might change her mind? Had I made some mistakes that I could now correct? The first mistake that came to mind could not be corrected: I should have stayed in Vermont for the extra week proffered by Constance. The other was my not being more articulate during those August days together in New Jersey. I should have told her about the intensity of my feelings, and about my desire to marry her. If I were home now, I would try to remedy that in person; but being in Europe for another ten months meant doing it by letter, quite a different matter. I would be approaching with hat in hand, in effect "telephoning from jail." After all, a relationship like this was supposed to be fun, but if one of the two persons did not want it, what was the use? I'd think about it more the next day. Meanwhile, I had a "must" social event on that evening. One decision I had made was not, as they used to say in Paterson, to "sing Ramona" to my colleagues. During and just after World War II so many servicemen had received "Dear Johns" that friends would think I was being jejune to ask for sympathy under the guise of seeking advice.

Sunday was a beautiful day in the Neckar Valley, and I headed up to the Philosopher's Walk high above Heidelberg with its terrific views and plenty of spots to sit and contemplate. I had about concluded that no matter how I felt, I could do almost nothing. Scott

Fitzgerald was probably right in this kind of situation: "There are no second acts . . . ." It was not the end of my loving her but of my seeing her. Distance, though, would not change the memories of our shared experiences: June Week with my high school sophomore; a year and a half of correspondence that, especially in the combat period, had meant so much to me; and the two wonderful weeks together this past summer. Of one thing I felt certain: no one could love like that twice.

Monday, September 30, as I headed out to work I remembered the Army wife's encouraging statement: "Don't worry, you'll get over it in a week, or two weeks, at most." But I didn't get over it in a week, or two weeks—or ever.

"Defendant Hermann Göring, the International Military Tribunal sentences you to death by hanging." It was mid-afternoon October 1, 1946, and the speaker was Sir Geoffrey Lawrence, president of the Nuremberg tribunal. Eleven of the defendants were sentenced to death, three were acquitted, and the remaining seven received prison sentences of varying lengths from ten years to life. The tribunal that Rudy and I visited the previous November had finished its work. The sentences of death by hanging were carried out during the early hours of October 16, but with one exception: Göring had committed suicide less than three hours before his rendezvous with the hangman.

Obviously, at that time no one could judge the long-range significance of this 1945-46 tribunal, but even then controversy arose, particularly over the question of whether a trial could be valid based on ex post facto law. Senator Robert Taft called the death sentence "a miscarriage of justice." A reporter asked Ike, "If the war had gone the other way, do you think they would have hanged you?" "Such thoughts you have, young man," the future presidential candidate answered. Churchill's feeling—that the Nazi leaders should have been shot outright, never mind the trial—had a certain rough appeal. Most of my colleagues believed that the trial was the best course of action available, considering that four nations of varying views sat in judgment;

moreover, the world needed to know the heinous nature of the Nazi crimes.

Completing the trial of Nazi leaders that fall of 1946 was another milestone in the passage from the war period into a future not clearly discernible. Though emerging as the most influential nation in the postwar world, the United States faced a multitude of problems at home and abroad. On the international agenda a pressing matter was how to achieve the goal of a unified Germany as agreed upon by the Big Four at Potsdam. As the fall moved along, though, the Soviets showed no interest in negotiating to achieve that result; in fact, they were busy establishing a Communist state in the zone of Germany that they occupied. By late fall frustrated British and American officials, convinced that unification was the only way to rehabilitate Germany, did the next best thing: they agreed to merge their zones economically under the rubric of Bizonia. In effect, this action divided Germany into eastern and western countries, thus accepting the concept of a divided Europe.

At the Europa bar I often chatted with Bob Murphy, a bachelor classmate also assigned to Third Army. One evening that fall we began discussing trips we would like to take during our remaining time in Europe. Agreeing on Britain, we followed up our bar talk with action. On Saturday, November 30, after a rough channel crossing, we began a two-week leave at a London American Express hotel. Our tour would also include several days in Dublin and Edinburgh.

That cold December we visited most of the well-known tourist stops in all three cities, finding them interesting, sometimes exciting, and generally fun. Some examples: Edinburgh—and its esplanade, which, though cold as hell that day, provided a terrific panorama of the Firth of Forth and the country beyond; Dublin—an Abbey Theatre presentation of one of John Millington Synge's comedies; London—Sir Thomas Beecham conducting Frederick Delius's *A Mass of Life* at Royal Albert Hall. Sitting next to us was a conservative British gentleman paying rapt attention throughout who, at the end of the concert, provided us with a British Moment. When Sir Thomas took his bows, my neighbor leapt to his feet applauding wildly and simultaneously turning to me with a delighted smile, saying, "Isn't he a horse's ass!" while continuing his enthusiastic applause.

Early in our London stay I boarded a train to Surrey to spend the day with George and Amy Forsythe, friends of my Aunt Dick's. After meeting me at the Staines station, George acted as a guide for a tour that included Windsor Castle, Eton, and Runnymede, site of King John's sealing the Magna Carta. Then we stopped at the bar of his club where he and some other members were pleased when I turned down my authorized allowance of two scotches. George had one of these, and the others matched for the second. "Why are you limited to two?" "Rationed like everything else, Captain."

The Forsythes lived in a nice but crowded cottage which was the gatehouse of Town Green Farm. The latter was formerly their home, which they had lost due to taxes. During dinner when I told my hosts that my next stop would be Dublin, their eyes lit up. Could I stop by a Dublin butcher shop on Essex Street and give the owner an envelope from them? Yes, of course. "Don't let Customs see it!" Now I knew how they acquired their meat. Remembering as well the comments at the bar, I was curious to find out more about shortages. Yes, the food was indeed in short supply; so were other items, such as materials for making clothes.

From then on, when possible, I deviated enough from the normal tour routes to observe and, when appropriate, to ask about living conditions of the three cities. London was in the worst shape, while Dublin, capital of a neutral country during the war, was closest to its normal lifestyle. Many London homes still lay in ruins, a substantial portion temporarily replaced by Nissen huts. With limited electricity supplies, no one was looking forward to the winter about to descend. England's situation what December was totally different from the one I had observed in the United States the previous summer. Both nations had won the war, but England's victory had merely brought survival and not much more.

Back in Heidelberg the American community prepared for its first Christmas with families. The post exchange was teeming with last-minute shoppers, including those of us trying to meet mailing deadlines for home. Community events abounded, but those with families present understandably celebrated at home their first holidays together since the war. They still remembered others, too; every bachelor I knew received an invitation to spend Christmas Day with one of them. Absent, though, was the fun of the Dillingen Christmas period with its many events involving Germans, displaced persons, and, especially, the children. Instead of being in a visible command role in Dillingen, I was now an anonymous staff officer in a large headquarters. The holiday period for me was one endless longueur, but I had only myself to blame; my chief New Year's resolution was to do something about it by getting more involved socially.

The new year began with that terrible winter of 1947. Temperatures remained below zero for weeks. Reports from England told of a paralyzed country hit with record blizzards and industry shutdown. Our own troubles in Germany, such as cold offices and hotel rooms day after day, were minor compared to those of the Germans themselves. In the first days of January I ended up in the 130th Station Hospital with severe flu. Toward the end of my stay I decided to try out my legs, and, donning a bathrobe recently purchased at the post exchange, I headed for the hospital library. No sooner had I picked out something to read and seated myself, when the woman in charge appeared and told me I was not allowed in the library. Puzzled, I asked why. "Well, you are in the V.D. ward, are you not?" "No, of course not." "Then why are you wearing a red bathrobe?" Needless to say, I changed into one of the hospital blue robes tout de suite. Only in the Army!

One American facility that remained comfortably heated was the Third Army movie theater in Heidelberg. Like many others I abandoned my normal routine to become a regular attendee. One new film shown during that period, *The Best Years of Our Lives*, subsequently became a movie legend, winning seven Oscars, including best picture, and is now a part of American folklore. Intrigued with the movie and what I thought might be its message, I returned later in the week for another look.

The story line centers around three World War II veterans who meet while returning to the same home town. Subsequently, though they differ in age and background, they develop a friendship, and their lives, problems, and (indirectly) love interests intersect. Al (Frederic March), an infantry sergeant from the Pacific, is a banker at home; Fred (Dana Andrews) is an Air Force hero from Europe and a former drugstore clerk; and Homer (Harold Russell) is an armless Navy veteran, previously a student. The movie clearly depicts the times in its characterizations, in the look and feel of its scenes—some unforgettable—and in its successful focus on the concerns and issues of that brief period we were then living through. The wartime past was gone but our future, individually and collectively, was still uncertain.

The subtle, possibly ironic title of the film captured the tenor of the times—apprehension mixed with optimism. We knew that our wartime experiences had given, as well as taken, some part of our best years. The question remaining, though: Was the present what was left of those years, or was it our optimistic hopes for the future that made these seem the best years? For me no movie before or since *The Best Years of Our Lives* has been as provocative in causing me to think about my own situation.

During the second week in February the weather began to improve in our area of Germany, and life resumed its normal tempo, but it was also a time of change. Third Army, which would always be associated with George Patton, the most colorful and famous of American field generals in World War II, had now completed its tasks as an occupying army and was passing into the history books. On February 14 at dusk, with many of us watching, its flag was lowered for the last time in Europe.

The highest-level occupational command would now be the corps-sized U.S. Constabulary, whose headquarters would replace that of Third Army in Heidelberg. We had known about their coming for some time and had also heard that all company-grade officers in our headquarters would be sent to troop units. This did happen to my colleague Jack Gibson, but I was retained in the branch, along with Mr. de Coursey. This suited me fine, as I had no desire to start a new job during my last five months in Europe. Meanwhile, Talbott and a number of others had left for Vienna, accompanying General Geoffrey Keyes, the last Third Army commander and newly appointed High Commissioner of Austria.

About this time I began to think about redeeming my New Year's resolution to get more involved socially. The center of public social interaction for officers, though still partly in the Europa, had shifted to the Molkenkur. This former German restaurant, overlooking castle and river from a perch high above town, was now an officers' club. After going there a few times with bachelor friends, I realized that to feel part of it I needed a date. Watching the dancers on these occasions, I noted that the good-looking gals—army brats and civilian employees—had been picked off on arrival by officers who had been in Heidelberg during the summer months.

One of these, Kitty Clayton, daughter of the Heidelberg post commander, was attractive, personable, and a damn good dancer. Every time I saw her she was with Willis Crittenberger, an army lieutenant colonel in G-3, with whom I had worked closely since the early Bäd Tolz days. Knowing that Crit had orders to Washington and would be departing shortly got me to thinking. One day at the end of February I ran into Kitty at the post exchange and on some pretext engaged her in conversation. My timing was good, for I ended up with a date and, as it worked out, became one of the two officers that she dated routinely once Crit left; the other was a medical captain. It turned out to be a good arrangement. She was involved with Crit long distance, and I was involved with not wanting to be involved! Kitty, who was great fun, and improved my dancing to such a point that I could handle numbers like the then-popular "Route 66" and "Managua Nicaragua"! One of her musical favorites, which I could have done without, she hummed and occasionally sang was "In Love in Vain"—". . . it's just my luck to be in love in vain."

My five months on the Constabulary staff with its focus on operations differed from the Third Army experience. What I found really instructive was the manner in which the G-1, Colonel Bill Craig, ran his shop. Talbott's replacement, Major Don Harrison, was my branch chief, but Craig dealt directly with whoever was working on a problem in which he had a personal interest. Two or three times a week I found myself discussing a paper or briefing him on a project. If he needed more information before attending a meeting, he might appear at my desk. In time I developed a close relationship with Craig, totally different from my experience with P. M. Martin, his Third Army predecessor, who talked only to God. He also led me into personal relationships with his deputy, a 1934 West Point classmate of his, Colonel Bert Spivy, and with the G-3, Colonel Earle Wheeler. I sensed that all three were on a track to higher Army rank. The Constabulary experience was, thanks to Craig, no end of a lesson in how to get the most out of subordinates in a staff environment.

On March 12 the Frankfurt armed forces radio news mentioned a foreign policy address by President Truman to a joint session of Congress. The President proposed that the United States provide Greece with military and economic aid to cope with Communist-led terrorist activities. And, though the threat to Turkey was not so clearly stated, it, too, would be a beneficiary of this program. At first the significance of the news item escaped me. In reading the address in the Special Services library a couple of evenings later, the text struck me as poorly written and not coherent. One sentence, though, did catch my attention: "I believe that it must be the policy of the United States to support free peoples who are resisting subjugation by armed minorities or by outside pressures." This single sentence would afterward be known as the Truman Doctrine.

At that point none of us was aware of the event that had controlled the timing of Truman's address. The British government had sent our Secretary of State two notes less than three weeks before. One stated that Britain could no longer provide economic and military assistance to Greece. The other note contained a similar message concerning Turkey. In fact, Britain itself was on the verge of collapse; that awful winter dealt the final blow to the inevitable, the end of Pax Britannica. Even though Truman's announced goal was to provide vital support to Greece and Turkey to shore up the two countries, some observers came to believe that we were assuming a commitment whose limits were not yet knowable. Also implied in all this was a potential conflict with the Soviet "empire," on whose periphery lay Greece, Turkey, and other countries not yet identified.

When spring came again to the Neckar Valley, this young man's fancy turned to his next assignment. Helping to stimulate me to action was a recently published War Department circular that solicited applications for participation in a small program of graduate schooling in unnamed universities. Final selection from among the applicants would be made in Washington. A year of graduate work sounded great to me, primarily because of its flexibility; it would help decide where-from-here in my own life. On a trip to Frankfurt with Colonel Craig I mentioned my interest in the program; he encouraged me to apply and asked that I send him a copy of my application. Eventually, I received back a copy of a letter he had written to a friend on the personnel staff in Washington. It included "Please see what you can do to get this assignment for Captain Kinnard." I was impressed that someone at his level would take that much interest in a subordinate. Becoming optimistic about my chances, I hoped at the same time that, if I were selected, the unnamed university would not turn out to be some prize like South Dakota State or Colorado School of Mines.

One evening while waiting for Kitty at the entrance to the Molkenkur I spotted two familiar faces. One was General Phil Gallagher, chief prosecutor and judge for the so-called hazing episode in 1943, which propelled me onto the area for my last eight months as a cadet. The other person with him was none other than Lieutenant George Daoust, who had shared that experience with me. However unlikely it seemed, George was now aide to our former inquisitor. He introduced me to "Uncle Phil," who obviously did not relate us to any past event. I couldn't resist: "General Gallagher, last time we met you launched me on an eight-month career as an area bird and arranged for your aide to join me on the first six." He looked a bit taken aback, then said, "Well, it doesn't seem to have hurt either of you—harrumph." At that point Kitty arrived and I returned to the present.

One long weekend Kitty and I, accompanied by married friends, took a trip to Liège, Belgium, and to Luxembourg City, where, about three miles outside the latter, we visited one of our World War II cemeteries. Located on a gently sloping hill of perhaps fifty acres, it contained thousands of graves of our comrades killed in the Battle of the Bulge or in the Rhineland Campaign. Each was marked with a simple white wooden cross and the name of the person buried there. I took a picture of one marked "Geo. S. Patton Jr., General 3d Army," buried where he would have wanted. Though his grave was like all the others, he could rest in peace because glory sought all his restless life was his forever.

Events set in motion by Truman's March 12 message expanded in the course of that spring and early summer well beyond aid to Greece and Turkey. On top of Europe's ever-increasing danger of collapse, came the developing political tension between the Soviets and the West. At our level, we knew few of the details of the issues beyond official announcements, but we were well aware of our physical proximity to Soviet forces in Eastern Europe and beyond.

On June 5 Secretary of State George Marshall, speaking at the Harvard commencement, focused his address on the economic problems of Europe. American policy, he said, was to assist in solving these problems as part of a joint effort with the Europeans. I doubt that any in Harvard Yard that day (including perhaps Marshall himself) fully realized where that speech would lead us. Certainly, those of us in Europe, learning about it in newspaper accounts, did not understand the full implications of what was to become the Marshall Plan.

Later that month the Russians in their role as a European country attended a preliminary meeting to decide how to go about developing Marshall's idea into a reality. On July 4, however, they walked out of the meeting, taking with them the Eastern European countries under their physical domination. From that point on, Europe was divided into two hostile camps, East and West, as Germany already, in effect, had become.

That same month, about a week before I left for home, I came across the July 1947 issue of *Foreign Affairs* in the library. The key article, "The Sources of Soviet Conduct" authored by "X," later became famous. Obviously this article was authoritative, setting forth in conceptual terms what would soon be publicly accepted as American policy toward the Soviet Union.

...a policy of firm *containment*, designed to confront the Russians with unalterable counter-force at every point where they show signs of encroaching upon the interests of a peaceful and stable world.

Later that year the struggle between Eastern Europe, headed by Russia, and Western Europe, headed by the United States, was given a name—the Cold War.

As spring moved toward early summer we attended more and more farewell parties as friends completed their required thirty months in Europe. A few succumbing to the good life, Heidelberg version, or more likely to the charms of some fräulein, had extended their tours. Most received stateside assignments such as an understrength troop unit, an army school, ROTC duty, a Washington assignment (usually duty in that new five-sided building near the Potomac called the Pentagon). None of these appealed to me. After seven years of "yes, sir—no, sir" I was ready for a year's sabbatical. Fingers crossed, I waited to hear from my request for graduate schooling, which would give me the freedom I wanted for a while.

During that period Kitty and I took in many social events at the Molkenkur. One of them, a demotion party, was so unique that I can still recall the details. The hosts were Colonels Craig, Spivy, and Wheeler, who were among a large number of colonels and generals being reduced one rank to fit into the structure of a small peacetime army. About midway into the evening they and their wives moved into the middle of the dance floor. As the wives removed the eagles, symbols of their rank, from their husbands' uniforms the orchestra played "Till We Meet Again." We all felt certain that they would meet again (in fact, the three of them acquired a total of ten stars and one became Chairman of the Joint Chiefs of Staff). Then, as the wives pinned on the silver leaves of a lieutenant colonel, the band struck up a raucous version of "Roll Out the Barrel."

In mid-July I received orders to be at the Frankfurt airport on the 24th for a flight home. The orders took me as far as Westover Field near Springfield, Massachusetts, and a thirty-day leave. After that? I was scheduled for the afternoon of the 23rd to pay Colonel Craig an exit call, which he preempted by sending for me that morning. When I walked into his office, he was all smiles and handed me a paper. His friend in Washington had sent this message:

> Captain Kinnard has been selected for the civil schooling program. His orders will be mailed to his home address. He has been accepted for admission by the Princeton Graduate School, Department of Politics, reporting September 1.

Princeton! What images from boyhood that conjured up: F. Scott Fitzgerald and all that jazz; Richard Halliburton strolling near Lake Carnegie on a lilac evening before heading out on his "Royal Road to Romance"; and strong-jawed sons of Old Nassau singing in the quad. Of course, I knew the reality; my colleagues would be veterans on the GI Bill, and all of us would have to work like hell. But a more important reality was that I'd be near home and New York City, in short, where I wanted to be. I thanked Bill Craig profusely and walked into the future a damn happy guy.

So I was going home to New Jersey where it had all started two decades earlier with a ride in a taxi. Those two decades turned out to be critical ones for America and the world, spanning as they did the Great Depression and the Second World War. They were also the formative ones for those of us who are part of what became known as the G. I. Generation.

Looking back at the end of what is now called the American Century, this, as I remember it, is the way we were.

Author's Notes and Acknowledgments

These notes are being written in the year 2000, the year of my seventy-ninth birthday, a fact I find a bit hard to believe. From the perspective of age, though, we can look back at the years of our lives, seeing how they were interwoven with those of others and with events of the times. Distance also softens and, often removes illusions and passions, permitting one to view most events with a certain detachment and humor.

The years covered in this memoir, 1926-1947, though they seemed endless at the time, now are a relatively short span after living almost eight decades. These were the pivotal years for my generation: we were old enough to experience firsthand the effects of the Great Depression but young enough to carry America's combat burden in the Second World War.

I wanted this to be a true memoir, that is, to focus less on the author and more on the time's events and personalities; in effect, to portray the zeitgeist of the period. Still, all memoirs must be partially autobiographical, reflecting the times with a real personality who selects the events and people on which to comment. In the process the author must make value judgments that are conditioned by one's life experiences. For that reason, and to satisfy readers who might be curious, let me relate what happened to me after I left Heidelberg in the summer of 1947.

The fourteen months at Princeton were enjoyable and intellectually stimulating. Quite by chance, my living arrangements were in the Nassau Club, a "gentlemen's club" just off the campus. Though members of all ages ate there, I was the youngest of the dozen residents by a couple of decades. Most of the others were retired, and over half merited a *New Yorker* article in the Evelyn Waugh mode.

As time went by, I began to envy my Politics Department colleagues as they pursued Ph.D.s and academic careers. In the end, though, I decided to stay with my Army career, at least for the nonce. Since I no longer had any personal compulsion to remain in the East, I opted for a return to my branch, specifically to the faculty of the Field Artillery School at Fort Sill, Oklahoma.

A peacetime army post in Oklahoma, after two and a half years spent in Heidelberg and then Princeton, was a culture shock. By spring I began to adjust, thanks largely to an "across a crowded room" experience at a social event—a local lawyer's daughter, Wade Tyree, a blonde beauty whose picture I had seen in the newspaper not long before being crowned Miss Oklahoma University Freshman. Two and a half years later—after surviving another Dear John, this time from her—we were married and still are forty-nine years later.

The summer of 1952 brought an assignment to Korea for what turned out to be the final year of that war. By now a major I served as Operations/Intelligence officer of the IX Corps Artillery, a force of about fifteen battalions. Our primary mission was to coordinate and control fire support, including air, on the west central portion of the Eighth Army front. My own work involved visiting some of our thirty-six or so observation posts along the front each day, fire planning and coordination, and evaluating the effectiveness of our firepower in disrupting and destroying the opposing Chinese forces. In a strange ending to a strange war all action ceased on July 27, 1953, with an armistice that is still in effect. I returned home about a month later.

After commanding an artillery battalion at Fort Lewis, Washington, and attending the Army's Command and Staff College in Kansas, I ended up as a staff officer in the bowels of the Pentagon. Things changed dramatically for me in the spring of 1957 when, along with a number of Army majors, I was promoted ahead of my contemporaries. Reassigned to the office of the Army Chief of Staff, General Maxwell Taylor, I had as my immediate boss Major General William Westmoreland. During my two years in that office the central issue for the Army Chief was the policy-strategy-budgetary battle with the Eisenhower administration (and the Air Force) over Ike's nuclear-heavy New Look strategy. The Army wanted what Taylor called a strategy of flexible response, putting greater emphasis on ground forces. After losing this battle, at least for the time, Taylor retired in 1959 to head Mexican Power and Light until called back to Washington by the Kennedy administration two years later. By the end of my assignment in Washington I had learned much about the world of defense politics while also observing at firsthand the senior civilian and military leadership in the Washington milieu of that time.

After the Pentagon came another command, this time to a surface-to-surface missile battalion in Colorado, followed again by a student year, this time at the Army War College at Carlisle, Pennsylvania. In the summer of 1961 I returned to Europe for an interesting assignment in a great location: Special Assistant to the Supreme Allied Commander Europe (SACEUR) in the Paris area. The commander was then Air Force General Lauris Norstad, the fourth person to have held that position (Ike was the first in 1950) and, as it turned out, the last to play the role of proconsul. In 1961 NATO and Norstad had plenty of problems: the Bay of Pigs fiasco in the spring; Khrushchev's confrontation with Kennedy in Vienna in June; the Berlin wall in August. The following year came the Cuban Missile Crisis. None of this, though, was the cause of Norstad's forced retirement at the end of 1962; rather it was his struggle with the

Kennedy administration over NATO's nuclear strategy to include the control of nuclear weapons. Again, I had a truly educational experience watching the interaction between the Supreme Commander and Washington. As for social life, who wouldn't want to live in Paris at an international headquarters with representatives of fifteen nations as colleagues?

I was already acquainted with Norstad's successor General Lyman Lemnitzer, who had been Taylor's vice chief, and the second half of my tour at Supreme Headquarters turned out to be even more rewarding because of the projects assigned to me. In the summer of 1963, when the Army selected a number of officers to be promoted to colonel ahead of their contemporaries, I was one of them. As a result I went the next year to command the 24th Division Artillery in Munich, Germany. One year previously, this had been a brigadier general's job; my doing it as a lieutenant colonel on the colonels' promotion list required plenty of chutzpah.

Now the news out of Washington and Vietnam predicted that the U.S. military would be getting more involved in Vietnam. In my case this meant returning to Carlisle for a year on the faculty of the War College with orders to Vietnam afterward. During that time our son was accepted at Deerfield Academy for the following fall, so Wade decided to locate near there in Amherst, Massachusetts. She also enrolled as a student at the University of Massachusetts.

My Vietnam assignment turned out to be in Westmoreland's headquarters (MACV) then located in downtown Saigon. Living in the "pearl of the Orient" was in itself an experience, but my job as Chief of Operations Analysis—a branch in J-3 (Plans and Operations)—was an eye opener. Only by writing at length could I recapture the tenor of the 1966-67 phase of that tragic war with its multidivisional search-and-destroy operations; its body count litany; briefings for Robert Strange McNamara on his periodic visits; and news from the home front—especially Wade's letters from the college town of Amherst—about the increasing antiwar sentiment. My job included responsibility for a monthly "Measurement of Progress" report, which soon showed me the mess that "the best and the brightest" had gotten us into. My own sentiments are summed up in my notes on the trip home in 1967 at the end of my tour. "The plane roared skyward from Tan Son Nhut at 6:45 p.m. on July 6, stifled by the greater roar from all the happy troops on board including me. I thought, Thank God, that's over. I'll never be back here." How wrong I turned out to be!

Returning from Saigon to Amherst, seething with antiwar sentiment, was a dramatic change. Then, a few days after my arrival, came a real surprise: a telephone call from Washington stating that the President was sending my name to the Senate for confirmation as a brigadier general. A new assignment would come later; meanwhile, I was to proceed to the Pentagon's Office of International Security Affairs (ISA). Not knowing our eventual location, Wade decided to accept a graduate teaching fellowship at the University of Massachusetts, thus remaining in Amherst for another year.

That fall my Pentagon job in NATO nuclear planning called for me to travel to Ankara in support of Defense Secretary Robert McNamara, who was participating in a NATO Nuclear Planning Group meeting. During the meeting something not on the agenda came as a bombshell: Turkey proposed placing atomic demolition munitions on its eastern border with the Soviet Union! On return home I was designated to chair an American working group (including representatives of the Joint Staff and State Department) to study the proposal. My off-the-record orders were to kill the idea: "Would you believe helicopter pads?" was the thought passed on to me by an Assistant Secretary of Defense. Still, some military members of the group took the proposal seriously and went to the Turkish eastern front on a survey—an exercise from which I excused myself because of a subsequent invitation. In the end we received help from an unexpected source. In December without explanation the Turks suddenly withdrew the proposal. Much later we discovered that when hearing of this Top Secret proposal the Soviets had told the Turks to knock it off.

My assignment as a brigadier general turned out to be Deputy for Plans and Operations of the Continental Army Command at Fort

Monroe, headquarters for Army activities in the United States. This historic post in Tidewater Virginia was notorious for its large contingent of colonels awaiting retirement. I was then the youngest general in the Army, one of three from my class. This was heady stuff, but at Fort Monroe I was the junior of the thirteen generals stationed there and very much aware that, as the four-star in charge put it, I was a "buck general." Looking at him, I found popping into my mind Peggy Lee's theme song, "Is That All There Is?"

One responsibility that I did not savor was planning for federal troop involvement in domestic civil disturbances. On Thursday, April 4, 1968, Martin Luther King, Jr., was assassinated; within minutes a call on my direct line from the Pentagon ordered activating our operations center—a unique event for a laid-back headquarters at sleepy Fort Monroe. The next nine days were a haze of moving troop units to Washington and elsewhere, along with endless briefings and orders to be sent to units. At one point the firestorm in Washington was seven blocks from the White House, and LBJ was raising hell. In the weeks and months following this crisis, which ended for us on April 13, intense civil disturbance planning took place under the code name Garden Plot. This worst-case scenario meant the simultaneous commitment of ten thousand troops to each of twenty-five American cities, including Paterson, New Jersey! I wondered if a contingency on this scale would be a civil disturbance or a revolution?

Nineteen sixty-eight was a year of upheaval. Besides the King assassination, the Tet offensive in January had shocked the American home front; then came LBJ's "abdication" speech at the end of March, the assassination of Robert Kennedy in June, and the Soviet invasion of Czechoslovakia in August, the same month as the Chicago riots during the Democratic National Convention.

The ambience of that year accelerated a decision I had been thinking about for a long time—retiring from the Army and pursuing an academic career. It was not an easy decision, for my early promotion to general pointed to more promotions and more responsible, prestigious positions. At that point in the fall of 1968 I visited the Politics Department at Princeton. The only professor left there from my student days of twenty years before was Harold Sprout, whose writings with his wife Margaret had had a profound impact on the discipline of international relations. An open and enthusiastic person, Harold listened to my story and agreed to help. He did caution me, though, that getting one of the limited fellowships would be highly competitive.

On the following March 8 a major complication arose, thwarting my "secret" plan. A back-channel message from Army Chief of Staff Westmoreland informed me that I would return to Vietnam in May as Commanding General of Second Field Force Artillery. As my boss at Fort Monroe said, "This will sew up your second star." My idea of retiring, which I now discussed openly, did not go over well at the four-star level. Finally, I realized that I had no choice. It was made clear that Chief of Staff Westmoreland would not give his approval.

When April brought Princeton acceptance and proffer of a fellowship, I traveled there again to determine whether they would hold their offer open until I returned from Vietnam in about a year. They agreed and had a remarkably simple solution: since those who were drafted after Princeton acceptance received delayed entrances, why not put me in the same category? As far as I know, I was the only general in Vietnam on leave of absence from a graduate school. During that year Wade and our son decided on a Swiss interlude—he with a scholarship to a school in Lugano and she as a teacher there.

The artillery command consisted of about eight thousand troops located in the eleven provinces surrounding Saigon and dispersed in approximately sixty fire bases stretching from the Cambodian border to the South China Sea. Whatever my personal feelings about the war at that point or my future plans (unknown to my colleagues there), my primary concern was the job at hand, in particular the welfare of the troops. Back at home the newspaper headlines trumpeted Woodstock, war protesters marching on Washington, and the emerging story of the My Lai massacre of twenty months before. This year, 1969, also marked the beginning of the drawdown of the American military from Vietnam—what Nixon called "Vietnamization."

After six months in command I was assigned as Chief of Staff of the Second Field Force, which had overall responsibility for all U.S. forces in the area. Since we were without a Deputy Commander, for several months, I handled both jobs. My daily helicopter trips were no longer to fire bases but to the divisions and South Vietnamese provinces and districts. About the time of the job shift I took a wonderful seven-day leave in Lugano with my family—what a different world. As my final major task I was in charge of field force planning for the Cambodian incursion that began April 30, 1970, and spawned a whole new set of headlines; recall Kent State! The following month I began the journey home, this time via Switzerland with Princeton the final destination.

My many memories of personalities and events of this second year in Vietnam would take several chapters to do them justice. Perhaps I can best convey the complexity of that second Vietnam experience with musings jotted down on that May day in 1970 as the plane headed for Madrid, where Wade was to meet me.

> It is high noon on a typically hot, bright day late in the dry season. Now I can barely see this beautiful land in which I have lived for two years. Only a short time ago a new phase of the war began with our invasion of Cambodia. I am leaving at an exciting and controversial time, but for me it is time to go. What memories will linger? Will it be the endless charts and briefings, or the daily helicopter trips over the jungle to remote firing bases or to the small villages and hamlets, or will it be the face of a South Vietnamese soldier expecting a VC attack that night, or the body bags sometimes containing the remains of my own soldiers, or the intrigue and magnificent squalor of Saigon, or, if I am fortunate, the view from the helicopter not of a jungle landscape but of rice fields being planted, and white swallows flying far below.

The rest of the story from 1970 until today has been of an academic cum authorial, and sometimes government official, role. Though this part of my life has been less dramatic than the earlier, especially the war periods, I have found it exciting and fulfilling for a number of reasons; in particular because I was able to do it my way. Perhaps we should let it go at that with one final thought.

Reading Chapter 18 of William Maxwell's *The Folded Leaf* on that Cannes beach over fifty years ago, I was impressed with his underlying philosophy; still, it took reflecting on the years of my life covered in this book to understand the real significance of his words, "To live in the world at all is to be committed to some kind of journey." I had always assumed that the journey beginning at the Paterson Station would end at a final destination, that is another station where I would achieve my goals. Now I have come to realize that this was an illusion. To paraphrase Robert Hastings, there is no final station awaiting us. The journey is the goal—life and love must be experienced and enjoyed as we move along. As the psalmist tells us: "This is the day which the Lord hath made; . . . rejoice and be glad in it."

It is not possible to list all the people who have helped me relive this twenty-one-year journey, but there are some who have helped in one way or another that I should like especially to thank. Beginning with the Paterson years: John and Nelda Federici Burke, Jim Farrell, Walter Kennedy, my sister Helen McBride, Curley Jackson, Carl Blumberg, Francis Walters, Vincent Waraske, and Marjorie Nenadich.

For the cadet years: Bill Banks who shared the Coast Guard experience; Ken Rothwell for the Stanton interlude; and for the West Point years Jim Connell, George Maxon, George Daoust, Jan Pardee, and Jim Douglas through his excellent chapter on our academy years in the class of '44 fifty-year book. Beginning with this period and continuing through the remainder of the book: Diana herself on factual matters. She would want me to stress that the interpretation and description of events of our four-year relationship are the author's.

For those unforgettable sixteen months with the 71st Division, Dave Ott provided help on technical artillery matters; from the 608th

Field Artillery Paul Webb and Milton Small; and from B. Battery Ed Kortnik, Gerv Nash, Charles Wheeler, and Rudy Kehren. Pete Sims' precise trace of the 14th Infantry's combat period in *Blue Mike* was invaluable, as was Gerald McMahon's *The Siegfried and Beyond*. For the trip through German lines and return with the Commander of German Army Group South I am indebted to Ed Samuell. Krystyna Sims provided me a copy of her husband's wartime diary which traced the Division Artillery's wartime experiences. She also provided both information and illumination on our occupation days in Dillingen, where she served as a nurse in the displaced persons camp.

Help on the Third Army period in Bäd Tolz was provided by Willis Crittenberger in the form of recollections and documentation, and by Orwin Talbott. Finally, George Daoust was very helpful with materials and background information on the Constabulary period in Heidelberg.

Working closely with me throughout the project were four persons: Paul Miles was particularly helpful with his constructive comments on Part II of the manuscript; Joanne Garland deciphered my sometimes illegible handwriting and produced a manuscript; Mary Mitiguy, who has worked with me on several books was both editor and adviser. My wife, Wade Tyree Kinnard, is to be thanked above all—for serving as senior editor and critic and for encouraging me to go ahead with the project at the outset.

Douglas Kinnard
Alexandria, Virginia

Printed in the United States
5234